UNDOCUMENTED

UNDOCUMENTED

HAROLD FERNANDEZ, MD

MALEVOLENT BOOKS
Santa Monica, California

UNDOCUMENTED. Cover and text Copyright © 2017 by Harold Fernandez, MD. All rights reserved. No part of this book of this book may be used or reproduced in any manner whatsoever without written permission except in the case of brief quotations embodied in critical articles and reviews. For information, address Malevolent Books, a division of Quattro Media, 171 Pier Avenue, Ste 328, Santa Monica, CA 90405 USA.

The opinions expressed by the author are not necessarily those of Malevolent Books or Quattro Media.

Malevolent Books may be purchased for educational, business or sales promotional use. For information, please write: Special Markets Department, Malevolent Books, a division of Quattro Media, 171 Pier Avenue, Ste 328, Santa Monica, CA 90405 USA.

Cover design by Kate Stearman
Interior design by Blake Brasor

FIRST EDITION

Library of Congress Cataloging-in-Publication-Data is available on file.

ISBN: 978-1-936573-12-7 Trade Paperback
ISBN: 978-1-936573-13-4 Hardback
1. Biography & Autobiography, Personal Memoirs
2. Biography & Autobiography, Cultural Heritage

americanforests.org
GLOBAL
RELEAF

Malevolent Books, in association with Global ReLeaf, will plant two trees for each tree used in the manufacturing of this book. Global ReLeaf is an international campaign by American Forests, the nation's oldest nonprofit conservation organization and a world leader in planting trees for environmental restoration.

10 9 8 7 6 5 4 3 2 1

DEDICATION

Brandon, Jasmine, and Sandra—
My son, my daughter, and my wife,
My light, my jewel, and my sweetheart.

ACKNOWLEDGMENTS

A hundred times a day I remind myself that my life depends on the labors of other men, living and dead, and that I must exert myself in order to give, in measure as I have received, and am still receiving.

Albert Einstein

This book has been in the making for several years. I feel strongly that it will be a timely addition to the current debate on our immigration dilemma.

In the silence of a small room in the basement of my house, I worked on the first version of the manuscript. This was ready for publishing in 2007. I was not able to bring it to print, even though I had the help of a great literary agent, Tina Jacobson. I want to thank her for her support and belief in the importance of the message.

Next, I worked with a great, *New York Times* reporter, Joseph Berger, on the second version of the manuscript. I thought that it was an improvement because it added more detail, including a vivid description of some of the events and the characters. However, we could not find a willing publisher then either, although we had the assistance of another great literary agent, Jane Dystel. I would like to thank Joe and Jane for their time and effort. Although the second manuscript was an improvement, one of the comments I received was that the writing appeared more like a journalistic account of events, rather than a story. Ms. Erika Goldman from Bellevue Literary Press was kind enough to read several chapters and give me some valuable insight. Briefly, the idea was that I had to tell my life as a story.

So this is what I attempted to do on the third manuscript. I kept the original account of events, since, after all, the facts are the same; but I re-organized it and did some more writing in a way that makes the narrative flow more as a story. Each chapter is a story that describes a specific part of my life.

I also want to express my gratitude to Joanne Asala from Compass Rose Horizons for her great effort at editing the initial copies of the manuscript. She has spent countless, mid-night hours working on improving the grammar and structure and making very useful suggestions and comments. This has not been an easy task because I am not a writer by training.

Several people have been instrumental in reading different parts of the manuscript and providing useful comments. Professor Arcadio Diaz-Quinones, Enrique Saez, the nurses in the Intensive Care Unit of St. Francis Hospital have all been invaluable in providing useful comments suggestions and words of inspiration as I undertook this monumental project. My infinite gratitude for your love, support, and encouragement. So, as you can see, this final manuscript has been the combined effort of many people, and I want to express my deepest gratitude for their honest work.

My inspiration to write this story has been the daily struggle of many families and students who are currently living in America as undocumented immigrants. I hope that some can identify with my story and find comfort inside the pages of this book. I also hope and pray that a better understating of their struggles will bring America closer to finding a humane and practical solution.

Last, but certainly not least, I would like to acknowledge the sacrifice, hard work, and struggle of several members of my family and their willingness to share this story with you. My parents and my family have been infinitely supportive. In these pages, we have shared many intimate details of our personal lives with you, some of them excruciatingly painful. I feel greatly indebted to them, my wife Sandra, Johana, my aunt Gilma, my parents, and my grandmothers.

TABLE OF CONTENTS

Waiting on a Letter 13

A Secret Wedding 23

A Glimmer of Hope 35

A Single Bullet 45

A Mother's Love 55

The Bermuda Triangle 67

Two Bicycles 79

A New Language 89

Smoking in a Room 99

A Friend 107

Going for the Gold 117

Studying with Mice 127

The Young Scientist 137

PHOTOS 151

Dwelling in the Shadows 159

Spires and Gargoyles 167

A Day of Gloom 179

American Compassion 189

This Side of Paradise 201

The Girl in the School Uniform. 217

On My Way to Harvard 227

The Making of a Surgeon. 243

Losing a Patient 261

A Bouquet of Flowers. 273

A Childhood Dream. 281

WAITING ON A LETTER

On a sunny afternoon in March 1985, I returned home from my high school after an exhausting track and field practice. I shuffled into my room, dropped my books on my desk, and hastily greeted my mother.

"Mom, have you picked up the mail today?" I asked.

She hadn't. She was avoiding the mail because she was even more nervous than I was. She preferred to hear the news from me. She had noticed that I had been very tense over the last few weeks as I waited to hear from the university that I had always dreamed about. She thought that I would have been devastated if I received a negative response. During the few weeks prior to this, I had waited anxiously to hear from each school, and one by one the letters had come in. I was turned down by the California Institute of Technology, but the letters from Rutgers, R.P.I., Cornell, Brown, and Yale all offered me a place. Still, the letter I was waiting for the most had not yet arrived. I had been thinking about this all day. I had a feeling that today I would find out.

I picked up the mailbox key and scrambled downstairs to the vestibule of our building. Before I opened the mailbox door, I peeked in through the small opening in our mailbox and noticed that there was, indeed, some mail. Although it was hard to see, I could even make out a small white envelope with the black and orange logo of Princeton University. As I held the letter in my hands, I was disappointed because it felt very light. From my experience with the other letters that I had already received and also from hearsay from my friends, I had come to believe that acceptance letters are usually thicker because they contain lots of other papers a student has to fill out— financial aid forms, housing forms, etc. Letters of rejection are single pieces of paper with just a couple of paragraphs and begin with the words, "The admissions committee regrets to inform you..."

I could not muster the courage to open the envelope immediately. I went upstairs, came into the apartment, and as I silently walked through the kitchen, I put the Princeton letter in my right hand. I handed the rest of the mail to my mom. My mom also feared the worst; she could see that I didn't look happy, but she did not ask me anything. I walked into my bedroom and closed the door. I needed some time alone. My poor mom just waited outside the room, wishing she could be there with me to console me if I was not accepted.

As I sat on the edge of my bed, holding this small, light envelope in my hands and thinking that it was a letter of rejection, I could not resist the temptation to reflect on my work during the last few years. I wanted to know if there was anything else that I could have done. I thought about my work during my few years in America, and I started to realize that I had done well. I had adapted to the intricacies of life in America as a troubled teenager. I still had a heavy accent, but I had reached a level of comfort with spoken English that allowed me to be pretty much at ease with my schoolmates and teachers.

Although I had pride in the Colombian culture that ran deep in my heart, I was also captivated by American traditions and American society. I had become successful at many other endeavors. I was an Eagle Scout. I had been selected for the all-county teams in three sports. I was the top student in my grade and had achieved A's on my computer courses at R.P.I and third place in the science fair. I had even—insignificant as it may seem—been named newspaper carrier of the year by doing a job I'd needed to make some pocket money. I had certainly come a long way since my days as a young teenager in my native town of Medellín, where I was hoping to learn how to smoke and had started taking sips of hard liquor. Undoubtedly, my outlook on life appeared infinitely more positive since my adventurous mid-night voyage across the treacherous waters of the Bermuda Triangle.

However, did Princeton see my accomplishments in the same light? Did they understand, for example, that my verbal score on the SAT was low because I had just recently learned English?

As I thought more about this letter, I realized that even if I was not accepted, I had already gained acceptance at other great universities. This, by itself, was a huge accomplishment. No one in my family had ever finished high school, let alone attended college.

I was advised by my guidance counselor to concentrate my efforts on some of the local colleges in northern New Jersey. But like many of my classmates, I had bigger dreams. I wanted to win acceptance to an Ivy League college. The rich and ancient traditions of scientific discovery, of a code of honor that mingled academic and athletic accomplishment, of sheer exclusivity—all embellished by portraits of those campuses in literature and the movies—exerted a pull on many Americans, especially new immigrants such as me. I realized that I should not really be afraid to open this letter, since I already had been admitted to an Ivy League school. Yet, I could not understand why my hands trembled as I started to open it.

"Why is Princeton my first choice, anyway?" I was asking myself. All the other schools that I had been accepted to were just as great. The reason is probably that I had actually seen the campus and had spent some time there competing at Princeton's gym in indoor track and field meets. I had already fallen in love with its beauty. It was love at first sight. I also was aware that

Princeton was the university that Albert Einstein had selected when he decided not to return to Germany after learning that Hitler would be in power. During my application period, Princeton was also getting a share of attention because it had been the choice of a young Hollywood star, Brooke Shields. My parents were thrilled; my father had heard of Einstein and was overjoyed by the association.

As I was taking out the letter, I started to come to my senses. "Who am I kidding here?" I asked myself. I should just be grateful that I had come this far. Thinking back to just a few months before, I did not know how I was even going to apply to college as an undocumented immigrant in America.

When I initially entertained the idea of attending college, I sent out letters to many top schools to request applications and quickly realized that there would be two insurmountable hurdles to my dream: money and documents. The costs for tuition, room, and board at Princeton, for example, totaled more than my father's entire annual salary. How could I possibly afford this expenditure? I had heard of scholarships, but how generous could these schools possibly be? I decided not to worry about this impediment for now. At times, I thought that the chance of my getting accepted to an elite school was so small that I really would not have to worry about money.

But there was a second problem—one that seemed even more complex. Each application requested my social security number and a photocopy of my green card. Most kids in my class were concerned about their SAT scores, transcripts, and letters of recommendation; I was mostly concerned with getting a green card and a social security card. As a family, we sat around the kitchen table every night, discussing what we might do. In the quiet and the darkness of the night, before going to sleep, my parents agonized about their fears that their undocumented son, who had surprised and delighted them by becoming an academic star at an American high school through hard work and determination, would not be able to continue with his studies because he was undocumented.

They had sacrificed all they had but felt helpless. They had even risked our lives by bringing us through a daring voyage on a small boat across the high seas. The original sin, my entering the country without documents, had still not been rectified; it lingered like a dark secret, and was going to hinder my chances to advance any further in this society. In low moments they asked themselves why they had even bothered. But they had also seen how hard I worked, had seen that each day I was the first one to get up to complete a paper route on the run, and that, due to studying and reading, I was always the last one to go to sleep. How could they deny this son the chance to fulfill his promise? They had no choice. Although they feared the worse, they would obtain falsified documents.

And that was how I wound up obtaining a forged social security card and green card that I used on all my college applications. I was not proud of having done this; the doubt and guilt about what I had done never stopped gnawing at me. But I was not ready to give up on my dream of an education.

So after a long period of reflection, and realizing that I really had nothing to lose, I ripped the envelope open, slipped out the letter, unfolded it, and was startled by the opening words: "The admissions committee at Princeton University is pleased to inform you..."

"Oh my God!" I yelled loud enough for the entire building to hear me. "I cannot believe this!"

I opened the door to share the news with my mother. She had been quiet this whole time, pretending that she was not aware of what I had been up to. She was equally ecstatic—and relieved. We hugged tightly. She said, "I love you, son. Your hard work has paid off." I felt at the top of the world, as if I had just won the biggest lottery ever. I was so overjoyed that I didn't even know what to do. Words could not describe the feeling of delight that filled my body. I changed into my running clothes and rushed down the stairs for a three-mile run. That was how I celebrated the admission to the college of my dreams.

When I returned from running, I had calmed down and realized that I had not even read the entire letter. I sat down with my mother at the kitchen table and translated the letter into Spanish for her. My mother—and later my father—were just as excited as I was, but their exhilaration was blunted by the fear they had of not being able to afford the expense of a Princeton education. Moreover, there was the pervasive uneasiness about what we had done with the social security card and the green card. In our silent thoughts, we all feared that this would one day come back to haunt us. However, we tried to put it out of our minds. The day we got the letter from Princeton was our day. Princeton had invited me to be a part of their community.

As testimony to how rare such an event was in our town, when my mother told her friends of my acceptance to Princeton, many of them didn't believe her and teased her with comments hinting that she was exaggerating the truth. My father was also accused by his co-workers and his boss of misrepresenting the facts. They would imply that perhaps the school I had been accepted to was actually some other community school in the township of Princeton and not the real university that they all knew.

During the next few months, I had to figure out how I was going to pay for my Princeton education. The beauty of the Princeton offer was that my admission did not depend on my ability to pay. Princeton had admitted me. Their financial aid officers would figure out what I could afford and Princeton would take care of the rest. So I submitted the necessary information: my parents' income tax returns and various financial aid forms. A few weeks later, Princeton replied with a package that included a large scholarship from the university itself and a combination of government grants, student loans, on-campus work assignments, a summer job, and a private scholarship from the Golden Nugget

Casino in Las Vegas that would be renewed each year, depending on my grades. In fact, Golden Nugget awarded me small bonuses every year for my high grades. My parents were expected to make a small contribution that they could afford. It was all written down on paper and signed by the dean of financial aid. The total package meant, as the Mexican slogan states, *sí se puede*, "It can be done." I was going to Princeton!

My high school graduation day was a triumphant and memorable occasion. On a blazingly hot, late afternoon in June, the 409 seniors at Memorial High School marched onto the field of the local football stadium, accompanied by our teachers, the principal, and members of the board of education. The stands were filled to capacity with family and friends, all wearing their best formal attire.

As I strode in, it felt as if it had been only a few months before that I was nervously heading toward the school for my first day of classes. Time had passed so fast, and we would never again be together as a class. For my family and I, the graduation would be especially unforgettable. I was the valedictorian and would address the stadium crowd. I was anxious at the thought of having to write a speech for such a moment—seven years before, I did not even speak English—and for such a distinguished group of people as West New York's mayor and the school board members. I worked hard on the words. Once I was on the stage, I gained my composure, looked into the section where I knew my parents were sitting, and spoke slowly and deliberately into the microphone. This is the speech that I delivered to the graduating class of 1985:

> Tomorrow we join humanity in its search for the ultimate truth—that which is the key to an ideal society where there is no evil and no fear of war. Let each graduate take a step towards the ultimate truth by developing his or her own character. Let free that part of our minds that hungers for

knowledge, and let free those cells in our heart that hunger for justice and love. Character is the soul of happiness, just as "brevity is the soul of wit." It is that unit that measures how close we are to real success. Tonight, we should also reflect on our performance at Memorial. Even though some of us have not worked to our potential, we still have an opportunity for a new beginning—a commencement. The mistakes we may have made in our last four years can be utilized to our advantage. Trying to reach the best of our abilities is all we can ask of ourselves, for human resources are endless, and our best is always enough. I hope that each student graduating here tonight never gives up, for failure only exists in the mind. Thank you.

My speech had a subtle message that I hoped some in the audience would decipher. The legality of immigrants was being debated around the country in 1985 and even more so in West New York. I wanted everyone to understand that although my family was undocumented, I had worked tirelessly to accomplish my goals and become the number one student at my school. Yet I felt a great agony inside because I was going to the college of my dreams with forged documents. I realized that many would not approve of this, and some would even want me to be prosecuted or deported. Yet, I had confidence that if people saw my struggles—if they saw that I had spent almost every minute of my life trying to be a better person, to improve myself so that I could go to a college like Princeton so I could become a doctor to help others just as my grandmother had wanted me to do—they might have second thoughts. If people realized all this and "let free those cells that hunger for justice and love," they would feel that maybe, just maybe, I deserved a second chance.

At the end of my speech, all my classmates applauded; however, I was not finished. Since many of the parents did not speak English, I wanted to share a few words with them in my native language—if only I could muster the courage. I did.

Desde el fondo de mi Corazón, quiero agradecerle a mi madre, a mi padre, a mi abuelita que está en el cielo, y a mi abuelita que está en Colombia por todos los consejos y el apoyo que me han dado. También quiero felicitar a todos los padres que están reunidos esta tarde por el buen trabajo que han hecho. Para concluir quiero repetir que mi deseo es que ninguno de los estudiantes que hoy se gradúan se dé por vencido, porque la palabra 'fracasar' solo existe en la mente. Muchas gracias.

That part of the speech wasn't very lengthy, but it gave me the opportunity to thank my parents and my grandmothers, and to translate some of the thoughts from the English version. My few words gave the afternoon an extra glow for the crowd's Spanish speakers. Their applause was exuberant; many of the parents were crying with pride and hope.

Two days later, my family and their friends celebrated in our tiny apartment with a special mass to thank the Lord for all the blessings that we had received. "Mijo tenemos mucho que celebrar, y le tenemos que dar gracias a Dios," my mother said. "My son, we have much to celebrate, and we need to thank God, our lord."

In just a few years, she and my father had witnessed what they considered a miracle from God in the same apartment where they had agonized and cried for several days because they feared that my brother Byron and I would not make it through the mysterious waters of the Bermuda Triangle in a small boat. We could now gather to celebrate the first member of the family to graduate from high school and the first to go on to college. My parents could not afford to rent a hall or anything grander, but my mother invited a priest from the local Roman Catholic Church to recite the solemn mass, and afterward, in that cramped apartment, we rejoiced with music, Spanish dances, and lots of boisterous conversation. My father made sure that all guests were well served with food and drinks, and my mother walked around the apartment with a gracious smile on her face as if she had just won the lottery.

I remember thinking at the end of the night about how great everything was. It was all so perfect. On the surface, it appeared that there was much to celebrate. I really thought that life could not get any better than this. I was on my way to Princeton. What else could anyone ever want?

On second thought, however, there was much to worry about. This was really only the beginning of a lengthy, uncertain, and arduous journey through the shadows of life as an undocumented person in America, or as many other people like to say as an "illegal alien." Through hard work and dedication, I had just graduated from an American high school as both the valedictorian and also as an undocumented student, but there were many obstacles ahead on my way to achieving my goal of becoming a doctor. This book is about coming to the land of dreams, the home of the brave, and the most wonderful place on earth. My story is about the life, the struggles, and the dreams of an undocumented family in America.

A SECRET WEDDING

On the morning of October 3, 1964, my mother stumbled out of bed half an hour earlier than her customary time. She went about her habitual morning routine of taking a shower in cold water, organizing her room and her bed, and drinking a cup of coffee. She did everything exactly as she did every morning, so as not to arouse the suspicions of my grandmother Rosa; she wanted this day to seem like an ordinary day.

When she was ready, she kissed my grandmother on her cheek, said good-bye, and stepped out of the front door. She made a quick left, and headed up the street on her daily half-mile walk to her factory. On this morning, however, my mother was radiant with energy, excitement, and fear. Even in plain work clothes, she looked beautiful with big, round, green eyes, long, light-brown hair down to her waist, and a slim figure. At the first corner, instead of continuing straight down the road, she made an unexpected left turn. In the middle of the block, her friends were waiting for her in a car. She stepped in and proceeded to change into her wedding clothes. My mother was trembling with fear and excitement. She had made the biggest decision of her young life—one that would change the course of her future forever.

A couple of friends helped her to change into her wedding dress right inside the car and took her to the church, Cristo Rey, in the nearby town of Guayabal in Medellín, Colombia. My mother wore a white dress, cut just below her knees, that had been made by a local tailor, and her face was veiled in white gauze. She walked to the altar carrying a small missal in one hand and a rosary in the other. My mother had been imagining this moment for months, patiently waiting until the day that she would leave her home and start her own family. Fearful of openly defying her mother, my mother had left her house at 6 a.m., pretending she was simply heading off for another workday at Medias Crystal; instead, she had decided to wed the love of her life.

My father was patiently waiting at the altar. He looked sharp in a dark-green suit and tie and spit-polished black shoes. He had only worn that suit once before. Because my mother's family did not know of the wedding, the only people who attended were my father's relatives. The only person from my mother's side was her younger brother, Hernando. Soon after my mother had left, he was tipped-off about the wedding. He showed up at the church with a machete in hand, determined to stop this ceremony. As my mother and father were kneeling in front of the priest, my mother heard a commotion in the back and turned to see Hernando arguing with my father's uncles. They were armed with guns and persuaded him to allow the wedding ceremony to proceed.

"They truly love each other. There is nothing we can do." My father's uncle Mario told Hernando.

Nevertheless, as she absorbed this scene, my mother wondered if she had made a grave mistake, if she had rushed things, and if she should have waited until she secured her mother's blessings. The tears rushing from her green eyes during the proceedings were partly from happiness and partly from remorse that her mother and her family were not there. She thought about the pain and anguish that her mother Rosa would feel when she discovered that her oldest daughter was getting married without her approval.

The ceremony was followed by a party at my grandmother Alicia's house, but before going, my mother and father stopped at my great-grandmother Debra's house, where my grandmother Rosa lived, to ask for her blessings. When she saw them together in their wedding outfits, Rosa could not keep from crying.

"How could you do this without our permission?" she asked my mother. "We have loved you so much all your life. How could you disappoint us like this?"

My father also felt the anguish at the scene, and he stepped in to promise my grandmother Rosa that he was going to be a good husband. "Señora Rosa, I promise to make your daughter happy. I will devote all my life to her," he told Rosa.

It was not long before my grandmother's pragmatic instincts took over. She realized she had no choice but to accept what had already happened, and she reluctantly told them she would give them her blessings. The young couple spent their honeymoon night in a bedroom in Grandmother Alicia's house, and in the morning, Alicia brought them a warm cup of chocolate milk and some slices of bread. That was their honeymoon breakfast.

- - - - - - - - -

Both of my parents had left school at a very early age. They met while working at Medias Crystal, a small company that manufactured designer socks. Although this was a very low-paying job, their respective families were happy that they had any job at all. They dated for several months and impulsively decided to get married.

My mother's family did not approve of their courtship. They felt that she could do better. However, my paternal grandmother, Alicia Fernández, was pleased with her prospective daughter-in-law because she had green eyes, fair skin, a shapely figure, and she appeared to be a caring and honest young woman. My mother's family, on the other hand, was strongly opposed to their friendship. My father, although handsome and well dressed, had never been schooled beyond fourth grade and was often jobless. The best he could ever aspire to was to remain with his current job at Medias Crystal. My grandmother Rosa often warned my mother, "This is not the man for you." My mother, however, was deeply in love with him, even if her family did not support her. She was determined to become his wife at all costs. When my father proposed, she did not think twice. She said, "Yes, my love, I will become your wife."

My mother was a typical teenager growing up in a very poor home. She worked very hard at the local factory during the day; at night, she helped with the daily chores of the house. At the age of nineteen, although she lived in a very humble setting, she had big dreams of getting married and having a family of her own. She dreamed of children and not of a career. She felt deeply in love, and she wanted be get married and start a family with him.

My father Alberto was dark-skinned, had a reputation for having a bad temper, and was close friends to young men with criminal records. This was not what my grandmother Rosa wished for her oldest daughter. She wanted something better.

- - - - - - - - -

Not surprisingly, the years that followed the wedding were very difficult for my parents. They lived in that same bedroom where they spent their honeymoon, sharing the bathroom and kitchen with my grandmother and with my aunt Gilma and her family, who occupied another bedroom in the house. My grandmother slept in the living room. This overcrowding of relatives was not an uncommon arrangement in Medellín, but was often troublesome and complicated nonetheless.

The money my grandmother earned was the main support for the household. She made hundreds of *arepas* every day. These are the corn-based tortillas that are a daily staple in Colombia. She baked the *arepas* in a large, brick, coal-and-wood oven at the back of her house. She would start her day at two in the morning, and would prepare a thousand *arepas* to bring to the local shops, which sold them to men and women on their way to work. Single-handedly, she boiled and ground the corn, mixed in the tropical cheese and other ingredients, and baked the patties. She took off only two days a year, Good Friday and New Year's. Although my mother was eager to contribute, my father was too proud to have her work. He sometimes boasted of his aristocratic heritage. His great-grandfather had been a wealthy mine owner, a man of Spanish-colonial pedigree with pale white skin. But he had disowned his son for marrying a native Indian, consigning the future generations—my father among them—to poverty. Still, with that heritage and the pervasive code of *machismo*, my father felt that a wife of his should not have to make *arepas* for a living. So she helped my grandmother only occasionally.

My father insisted he was in charge of his household, and even demanded that my mother quit her job at Medias Crystal. She stayed at home and was only allowed to visit her family or friends with my father's consent. My father, on the other hand, kept up his routine of hanging out with his friends at the local bars after work and on weekends. This was a too-common arrangement for a husband and wife in the culture of Colombia. The woman stays at home; the man spends all day out in the street, at work, or befriending other women.

But one day, my father was humbled, almost humiliated. He lost his job at the sock factory. The only income for the family was from *arepas*. While my grandmother took care of the routine expenses and even provided some money for the young couple's weekend entertainment, the arrangement prompted tension between my parents and occasional fights. This went on for several months, until my father got a break. He was offered a job in an embroidery factory, but the factory was in Cali, a city about 200 miles to the south of Medellín. Like Medellín, it was also known for its rival drug cartel.

In Cali, my parents rented a small room in a house they shared with three other families. My father had experienced the pain of being unemployed, and he was determined to make a success of his new job. He quickly realized that he now had other people who depended on his labor. He worked hard and was rapidly rewarded with a promotion to supervisor. This made him happier, but he realized that this would probably be the highest position that he would ever reach. His past mistakes, especially his decision to drop out of school during fourth grade, would hobble him.

He clearly remembered the day when, at the age of eight, he decided that instead of going to class, he would sell coconuts, fruit, or newspapers on the plaza of his hometown on the outskirts of Medellín. At that age, this made him happy because he was earning some money.

My grandmother had been so involved in making and selling *arepas* that she only discovered several months afterward that her son had dropped out. When she did, she could not force him to return. Poorly educated herself, she did not realize how crucial education was, and, like many Colombian women, she had no husband to help her force her eight-year-old son to do what was right. The men in her life had been abusive and she never developed the courage to assert herself with her own child. Therefore, my father, at age eight, began a life of small jobs to support himself. He managed to stay away from selling drugs as his source of income, and he learned to read and write on his own by reading the local newspaper. That ability served him well as a supervisor because he had to read and sign documents and write notes to workers and other managers. He was proud of his well-printed letters and his tidy penmanship.

Although my parents remained quite poor, the promotion and a steady job stirred a new sense of optimism and a confident outlook that was enhanced when my mother became pregnant. I was born on August 1, 1965, at eight o'clock in the evening. Although my parents had wished for a girl—in preparation they had bought my first wardrobe in pink and yellow—they were grateful that the pregnancy and the delivery had been uncomplicated and that I was a healthy baby. Several relatives from Medellín traveled the 200 miles over mountainous terrain to see the new arrival, including both my grandmothers and my uncle Hernando. My grandmothers felt obliged to stay for several weeks to help the new couple to take care of their first baby. My father's feeling of security deepened. He had what appeared to be a relatively solid and secure job, and now he had company to assist in the care of the new baby.

At six months, I was baptized as Harold Alberto Fernández Londono. Alberto and Fernández came from my father's family and Londono from my mother's side. The choice of Harold was somewhat surprising, since it is not exactly Spanish. It appears that around this time in Cali, a well-known Jewish business-man named Harold Edder had been kidnapped by guerrillas. His name was so commonplace in the headlines that people devel-oped an affinity for it, and some named their new babies Harold.

But Cali was not to be my parents' hometown. They missed their families and friends too much and the meager money they had to live on from my father's job did not soothe their loneli-ness. My grandmother Alicia warned my father that there were no jobs to be had in Medellín, but he and my mother returned anyway. We lived for a time with my grandmother, who already was housing my aunt Gilma, her husband, Jose Chica, and the four children they had at the time (they eventually had eight). Jose had served honorably in the Korean War, losing a leg in combat in a Colombian unit that was supporting the American forces. My aunt Gilma mischievously liked to hide his artificial leg whenever they had an argument. Everyone in their family worked. Jose owned a small grocery and Gilma helped my grand-mother with the *arepas*. Even the young kids helped in the store and with the daily chores.

Because I was my father's only child, my grandmother Alicia showed a special affection towards me, and this made Gilma, my father's sister, resentful. The animosity climaxed when my mother became pregnant with her second child. There was an argument between Gilma and my grandmother over some missing cash. My father interceded and in the heat of his rage, he ended up punching Gilma in the face. Her husband, Jose, summoned the police.

My father did not go to jail, but Gilma demanded that my family leave immediately. And so we did, immediately. We rented a small room in a stranger's home a few blocks away. We didn't own much, so we carried our mattress, cooking utensils, and clothes to this new home. My grandmother Alicia even came with us for a time, telling Gilma, "If there is no room here for my son, there is no room for me." But she returned to her home, and along with grandma Rosa helped us pay our rent. In that small room, my brother was born on July 21, 1967. He was named John Byron Fernández, and almost from the start, everyone called him Byron.

So in one single room that was rented, my family lived—all four of us. My father did not have a job. We were supported by money from our grandmothers. My parents' economic situation could not have been any worse, and soon after my brother's birth, my father decided to take a friend's advice and make the trip to New York. By then, stories were filtering back to Colombia about the prospering lives émigré Colombians were leading in New York City.

In 1969, it was much easier to obtain a tourist visa to come to America, and without much difficulty, it could be converted into a green card, establishing permanent residency on a pathway to full citizenship five years later. The friend offered to lend my father the money to file all of his documents, including some fake ones that portrayed him as a vacationing businessman, as well as pay all the expenses, like the $200 round-trip plane fare.

My father knew that he would find work in New York, and that he would take in enough money to better support his family. Because nothing in life is free, the cost of this opportunity would mean leaving his family behind—his young wife, his two sons, and his mother. The decision was a necessary one, he felt, but it filled him with dread and anguish. I was four years old, and my brother Byron was two years old. My father was desperate. He had to do something.

My parents spent hours trying to calculate how long it would take to earn enough money in New York so they could buy a house and put a down payment on a small business. They thought of friends who were able to return to Colombia after a few months in New York with enough money to live well and buy luxuries, like a car. But these people did not work for a minimum wage in New York's factories. Many of the people who made the quick fortunes were involved in the drug trade. It would be years before my father could return to Colombia.

My father arrived at JFK International Airport on April 6, 1969. Two of his friends from Barrio Antioquia, Carlos Grajales and Gabriel Jaramillo, took him into their one-bedroom apartment at 475 Riverdale Avenue in East New York. Soon after, two other friends, Luis Morales and Alejandro Foronda, joined them. All were down-to-earth men who wanted to save their money so they could help their families back in Colombia.

My father quickly got a job twenty blocks away in the Perey Corporation, which manufactured turnstiles used in subways, buses, and arenas like Madison Square Garden. He was hired as an assistant carpenter and his job was to make the wooden containers that were used to ship the turnstiles around the world. He earned $1.65 an hour and brought his weekly take home up to $107 by working twelve hours a day, six days a week. He supplemented his income on Sunday by working as a handyman at the home of his foreman. He decided on his first day at work that he would walk the twenty blocks to his job every day and save the fifteen-cent subway fare. With thrift like this, he was able to send eighty to ninety dollars each week back to Colombia through a "giro postal" at one of the money transfer shops.

There were weeks that, after paying the rent, he lived on $15, nourishing himself with hot dogs and boiled eggs. His friends all did pretty much as he did, working similar jobs, and sending most of their money back home.

— — — — — — — —

Life in East New York was ruthless. Almost daily, there were vicious fights between young blacks and Puerto Ricans, and the police were often called. My father heard of several rapes. He had never imagined living under such circumstances and decided that he could not bring his family to that neighborhood. He didn't see too much difference between the anarchy in Barrio Antioquia and that of East New York. Thieves broke into his apartment three times. So each day, my father carried with him everything precious that he owned. He and his roommates had few possessions, the most valuable a small black-and-white TV that they chained to the wall. However, they were worried that thieves would ruin the locks on the door. So they came up with the clever idea of simply leaving the door open!

My father's only indulgence was an occasional movie and his only refuge from loneliness was in the connections he felt in the letters we wrote or in the photographs my mother would send of Byron and me. Once a month, he would travel to an international calling center at Grand Central Station and go into one of the long-distance booths.

"I call to Colombia," he learned to tell the operator.

He on his end and we on ours would shout into the phone as if our voices had to carry the thousands of miles separating us. Whichever way we communicated, the separation was growing intolerable.

"This is terrible," he wrote in one letter. "I can't live without the boys. I need to go back."

I was very young and felt his absence deeply, but I also somehow felt that he was with us during those years. My mother made sure to keep us informed about what he was doing and the hundreds of letters that he wrote to us made it seem as if he conversed with us every day. Every night, I could feel his lonely heart swollen with love for us.

A GLIMMER OF HOPE

On a sunny day in late September of 1972, I received the best news of my life—my father was coming home. My mother got dressed up in her best dress. In a frenzy, she was hurrying me and my brother to clean up, get dressed, and get ready. "Come on, kids! We need to go to the airport. You need to look your best. Your father is coming home today." My mother had informed us a few weeks before, but it just seemed like it would never happen. Now the day was here, and I would finally see my father.

I was only seven years old, and I had not seen my father for four years. I really did not remember him at all. I knew my father from the photographs that he would send from New York, and from the brief conversations that we had on the telephone. As the minutes approached to go to the airport, I could not believe that the time was approaching to have our father in front of us so that we could put our arms around him and kiss him.

After three years and nine months of hard work and sacrifice, my father had raised enough money to buy a humble house in Colombia and a small business, and now he was returning to Colombia to a hero's welcome. Although I was very young, I still remember the excitement and sense of relief that surrounded his return. He would fill that empty vacuum that we had felt for so long.

The entire family journeyed to the airport. There were so many of us that we had to rent a bus. When my father walked into the terminal, his friends and neighbors burst into cheers. My mother embraced him tightly and gave him a long, passionate kiss with everyone gazing on with pleasure. He had returned from the United States.

We celebrated late into the night with tangos from Argentina—his favorite music. The door to our home remained open and neighbors stopped by until two or three in the morning to celebrate. As they walked into our living room, my father would offer them a drink of *aguardiente* (fire water) or whiskey. The conversation of the night was the wonders of life in America. I remember thinking that my father had come from paradise by his descriptions of so much wealth and beauty. I remained closed to his side, taking in every one of his words. I gazed at him as a hero of gigantic proportions. He did not describe the hardships of his condition there. I guess he must have been happy that although he had sacrificed so much, he was now back with his family, and he had saved enough money so that he could dream of having his own business in Colombia.

With the money he brought back with him, he was suddenly important. Everyone was astonished that he had turned his life around. This was the same person who just a few years earlier had been thrown out into the street with his pregnant wife and son and a small collection of personal belongings on hand. Just before we got into bed, he opened his suitcases. We almost fainted at the sight of so many toys and gifts, including a remote-controlled car, a radio-controlled airplane (that never worked), several pairs of sneakers for Byron and me, and dresses and jewelry for my mother. Life could not have been better; my father was home where he belonged.

Upon reflection, America had given us our first hope. As a family, we started to think that our lives would be different. We started to dream of a better tomorrow. It seemed that the sacrifice that my parents had made of splitting up the family would pay its dividends. Although the family had been split for several years, my parents were able to save some money. My father had been laboring tirelessly as an undocumented immigrant in the ghettoes of New York City while I, my brother, my mother, and the rest of the family had remained living in the daily conflict and uncertainty of the escalating drug war in Medellín. But now my father was home with us. Life could not have been any better.

The next two years were a time of contentment that I had never experienced before. My father started a small trucking company with a beat-up truck he bought. He transported barrels of fish oil, cattle, and corn from the coast into the countryside. He did not have to work as hard as he had in the past. He owned the truck and he was able to employ drivers for overnight trips, except when he had to accompany a driver on a new route to ensure that his directions were being followed.

We soon moved into our own house at *Carrera* 58, *Numero* 28-44 (58 was the avenue and 28 was the street number). At first, we rented the house, but my father soon made enough to buy it for about US $2800. It was a one-story, brick-and-wood house, which we fixed up over time. It was small but far more comfortable than the single room that we had rented before. My brother and I even had our own bedroom. My parents enjoyed each other's company as if they were newlyweds.

We lived modestly but never went hungry. We had enough money to buy clothes and the books that Byron and I needed for school. We had enough money for shoes—not a small distinction, since I had friends who had to walk barefoot through the streets. Sometimes I would be asked to take my shoes off in a soccer game so I would not have an unfair advantage over the many other kids who did not have shoes. I felt carefree, and not only played countless hours of soccer, but now I could enjoy many of the activities with friends on the street. One of them was racing little go-carts known as *carros de rodillos*, which we made out of planks and ball bearing cylinders that we picked up from the local truck repair shops.

Despite the dangers of daily life in our town, we felt more protected with our father in the house. We even gained confidence in the street as we interacted with other kids in the neighborhood because we now had our father who would back us up. This was a more normal childhood. My father looked at our homework assignments at night. He signed our tests. He stood on the side of the street as we played soccer with our friends and provided guidance. "Harold, you cannot be scared of the ball. Don't close your eyes when you head the ball."

But those two years of contentment also came to an end when my father's amateur enterprise failed. My father had always worked for someone else and did not have a background in running a business. While the trucking profits were adequate, he did not lay away enough for unexpected expenses. There were a series of accidents on the road and the old truck developed mechanical problems that were expensive to repair. When two tires on the truck wore out, my father did not have the money to replace them. Contracts were canceled and soon it dawned on him that he was bankrupt.

The job market in Medellín at this time was deplorable. My father realized that he would not be able to find employment. The only viable option in his mind was to return to America and start all over again in the factories of New York. As difficult as this was in his mind, he realized that he needed to do this. He had seen life in America. He was confident that he could do it again. He had the confidence that if he worked hard, he could help us in Colombia and live with dignity again.

He was able to sell the truck for enough money to pay for this second trip and obtained a visitor's visa through the American Consulate in Bogotá. I was now nine and my brother was six.

We were all very sad to see our father leave for a second time. My mother and my grandmothers were in tears. We had no idea how long he would need to be away. Our brief time together as a family was about to end.

My parents had many arguments and discussions about what to do. After they made their plans, she gave him an ultimatum. "This is not good for the boys," my mother told him before he left. "If you are not back within one year, you'll also have to bring me and the boys to New York."

My father returned to the same job at the turnstile factory, sending most of his paycheck back to Colombia. He saved every dollar that came into his pocket by again sharing an apartment with two compatriots. This time, the apartment was a studio on 42nd Street and 10th Avenue in Manhattan. The rent was $62.50 a month. My father had wound up in the heart of New York City, on the 42nd Street of song and legend, which at that time was plagued with drug dealers, prostitutes, thugs, and robbers. He enjoyed his free time taking walks in Central Park or going to the cheap theaters that showed American movies dubbed into Spanish or Spanish movies featuring the Mexican actor Cantinflas. At times, he was so lonely that he caught three movies in a single day. After a few months, he found himself a better-paying job in an embroidery factory on the night shift and started commuting to West New York, which is a small town in northern New Jersey.

- - - - - - - - -

Back in Colombia, I missed my father desperately. I dreamed that he was around so I could play soccer with him or that he could watch me play soccer. I wished that I could ask him questions about UFOs, spirits, and the devil, all the myths that were the talk of the other kids on the street. I wished that I could ask him questions about how to handle girls, romance, and peer pressure. I wanted someone to protect me whenever I had a street fight. I even started to fear that our house was vulnerable to thieves and had trouble falling asleep at night.

Meanwhile, my mother seemed excessively strict with us, as if she needed to compensate for the absence of a male disciplinarian in the house. Several times, I wrote to my father, complaining about how tough she was with me. Oddly enough, she threatened to appeal to him whenever we were out of line, playing soccer too long or not doing our homework.

"I'm going to tell your father when I write to him tomorrow," she would say.

When she was too harsh or would punish us, I would run to the photograph of my father in the hall and sob next to it as if I was pleading for him to come back and take control. I missed him terribly.

Two years after my father returned to America, things got even worse. My father was away, and now my mother was leaving as well. In September 1976, my mother left our home to join him in New York in his 42nd Street studio. She was able to gain admission to the United States with visitor's papers that described her as a microbiologist. She knew my father needed a companion, and that any more years apart would not be healthy for their marriage. She also knew that it would be difficult for him to find work in Medellín if he came home.

"Yes, Alberto, I know it is difficult and expensive to make the trip to New York, but we need to be together as a family," I heard her tell him on a call to New York just a few months before her departure.

Her long-range plan was to join him and then bring her sons over. However, the downside was that we would be apart from her for several months, and probably much longer, and we needed her. Though she trusted her mother to care for us, she had never been away from us for more than two or three days.

"My sons, I will only be away for a few months because I will bring you to America soon," she said. "I know we can make this happen."

Initially, we were very excited about the prospect of living under the tender and loving care of our grandmothers. However, as the day for my mother's departure approached, I started crying quietly in my room before falling asleep. Several times, my mother heard me, came into my room, laid next to me, and painted pretty fantasies of how wonderful life would be when we joined her in America. Imagining such fantasies of life in America was soothing and pleasing.

The day of her departure arrived and I wasn't sure how to act. She was on her way to join my father, so I did not want to ruin the moment for her. I wanted to stay strong. My mother looked particularly pretty that day. She had a light-green floral dress that was belted at the waist. Her green eyes were as bright as ever and she had just been to the hairdresser to look beautiful for my father. I was jealous of losing my mother. By the time we reached the airport, I stayed by her side until she left for the "passengers only" area. By that time, my mother's eyes were red and inflamed and she cried some more as she gave us our last kisses. With tears flowing down from her eyes, and a tight embrace, she said, "My sons, we will be together soon, I promise."

I repeated those words to myself as she disappeared into the "passengers only" area. Tears streamed from my eyes, and my lips trembled. I wanted to yell to her, "Come back!" But I restrained the impulse. It helped that Grandmother Rosa hugged both of us at that moment.

Although, in the weeks that followed, my grandmothers made sure we were well fed and well dressed, I missed my mother's smile and embrace. Over the next two years, our grandmothers were in command. Right away, they started to instruct us and teach us. Our grandmothers would advise Byron and me to work hard in school, stay out of trouble in the street, and obey her orders because our parents were slaving in their factories, suffering so we could have food on the table. "You need to do well in school to show them that their work and sacrifice are paying off," my grandmother Rosa would tell us.

Meanwhile, my mother suffered even more. Although she and my father had moved to a third-floor apartment in West New York and she was impressed with how safe the neighborhood was, she was not happy. There was not a day that went by that she did not cry. There was a television show on one of the Spanish channels where every night the announcer would ask, "Do you know where your children are now?" That would always bring her to tears. "We need our boys; they need to be with their parents," she kept telling my father. "There is no future for them in Barrio Antioquia."

Without their boys, their hard work seemed to bring them no reward. My father worked twelve hours a day in America's embroidery capital, from seven in the morning until seven at night, and many evening and weekends as well. My mother was also working very hard. Although my father initially opposed the idea of her working, he realized that the family needed her income. She taught herself to sew on a friend's Singer sewing machine and started working in a blouse factory. After working for ten to twelve hours a day under the same terrible conditions as my father, she came home to another job. Cooking, keeping the apartment tidy, and handling all of the daily problems and disputes kept her tremendously busy.

— — — — — — — —

Each week that passed without them seemed like an eternity. I thought that life was not being fair to us. I tried to get through my sadness by concentrating on school in the daytime and soccer in the afternoons and evenings. I entered school in the first grade at seven, skipping kindergarten because my mother had taught me how to read at home. Most children would not have been allowed to enter school until the age of eight. However, a friend of my mother's persuaded the principal, Don Luis, to admit me by visiting the school and offering him a home-cooked lunch she prepared. He appreciated the favor and disregarded the state rule.

The school, named La Paraguay, was in a one-story brick building with rooms radiating from a courtyard where we could play at recess. The structure of the teaching and learning was done around strict discipline and memorization. If children did something wrong, they would get their hands slapped with a ruler. When there was a serious lapse, Don Luis would gather the entire school in the courtyard, line everyone up, and lecture us about proper behavior until we were exhausted. At times, we would all be forced to stand with our arms up above our heads for several minutes. Reserved and quiet, I mostly kept out of trouble.

The classes themselves were regimented, with memorization being the standard approach to learning in every subject. We memorized a list of the world's significant animals, the anatomy of a pig, and Colombia's major imports and exports. I memorized the geography of Colombia and its regions so well I could draw a map of the country with my eyes closed. We would have a reading of two or three pages and I could memorize the passage and come into class the next day and recite it. Although this educational process was probably not ideal for developing problem-solving skills, my proficiency at memorization proved helpful in getting me through medical school many years later.

As my parents continued to labor in the factories of America and, at the same time, hide from the immigration agency, we attempted to live as normally as we could. However, every day seemed an eternity without our parents, and the same was true for them. My mother knew that this could not go this way forever. Something had to be done.

A SINGLE BULLET

One afternoon, as I was sitting by the sidewalk just outside my house to watch a soccer game on the street, a loud explosion suddenly interrupted my attention. I clearly recognized this sound. It was a single gunshot. Even at this early age, I had heard this sound before in the streets of Barrio Antioquia. I was supposed to get up and run to my house to look for the safety of my grandmothers. They had told me hundreds of times, "If there is a fight, you run to the house immediately."

However, this time it was different. I was so close. The sound was so loud that I was paralyzed. It only took one shot. In front of me, I could see that one of the older kids who had been playing in the game, Alvaro, was holding his side, trying to stop the blood from rushing out of his body. As I watched him being taken to the hospital, I was afraid that he might become another victim of the senseless violence afflicting the streets of my humble town.

Yet, strange as it may seem, to a kid like me and my friends, the town's broken, dangerous streets were just another field on which to play. This was our playground. The street is where I learned many lessons from friends. Most of the time, the streets were safe because many adults would be outside of their homes as well, sitting in front of their houses late into the night.

For all of us, the most important game was soccer. I would come home from school, change out of my school clothes, get through my homework as best as I could, then dash out the front door and start kicking a ball with my friends on the dusty roadway in front of my house. There was never a shortage of kids to start a game on the street. All you needed was a ball, and in my group, that ball usually was mine. That was because I had parents who were in the United States working in factories and so could spare money for such a luxury. In fact, I probably had the best soccer ball around.

Very often, the kids on my street waited until I finished my homework just so we could play with my regulation ball. For hours each day, we kicked the ball, weaved it between the other players, swiped it from opponents, and shot it through imaginary goal posts until the gathering darkness made the ball impossible to see. With Medellín's warm climate, we played year round, organizing our own tournaments and competing against other blocks in the *barrio*. We did not need grass fields or special parks; we played right on the street in the midst of the traffic. Although most of us could afford shoes, several kids did not have the means to buy shoes, and they played barefoot. Their parents were that poor, though some of the shoeless actually preferred that method of kicking a ball.

The older kids—those, say, between fifteen and eighteen—had their own games and I often enjoyed squatting on the sidewalk and watching their more expert play. Their games were more intense and physical, and fistfights were not uncommon. There was no official referee, so many of the regulations were enforced with fierce arguments and at times with fights.

Earlier that same day there had been one such situation. Alvaro, got into an argument with Marlon, a younger opponent, over whether or not a particular foul had merited a penalty shot. Marlon had touched the ball with his hand—illegal in soccer— but he argued that it had been unintentional.

"You touched it deliberately; it should be a penalty kick," Alvaro retorted.

"You must be crazy; the ball just hit me," Marlon insisted.

The argument heated up, and the two began to shove each other until the stronger, older Alvaro knocked Marlon to the ground. We gasped at seeing this because Marlon was a well-known *sicario*, a paid assassin for the drug gangs. Although he was only fifteen years old, he was already credited with several murders in the neighborhood, so we sensed this quarrel would not end well. Marlon got back on his feet, leaped into the air, and ferociously head-butted Alvaro. Then he slowly strolled away as if nothing had occurred.

The game resumed, with someone assigned to replace Marlon. A half hour later, as I remained sitting by the side of my house, taking in the game, it happened. I heard the loud gunshot.

I was in a state of panic at the sight of blood soaking through his shirt; I could hear everyone yelling, "Oh my God! Oh my God! He is going to die."

Ten yards away from where I watched, Alvaro stood, clutching the left side of his abdomen. He was trying to keep blood from spilling out by pressing both of his hands against his abdomen. Alvaro was a strong kid and appeared calm, probably because he had seen blood before while assisting his father, who was a local doctor. I glimpsed Marlon, who was not too far away, calmly ambling off with a gun in his fist, making no attempt to hide the weapon. No one made any attempt to stop Marlon. He had been in a rage, and he was armed.

Before Alvaro hit the ground, he was picked up, swiftly loaded into the backseat of a car, and driven to a hospital emergency room. Luckily, the bullet had missed his major organs, so the doctors were able to treat him and release him a week later. No one pressed any charges. No one had the courage to testify against a *sicario* for a powerful gang. However, as was usually the case with these teenage killers, Marlon did not live for long.

On a cloudy, rainy day less than a few months later, when the weather had briefly cleared, I noticed Marlon, who was dressed in a black fedora and a long, grey, canvas coat, hurrying down the same block and glancing behind him as if he were being chased. He appeared unsteady on his feet, probably because he was high on drugs. As he reached the corner, he ran into one of his enemies, a taller, older man, who shouted something at him.

This time Marlon did not have his gun, so he pulled out a long knife and waved it threateningly. The rival gangster had no weapons, but he was not drunk or high and picked up a rock in the roadway and flung it, dead-on, at Marlon, knocking him to the ground. He leaped on top of Marlon, punching him in the head repeatedly, then rose to his feet and kicked Marlon again and again. He finished the job by stomping him with the heels of his shoe. As he swaggered off, he left Marlon to lie in a thick pool of blood, slowly bleeding to death on that roadway.

There were several witnesses, but nobody interfered or rushed to help. It took an hour until we heard the wail of an ambulance, and when it came, the medics simply picked up the lifeless body. No one was ever charged.

As with other *mafiosos*, Marlon's body was laid out in his living room in an open casket surrounded by four candles—one on each side. The casket sat there for three days and nights while neighbors, friends, and relatives, all dressed in black, sat around the body, praying and weeping. The waxy smell of those candles became, for me, the smell of death.

Back home, my grandmother Rosa used occasions like this as a time to teach a lesson. "You see, this is what happens to all of them," she said. "Their bravery and greed always ends up in death."

Such brutality began to make violence a routine and accepted part of life in Barrio Antioquia. Ordinary squabbles between neighbors or disputes about politics would explode in violence. Life was not valued, and the threshold for what kind of violence would be tolerated seemed to get lower year after year. Wakes and funerals were becoming more frequent. Because the families were poor, the wakes were usually held in living rooms. A family would post a sign by the sidewalk identifying the dead person, his age, occupation, and the names of his parents, and the front door would be kept open so anyone could walk in or out. The neighbors enforced a code of silence in the blocks nearby; even soccer and music were forbidden. This was a common scene as I was growing up. I remember seeing many young men alive one day, and in the casket the next day after being violently murdered.

Then there was the funeral procession. This consisted of four or six men carrying the coffin through the middle of the road for the few blocks to the church, which was located just across from my house. Mourners dressed in black would follow, some screaming in anguish. Mothers would cry, "Oh, my God, why have you taken my son?"

I witnessed many of these wakes and funerals. Even if I didn't know the deceased, it was agonizing to see the relatives crying and sobbing. I would sit on the curb and watch the procession go by until my grandmother would pester me to come inside. She was worried another outburst of violence would occur during the procession. After all, it was not unheard of for criminals to visit a procession to avenge themselves on yet another member of a family. She would tell me with tears in her eyes to please study hard so that I would not end up like this.

This senseless loss of life in my town was heartbreaking. Most of the residents of Barrio Antioquia were honest and industrious people. They wanted prosperity, peace, and safety. They dreamed of a day when their kids could play freely on the streets without concerns about violence and drugs. Unfortunately, the ruthless actions of a few promulgated a far different and sinister image of Barrio Antioquia. The town became famous in Medellín for its criminal activity.

Underlying the surge in violence during the late seventies, eighties, and nineties was an epidemic of unemployment in what, normally, was Colombia's industrial capital. Drug-trafficking organizations, like the one led by Pablo Escobar, known as *El Patrón* (The Boss), exploited these jobless young men and women. *Barrios* like ours provided a steady supply of new leaders, *sicarios* (hired-assassins), and *mulas* (mules or drug carriers). While the assassins were usually young men, the *mulas* were often young women who would swallow condoms filled with cocaine and travel to the United States to deliver the drugs.

In the eyes of young people growing up in the *barrio*, the models of success were the *mafiosos*, the young men who entered the *mafia*, as the drug trade was called in Spanish, which borrowed the word from the Italian. These were the men who bought the best houses, married the most beautiful women, and had the fanciest cars and motorcycles, finest suits, and the grudging respect of other people. There were many examples of poor, young men who would suddenly turn their lives around by making a quick fortune overnight. They would suddenly demolish their modest house and build a fancy one in its place or drive around in a new car. These young men would disappear for a few weeks or months and return wealthy. Often, we learned that they had gone to the United States in search for a better life. These gangsters were not shy about flashing their newfound success.

One gangster we often saw on our block recruiting *sicarios* or *mulas* was "El Chino" Arles. He lived around the corner from where I grew up. He owned a fleet of motorcycles, dressed stylishly, and was always surrounded by swaggering friends and flashy women. His house was the grandest on the block, and in it, his mother lived comfortably. Each Christmas, he would give money to the neighborhood's poorest. Young and old alike respected him. People weren't sure what he did for a living, but we eventually learned he was involved in drug trafficking. He must have been implicated in many of Medellín's most violent crimes during the eighties. But just as Escobar had an early, violent death in Medellín, a rival gang killed "El Chino" Arles in Miami.

- - - - - - - - -

It may sound contradictory, but even in the real Barrio Antioquia, I experienced warmth, hospitality, and a sense of family values. While my parents were working abroad, my family still enjoyed the neighborhood's respect, and many residents, especially older ladies, would look after us. They acted as a network of informants who would inform our grandmothers immediately if they saw my brother and I engaged in any wayward activities or mingling with the wrong crowd. The neighborhood we lived in had an intimate culture, with neighbors curious about one another and sharing gossip. Everyone knew everyone else's troubles and joys. Every night, people would sit out on chairs and boxes and chatter while their children scampered about. If there was an argument or fistfight outside, everyone would peek through their windows or through the six-inch peepholes in the doors to witness the drama.

Barrio Antioquia was just one of many towns in Medellín, a city that many in America do not know well. For many of us, all we have heard about this place is that it is a city in conflict, a city in the midst of a violent drug war. However, many do not know that it is also a place of infinite natural beauty, which is home to people called *paisas*, who have a reputation for their pleasant, industrious, and honest personalities. The city is in the midpoint of a valley, surrounded on all sides by tall mountains that seem to touch the sky. At night, one feels as if the lights from the small towns hidden in these mountains are continuous with the heavens. But all that beauty meant nothing to Medellín's notoriety among the world's cities. For three decades and into the nineties, it was known as the planet's cocaine capital. Over the years, drug smugglers like Pablo Escobar and others in his cartel brought in million-dollar revenues each month. To keep their business thriving, they assassinated police chiefs, a presidential candidate, several supreme court judges, and newspaper publishers and editors. The thriving center of that drug capital was my childhood neighborhood, Barrio Antioquia. This was a small town consisting of about forty square blocks, with almost as many gangs.

I have often wondered why there was so much violence in my town, as compared to other poor towns in Medellín. The reason probably has origins in some of the historical events of the past. One of these important proceedings occurred in 1951 through a decision by its then mayor, Luis Palaez Restrepo, to open it as a "zone of tolerance." The city had been trying to control organized prostitution that seemed to be sprouting everywhere and the mayor's solution was to select one neighborhood where it would be legal. Municipal Decree 517 established Barrio Antioquia, strategically located near the city's center, as the city's red-light district. The residents of the *barrio*, led by their priests, put up a fight, but to no avail. In the months that followed the decree, trucks packed with prostitutes arrived daily from all over the city. Many houses became brothels, identifiable by the red lights that illuminated their entrances.

My great-grandmother, Debrah Ramirez, owned a bar in the *barrio*, which prospered as a result of the neighborhood's new traffic. It may have been a brothel as well. In this upheaval, many residents moved out, churches relocated, and three of the four schools closed, with one of them becoming a barracks for the extra police force required to enforce order in a neighborhood that overnight became a marketplace for sex. The fabric of the community began to unravel. Moral and religious values tumbled.

After a few years, under pressures from the priests and politicians, the mayor reversed his order, but Barrio Antioquia never recovered. The illicit activities that had sprung up during the years of tolerance—the drug dealing and the prostitutes—lingered on. Indeed, the police seemed to lose control. Not only were the prostitutes exploited, but also the neighborhood, once home to families, began to fill with single women and the children they had with their customers. The babies born during the years of tolerance and afterward often became the freelance drug traffickers who eventually formed the drug cartels. When my friends began to come of age, there were few examples of people succeeding as wage earners or in small enterprises, but there were many glaring examples of young people making a lot of money very quickly in the drug trade.

Despite the violence and the poverty, during the weekend nights, the streets would come alive. My block was flanked on one end by La Santisima Trinidad (Holy Trinity), the local church, and on the other end by a popular bar called La Oasis. My house was directly opposite the church's main entrance. La Santisima Trinidad was a plain, square, redbrick structure that might have been confused with a gigantic garage had its roof not been adorned with a large wood cross. The corner bar always had its doors open and passersby could peer inside. The music blasted through the open doors and could be heard the length of the block. Patrons would park their expensive cars or motorcycles just outside the bar. They and others with cash would pay for a table and sit with friends to have drinks and enjoy the music. Those who could not afford the bar's prices would sit on the sidewalk or stand at the corner into the early morning hours, drinking from their own bottles while listening to the same music. Many young and pretty girls would walk by in groups so that the men inside the bar could see them.

The background music of my early years came from the sound that was blasted from La Oasis, salsa from New York and Puerto Rico, *vallenato* from the coast of Colombia, tangos from Argentina. The music, sometimes upbeat, sometimes sad, poured out while we were playing soccer in daylight. At night, we learned to dance to this music.

The lyrics dealt mostly with tragic themes of crime and imprisonment, the mythic tales of our daily life in Medellín. They mixed violence and desolation with romance, passion, and bravery. "*El Preso*" (The Prisoner) was the story of a young man who laments the knowledge that he will be entombed for the rest of his days by the four walls of a jail. "*La Virgen de las Mercedes*" was about a young imprisoned drug dealer who prays to the "Virgin of Prisoners" for forgiveness and promises to reform so that he can finally see his suffering mother. Those songs were popular because many locals had spent time in jail or had a relative or a friend who had. A third song, from the Panamanian songwriter Rubén Blades, was the story of Pedro Navaja, a young man of the *barrio* who is looking for a victim to rob and meets up with a prostitute. Pedro pulls out his knife to stab her, but she is quicker and pulls out a gun and shoots him to death. "*Sorpresas te da la vida*," ("life has many surprises") goes the chorus.

As the music played in La Oasis, we would become immersed in the rhythms and the lyrics while admiring and pining for the gangsters' cars and motorcycles and hoping that some day we could own such luxuries. Some kids did get their wish; all of them did so at the expense of their lives, ending up dead or in jail.

A MOTHER'S LOVE

On a cold morning in the winter of 1978, my mother came to her job at the clothing factory on 64th Street, determined to make it a productive day. She punched her card at the entrance and silently made her way to the sewing machine in the back of the room. As she picked up the first bundle of blouses that was lying on the floor, her eyes welled up, and she was soon sobbing with anguish and pain. She'd had a difficult night and had been crying all night thinking about her two young boys growing up in a distant place and dwelling in the increasing danger on the streets in Barrio Antioquia. She could not hold back her tears.

Her friend Josefina, who was next to her, was deeply moved by the sight of my mother crying, and said, "What is wrong, Angelita? How can I help?" Her friend knew exactly why my mother was crying. This was not the first time it had happened. Josefina was also an undocumented immigrant and lived with the daily anguish of having her daughter far away in Colombia. She had also cried many times over the pain of being away from her family. This time, she said to my mother, "Don't worry, Angelita. Let me tell you of a plan so you can bring your sons to America to be with you. They can come with my daughter, Marina, and they could be here in three days." My mother looked up at Josefina with wonder and hope. She wanted to listen to what Josefina had to say.

This was not the first time that my mother entertained the idea of bringing us to America. During the early months of 1978, my parents realized that they had to make a decision concerning our future. There were two realistic choices. One option was for them to return to Colombia. The other possibility was to bring my brother and me to live with them in America. As you can imagine, this was not a simple decision. This was a crucial decision, as it would have a great impact on the rest of our lives.

They felt that America represented the opportunity of a lifetime, both for them and possibly for their children—one of those opportunities in life that rarely shows itself. This was the topic of conversation every night as they finally sat around their small table for dinner. My mother always brought up the conversation, often with tears in her eyes. During the day, they had been very busy at their jobs, but at night, they had some time, and each night, their memories would drift into thinking of their two boys in Barrio Antioquia. My mother would ask, "What if something happens to them? What if they meet the wrong person or get involved in some corrupt activity?" They had lived in Medellín and had become convinced that the situation was not getting any better. The streets were becoming more dangerous, the drug war was intensifying, and Barrio Antioquia was quickly becoming one of the most hostile places in the world.

My parents had always dreamed of providing their children with all their basic needs, as well as the opportunity of an education. Naturally, this would have been much easier in America. However, they understood that there were many obstacles that we would need to overcome. Over several years of working very hard, my parents had reached the conclusion that they would never be able to save enough money to ensure the possibility of returning to Colombia. The manual labor they performed was meagerly compensated. It was enough so that they could live here with dignity and support their family in Colombia, but it wasn't enough that they could make plans for a brighter future for their kids in our home country.

The prospect of coming to America is a dream for many people around the world. For our family, it was more than a dream; it was a necessity, both for us and for our parents. We had not seen our parents for several years. We had stayed in Colombia with our affectionate grandmothers. However, there is no substitute for the love and care of a parent. For many months, my parents struggled to make the right decision. Because they did not have legal documents, there was no possible way by which they could bring us here legally. Therefore, the only possibility would be for us to come in some other way.

The most common ways to immigrate to the United States from Colombia during this time involved one of three possibilities. First, one could attempt to get a visitor's visa from the American Consulate using a combination of false documents and bribing different officials who were officially involved in granting visas. With a visa, one could come in a plane in the usual fashion. Of course, this would have been the safest way for two young kids to travel to a distant country. This was not a realistic option for us because we were minors, and it was also more expensive than my parents could afford.

Another possibility involved coming through Mexico. As it is today, this was a very common way for Latinos to come to America, many originating from Medellín, as well as from many other cities in Central and South America. As we all know very well, this is not a straightforward trip. Although it involved traveling by land, the trip was long, dangerous, and complicated. It involved spending many days in a different country, making multiple contacts, walking across long stretches of barren land or desert, and avoiding the many people who would be trying to take advantage. In general, this was a preferred way for adults to make the trip, but not children.

The third way involved a journey across the sea—not just any ocean, but a little corner of the Bermuda Triangle. The most common way was to travel to a small island in the Bahamas called Bimini. From there, one would take a boat or a plane to the coast of Florida. This was supposed to be an easier trip. Typically, it involved having to make fewer plans and it would be quicker. This is the idea that Josefina was about to propose to my mother. Her daughter had come this way in the past, and it had worked perfectly.

In May of 1977, my mother had given birth to a third son in America. He was named Marlon. He was a cute little angel who became famous as a child for being very mischievous. Thus, he was nicknamed "Dynamite." My parents' friends thought that this was great. They would tell my mother that the birth of this baby would ease the pain of being away from the other two kids. Unfortunately, this had the opposite effect. As my mother raised Marlon and took care of him, her love for us grew more intensely. My mother missed us terribly. She could not get used to living so far away from her precious sons. She would cry several times a day, and wake up in the morning with red, swollen eyes. A phone call and letter only made matters worse. I was two years older and realized why my parents needed to be in America. But my eleven-year-old brother had no inhibitions.

"Come back, we need you." Byron cried to my mother on the telephone. "Mom, you've got to come back. I miss you so much."

"We *are* going to come back, but you have to wait a little longer," she replied, sobbing as she spoke. "We need to save money so that we can live well."

Sometimes, she would add, as a desperate bribe, "We need to work here so we can buy you toys."

No matter what she said, after these conversations she would fall apart. She would lock herself in her bedroom for hours at a time, unable to function. My father agonized just as she did, but his feelings were locked up and he would often be frustrated with my mother because she was unable to control her emotions. After much discussion over several months and tears and emotional outbursts, my parents decided to bring us to America. Now they just had to figure out a way.

After a careful review of the options, they decided my brother and I would come via the Bahamas. My mother asked Josefina for the name of the man in Medellín who could arrange the clandestine trip. His name was Uriel. The one danger, as they saw it, was the crossing of the high seas in a small boat. My parents had heard of people who had drowned or been seized making that crossing, but they also knew firsthand of people from our town, like Josefina, who had reached their destination.

"Everyone who departs from Medellín arrives in America three days later, including young kids," Josefina assured my mother. Since Josefina worked in the same factory as my mother, each day she would ask my mother, "Have you made a decision yet?" She also told my mother that her own daughter, Marina, who was now in Medellín, would be making the trip soon. My mother saw this as a great opportunity to finally convince my father to go ahead with the trip. This appeared to be the safest and most reasonable path.

Even so, my parents had some doubts. On one side, they longed to be with their sons. At times, my father discussed the possibility of returning to Colombia, but my mother realized that this was not a solution. She believed firmly that our future was here. She argued that this was the only place where two people without any education or training could possibly dream of a better life for their family. This was the place where a humble couple that worked in a factory could still feel the tranquility, self-confidence, dignity, peace, and liberty that we all desire for ourselves and our families.

My parents did not need a sophisticated education or an intricate knowledge of world history and affairs to realize that America was, in fact, a unique place. This is, in reality, what is at the center of the immigration debate in America. In general, immigrants have a great appreciation of how unique America is. We all love our native lands, but we feel passionate about America. Even my parents, who lived with the daily fear of being deported by immigration, realized that the only option would be to bring us to live here with them, even if this involved a high-risk journey across the sea. Through prayer and with the hope of a better life for their children, my parents finally decided that this was the best for all of us.

My grandmothers Rosa and Alicia were making all the arrangements. This was a busy time for all of us. My grandmother Alicia was very ill from complications of smoking and diabetes. She had recently lost a significant amount of weight. My grandmother Rosa was also ill from smoking all her life and from a condition that was diagnosed later as uterine cancer.

For several months, we attended multiple meetings with the person in Medellín who was in charge of organizing the entire trip. His name was Uriel. He lived in an upscale neighborhood in Medellín called El Poblado. We were able to make arrangements so that we could travel with Marina, Josefina's daughter. She would be the adult who would watch after us. Although she was a small woman in her late twenties and five months pregnant, she was energetic and fearless. She had spent several years in the United States until she was seized in an immigration raid and deported. Now, after several months of unemployment in Colombia, she wanted to return to the United States, even if it meant risking deportation a second time. She also wanted her baby born in America. She entertained us with glimpses of life in New York. "New York is wonderful," she would say. "When you get there, you'll eat something you can't find here—pizza. It's a big, delicious pie with cheese and tomato sauce. New York has pizza like no other place in the world."

The meetings at Uriel's house were frequent and intense. I often felt sorry for both of my grandmas to have to attend these meetings, which often lasted into the late hours of the night. We discussed every detail many times, similar to the way one would study for a final exam at Princeton University. Uriel organized every step, from getting all the documents necessary in Colombia to making all the hotel reservations and contacts in the various places. It seemed to us that each meeting brought us closer to finally making the trip that would bring us to America and to our parents.

During these gatherings, we discussed details such us how to dress, how to speak, when to talk, and what to say. It was similar to rehearsing for a well-choreographed play. We had to memorize several names and phone numbers of different contacts in different cities. They strongly recommended against writing down this kind of information because it could compromise the entire trip for everyone. We were often warned that failure to follow any of these instructions could result in being discovered. Most importantly, they repeated many times, "Do not tell anyone that you are going to New York." As you can imagine, the idea of being discovered and not reaching our destination was particularly alarming to us because it would mean not being able to see our parents at the other end.

I lost count of the number of meetings that we attended to plan every single detail of the trip, but in October of 1978, we were all ready and anxious to carry out the plan. Although I was only thirteen, I became immersed in the planning with the other adult travelers. At home, I reviewed different aspects of the trip with our grandmothers who used this opportunity to teach us many lessons about human nature and behavior. During this time, we grew closer together in our faith and understanding of God.

- - - - - - - - -

Although I received all the love, understanding, and direction that anyone would ever need, my brother and I took advantage of not having our parents around. With a group of friends, I had begun to follow the wrong path. I often missed school so that I could attend the practice sessions of my favorite soccer team, El Nacional. This was very convenient for me, since my school was located near to their practice facility. Numerous other times, I missed school to take part in some of the student protests and anti-government marches. Along with a few of my closest friends who lived on the same block, I started to experiment with drinking and smoking cigarettes. I was one of the good kids because I had not experimented with marijuana, as many of my friends had by this age. Although I had tried to keep these activities confidential, the neighborhood was very small and word of some of these actions was beginning to reach our grandmas and our parents in America. My grandmothers understood that this was only the beginning of a possible road to ruining our lives and our futures. They had seen it too many times. In fact, several of my close friends from childhood would later follow a life of crime in drug-related activities, and others were killed at a young age. Therefore, it was not surprising that both our parents and our family in Colombia sensed a feeling of urgency in making a decision to bring us into the care of our parents.

The days prior to the trip were very stressful for all of us. Our emotions were simmering with anxiety and anguish, as well as happiness. Our grandmothers were happy that we would be on our way to the land of opportunity for all. They had realized for a long time that our future in Colombia was not promising. At best, we would avoid a life of crime and live in a simple way, working in a local factory like Medias Crystal with just the basic education that everyone around us had achieved. This probably consisted of high school. The best-case scenario would be a college degree, leading to a low-paying profession. However, the risks and temptations of fast money and power were present all around us. There is no denying that many from Barrio Antioquia were the victims of this temptation and desire to achieve monetary success in the world of drug trafficking. This was the nightmare that my grandmothers were determined to avoid at all costs.

The last few days prior to the trip, we visited several people who had family members that had immigrated to the United States through the Bahamas. We spent time with them, heard their stories, and looked at pictures of relatives in the United States. With fascination and interest, we saw their pictures by places like the Statue of Liberty, the Empire State Building, the twin towers of the World Trade Center, the White House, and Coney Island.

Although we never discussed this, my grandmothers understood that if we reached our destination successfully, we probably would never see each other again. At thirteen years of age, this did not even cross my mind. At this young age, one doesn't consider such thoughts. Until this day, however, I can still feel the anguish and sadness of my grandmas as the day of departure grew closer. During the years that they had taken the role of our parents, we had grown very close. They pampered me and my brother like a pair of newborn babies. Each morning my grandmother Rosa would roll us up in a blanket as we made our way to the shower so that we would not feel the cool breezes of the morning.

– – – – – – – – –

Despite its imposing name, Olaya Herrera International Airport in Medellín was actually a single terminal building with only one major runway set among the green mountains. Entering the boarding area for international flights, I could not help but remember the times that I accompanied my mother or father before they left for what I knew would be years away in the United States. I never understood why my father had been away for most of my life. And when my mother left, I refused to cry at the airport, although I was in great anguish and despair inside as she gave us the last kisses and hugs. Now, as my brother and I showed up at the airport, there was no mother or father, though there was the hope that we would soon see both of them again.

Although we had been instructed to only allow a few people to say farewell at the airport, most of our family was there. My grandmas, aunts, several cousins, and friends came to share a few moments with us before we embarked on our journey. My grandmother Alicia was full of sorrow as she kissed and hugged us before we boarded the plane; it was almost as if she sensed with clarity that she would not see us again. "Be good to your parents," she told me. "Help them wash the dishes and take care of your little brother."

And in her last words to us, Grandma Rosa tried to keep up our spirits. "This is going to be great for you," she said. "You will have so many opportunities to go to good schools. And wait until you see the new bicycles your parents have bought for you, keep thinking of that."

Crossing the tarmac and climbing the stairs to the plane, I could see the broad terrace where relatives and friends stood to wave their last good-byes. I had been on that terrace before to see my father off and then my mother. Now I was on the other side, waving to those who were staying behind. I could not decide which circumstance was worse, being the traveler or the one left behind.

As we walked towards the plane, I could see my grandmothers crying, and waving us good-bye as best they could. My brother and I were also crying. We could no longer hold back our emotions. I wondered as I entered the plane if I would ever see them again.

As it turns out, we were not able to see in person or feel the warmth and love of our grandmother Alicia again. She passed away on December 1, 1982, after suffering the many complications of a life of poorly controlled diabetes. When I look back, I can clearly remember, as if it was today, her glance of sadness and desperation when she kissed and hugged us before we boarded the plane in Medellín just four years before her death; it is almost as if she knew with certainty that she would not see us again. Just over ten years after our trip, however, the Lord would grant us the opportunity to see our grandmother Rosa. With letters of support from Princeton, and a visitor's visa from the United States government, my humble grandmother was able to make the trip to America to be present at my graduation from Princeton University on June 2, 1989.

THE BERMUDA TRIANGLE

In the darkness of the early hours of October 27, 1978, my brother and I, along with ten other undocumented immigrants, were huddled in the bow of a small motorboat fighting against the ravages of the middle of the Atlantic Ocean—not a fair fight by far. As the boat forcefully rocked back and forth and left to right, we struggled to stay in place overtaken with fear and desperation. The darkness, the solitude of the night, and the ferocious movements of the boat were too much for us to handle. We all thought that we would die. I prayed and I begged the lord for another day so that I could see my parents. Despite our prayers, the force of the ocean seemed to get worse as each second slowly passed by in a time that felt like an eternity. One of the older ladies kept asking, "Oh my God, oh my God, how much more can this boat take?"

Our small boat was not just cruising through any sea—it was going through one of the corners of the Bermuda Triangle. Geographically, it is located between Bermuda, Puerto Rico, and Miami. It is an area of the Atlantic Ocean where a vast number of aircraft and ships have gone missing without reasonable scientific explanations. There have been many theories and explanations about the Bermuda Triangle, but in many cases, there has remained some element of doubt. One of the theories focuses on the waters off the coast of Bimini, where there is the existence of huge, underwater stone formations that may indicate the existence of an advanced prehistoric civilization: Atlantis. This is known as the Bimini Road. To some, the mystery of the Bermuda Triangle is just a myth; to others, it is an area with an unusually high rate of missing ships and planes due to unexplained forces. For us, on October 27, 1978, it represented the massive treacherous body of water that separated us from our destination; the yet-undiscovered force of the triangle was now fighting against our tiny boat. There was not much we could do, except to pray.

Except for a long delay and some minor distractions, the journey from Medellín to this point had been relatively uneventful. On the first day of travel, we stopped in Panama. There, we had a layover of a few hours. At this airport, an older man who was part of our group was held by the customs office in Panama. We never saw him again. There were rumors within the group that he may have been carrying drugs and that he was deported back to Colombia. We had also been instructed that if one person was detained, not to reveal any information that might compromise the plan for the rest of the group. We were all nervous because we knew that someone might weaken under the strain of being questioned by authorities.

From there, we boarded another plane, which made a quick stop in Jamaica before continuing over to Nassau, in the Bahamas. We spent about one hour in this customs office. We had detailed instructions about what to do and say if questioned. We were on vacation for one week. Fortunately, there weren't any delays at this airport. We were picked up by a taxicab and taken to a local hotel, where we already had reservations for the night. To keep costs to a minimum, about ten of us shared two rooms at the hotel.

The next morning we all rose early and pretended to go for a walk in one of the local markets. We had to give the appearance that we were a group of tourists enjoying the local scene. After a two-hour stroll around the town, we came back to the hotel, picked up our bags, and headed back to the airport. We then divided into two smaller groups and boarded small, six-person planes for a forty-five-minute trip to the island of Bimini, which is the farthest island in the northwest corner of this island nation. After an uneventful flight, we arrived in South Bimini at midday. We then took a taxi, followed by the boat that would bring us to North Bimini. Bimini is a set of islands located about fifty miles off the coast of Florida. It is so small that on most maps it is not even listed. The largest of the islands are North Bimini and South Bimini. North Bimini is about seven miles long and 700 feet wide. South Bimini is smaller and houses the airstrip. The downtown area in North Bimini is known as Alice Town. It consists of a small collection of shops, restaurants, and bars. Everything is connected by a single road, named The King's Highway. This was our "vacation" destination. This was the place that we had supposedly come to see. We had left Medellín to visit this tropical paradise, which Ernest Hemingway had once called home. It was the place where he had written two of his masterpieces, *The Old Man and the Sea* and *Islands in the Stream*. We had one-week tourist visas to visit this tiny seven-mile island. In reality, we did not have any plans to stay there for more than a few hours. This would just be a short stopover before proceeding to America.

After arriving at Alice Town in North Bimini, we walked half a mile to our hotel, where we had reserved two rooms. The hotel was a two-story house located in the middle of the island, right on the King's Highway. This is the only paved road on the island, which connects the main part of the island to the other places. We held a meeting and finalized plans for the remaining part of the trip. Everything was going as planned. I remember being very excited. I realized that a day later I would see my parents again.

Because Bimini is so small, you don't need transportation to get around. The leader of the group left the hotel to meet with the local contact. He had to pay this person the fee for this final part of the trip. It was about six hundred dollars per person. He collected the money from everyone and told us to stay inside until he returned with more instructions. The contact person lived half a mile from our hotel, located along the same highway. This person had already arranged to have her boat bring us to America that night. The trip had to be at night to reduce the odds of being caught by the U.S. Coast Guard as we approached our destination in Florida. Depending on water conditions, this trip would be about five to six hours. The excitement was building as we waited for the leader of the group to return and give us the rest of the instructions. This all changed when he came back with the news that we could not take to the sea that night. The weather conditions were rough and it would be too dangerous. The owner of the boat had explained how the month of October is, in fact, a very unpredictable time for the climate in this part of the world.

We did not need any explanations. We'd already had a brief opportunity to feel the strength of the sea when we had taken the small water taxi that brought us from South Bimini to North Bimini earlier that day. In fact, a couple of people in the group had become seasick during this five-minute trip. Nevertheless, we were all very sad and discouraged that our trip would be delayed. The more worrisome part of this situation, however, was that our contact did not know when it would take place. This would be dependent on a day-by-day evaluation of the weather conditions. Therefore, she arranged with the owner of the hotel for us to stay there longer and pay them daily.

It was already six at night. The local communications office, which was a short walk from our hotel, had closed. There wasn't any other way for any of us to make a call that night. Furthermore, we had been instructed not to make any calls to the United States. This might arouse suspicion amongst the local authorities. Our trip for that night had been cancelled and we had no way to inform anyone outside of Bimini. The next day, October 15, would have been our arrival day. Our parents were waiting for a call between six and nine in the morning from their friends in Florida to inform them that we had arrived safely and that they would buy our plane tickets for New York. The few hours waiting for that call and the next several days would feel like an eternity for them.

Instead, the call that they finally received was from Medellín. My grandmother Rosa had been informed that we were safe and that we were in Bimini waiting for better weather conditions. My parents and family in Colombia were also warned against attempting to get in contact with us because this might compromise the trip. We did have permission to make calls to Medellín occasionally, but not to the United States. The communications office in Bimini was a small room where any conversation was easily overheard.

- - - - - - - - -

The stage for what would occur during the next twelve days was set that first night. After having gone to bed that night, unknown individuals came to our rooms to offer their boats. They would knock on the door and tell us about different discounts they had. We had been warned that this might happen and had been told to tell everyone that we were there only for vacation and that we did not have any interest in crossing over to the United States. The people that came every night were Americans who owned small motorboats and were trying to make some extra money. If they took ten people a night, they could make about five to six thousand dollars. As time passed, and people became more anxious, some members of our group accepted these offers and departed.

We had been warned that in Bimini there were undercover immigration officers looking for people that were trying to cross over to the United States. We needed to avoid attention in the local community. The plan was simple. Every day we would get up and pretend that we were tourists. We would visit the local restaurants, beaches, and places of interest. Unfortunately, Bimini is a small island. After two or three days, we realized that we had seen most of the island. We also had a very limited budget. There would be no way for our parents to send extra money to this remote little island. My brother and I did the best that we could by skipping a meal each day and replacing it with a coconut. These grew in copious numbers in Bimini and were often just lying on the beach. We never ate at the expensive restaurants. We had our dinners at the same shops that cooked meals for some of the local workers in the marina.

Over the course of the next few days, we all got to know Bimini very well. My brother and I even started to make some friends on the island. There were a few local kids who enjoyed playing soccer out in the street. We did not speak English, and they did not speak Spanish, but we were kids and we could still play together.

After a week, our tourist visas expired. Technically, this meant that we could be caught and deported by Bahamian immigration officials. After the visas expired, we were instructed to spend most of our time indoors. This was, of course, much more difficult because it limited the way in which we could distract ourselves and forget the real reason for the trip. After spending nearly two weeks in this place, I had learned my way around. The locals were also learning too much about this group of Colombian visitors that had been there for more than a couple of days.

Probably one of the advantages of being a kid during this waiting period was that we were easily distracted by the beauty of the place. We were fascinated by the ocean. The eastern side of the island, where the boats were stationed, was calm. A few hundred feet away on the other side, it was rough, with huge waves continuously crashing against the shore. At night, however, both sides seemed to come alive, and the waters appeared ferocious. The entire night one could hear the constant noise of the waves reaching the shore. We had seen the boat that would take us on our journey. It wasn't very large. We all had somber concerns about such a small boat in these waters, especially when the boat would reach the high seas in the middle of the night. Perhaps this is the one reason that explains why we were content to wait until our contact decided that it was safe to make the trip.

In New Jersey, however, my parents were in a complete state of despair. In Colombia, my entire family was in a similar situation. My brother and I were on this tiny island, waiting for the weather to improve so that we could make the trip. We had called our grandmas in Medellín twice to let them know that we were well and to be patient. They would in turn inform our parents in New Jersey. Every day, they would wait anxiously by the phone, hoping to hear from their friends in Florida with the news of our safe arrival. For a total of twelve days, they sat next to the phone to wait for this call. All the while, they prayed and cried together. Many times, they wondered if they had really made the best decision. There was absolutely nothing that they could do. My parents were undocumented immigrants; they could not travel to Bimini and return. They could not call anyone for help.

Several times during our stay there, we were told to prepare for that night. There was not much that we really needed to prepare, since we only had two or three sets of clothes in our possession. Each time, our hopes would be shattered when the plans would be cancelled later in the day by our contact who had decided that the tide was still too high.

October 26, 1978, seemed just like any other ordinary day in Bimini. A beautiful sun and a gentle breeze, which is unlike any other in the world, lasted through the entire day. We all went through our daily routine. I was in charge of the finances for my brother and me. I counted the money in the morning. We were doing well. I had just over $1800 remaining. About $1200 would be for the expense of the boat trip. We did not get a discount for being kids. I would have six hundred dollars to help with getting a taxi ride from the place where they would drop us off to the home of our parents' friends. It appeared that my plan of saving money by skipping a meal a day had been helpful. I was not very popular with my younger brother for doing this. He would have preferred to eat at the local burger place, named King Burger, instead of surviving on coconuts.

At six o'clock that night, we received the confirmation that this would be the day. We also received all final instructions. The plan was as follows: Starting at midnight, we would leave our hotel room in pairs. There were ten of us left in the group. Each pair would stay together, walk two blocks south on King's Highway to the main entrance of the boat marina, turn left into its main entrance, and walk down about 200 feet to the end of the dock where the boat would be waiting for us. Each group would leave the hotel two minutes apart. It seemed simple enough.

In reality, it was probably the scariest short walk that I have ever taken. I was paired with my brother. We left as the third pair. The two people in front of us were far enough that we could not see them. Besides, the island was very dark. This is a small tropical island, and at night, most of the lights are off to conserve energy. There were just two small lamps at the entrance of the marina that we could use as guides.

When we reached the entrance, we were surprised to find a tall, black man with a dark coat and a large cowboy-style hat pointing us in the right direction. This had not been part of the instructions that we had received. Whoever had given us the directions had forgotten to tell us this minor detail. We had no choice; we followed his instructions. Although we did not understand what he said because it was in English, he did have a reassuring and comforting tone that put us at ease. We continued walking at a regular pace towards the end of the dock, where another person assisted us onto the boat.

The motor of the boat appeared to be off. There was only a small light on to assist with the loading of the passengers from our group. After a few minutes, we had all entered the boat and were sitting around a table in the bow of the vessel. In addition to the ten of us, two other people were already inside, and there were two people who would drive the boat.

The sitting area inside was full. The bow was big enough for the twelve of us to sit around a wooden table in its center. There was a small sink and a small room that had a toilet. No one spoke. It was very dark inside. You could not really make out the different people inside. This was probably helpful, because some of the people were clearly in a high state of panic and anxiety. The only people that could be heard were the two men out by the cockpit. They were busy making plans. There were a few small windows around the side that were covered by curtains. The small door that led into the bow appeared to be missing. We could scarcely see the outside from where we were sitting. At this time, there was not much to see. It was all darkness. This was the calm side of the island. Once inside the boat, however, you could feel that it was, in fact, not that calm.

After a few minutes, the lights inside the cabin came on. We were probably a few hundred yards away from the dock by now. I had a moment to reflect on the journey that had begun. However, it never crossed my mind that this voyage would one day take me to Princeton, Harvard Medical School, and, subsequently, into the operating rooms of a premier heart center in New York.

There was no going back. We were in this small powerboat headed in the direction of the mainland of the United States. We also realized that before reaching land, we would have to cross over this part of the Atlantic that was already famous for the mysterious disappearance of many planes and ships. In fact, some of the vessels that had disappeared were orders of magnitude larger than this tiny vessel that we were on. As I looked around at the faces of the people inside this boat, it was evident that we all feared the worst. I realized that the worst-case scenario was no longer getting caught by the American Coast Guard, but dying.

Probably the only one in the boat who did not grasp the gravity of the situation was my brother, who kept asking me questions about the boat. I initially would answer him, but stopped when I realized that I was becoming seasick.

All my life, I have suffered from motion sickness. In Colombia, I would often become carsick following any trip over an hour. The movement of this boat became unmanageable. Inside, it felt as a constant rhythmic cycle of upward elevation, followed by a sudden descent, and terminating with a loud bang that made each of us shriek in fear. Each time that we crashed against an oncoming wave, it felt as if this boat would split in half. Everyone inside the boat was praying aloud as much as we could.

We all became seasick and started to vomit. After a while, we did not even attempt to use the little room with the toilet bowl. We all just vomited everywhere. Most of us were sitting, with our heads down, praying in between the bouts of vomiting. We were all holding to something, or to someone else, to prevent from being violently thrown across the floor. Although I was severely ill, I was more fearful of the boat sinking. I had a sense of doom each time I felt and heard the sudden bang from the boat coming down against the waves.

Glimpsing outside was not reassuring. I could just see the darkness with the shadows of the white foam created by our boat. The two captains were obviously very busy trying to stay in control of the vessel. One was busy in the cockpit, and the other one using a bucket to empty some of the water that was getting into the boat. They clearly did not have any time to come down and speak to us or give us some words of reassurance. I often wonder whether this was just a usual trip for them or whether the vessel was really in danger of sinking. From my perspective—looking into the darkness of the sea in the middle of the night outside this small door surrounded by a group of people praying and sick—we were in danger. I thought of my grandmas and my parents.

As the hours passed, a few rays of light started to come in. On the other side of the small door where we had only seen darkness for several hours, light was making its way in. It was a clear day. The rocking motion of the boat decreased in its intensity. The loudness of the boat hitting the waves lessened. We all began to feel safer. We had become so dehydrated during these few hours that we could barely get up from a sitting position.

The waters were now calm, but the boat was still moving. As we approached the coast of Florida, the boat was constantly changing speeds; it would slow down at times and then rev up to very high speeds. We thought that this was probably related to attempts by our captains to avoid being detected as a suspicious boat by the U.S. Coast Guard.

Eventually, we slowed down, and some of us managed to stand up and look outside the side windows of the cabin. In the distance, I could see other boats and buildings. I realized that we were actually in American waters. For about an hour, the captains searched around for a safe place to dock. In time, we found a place.

We cleaned up our clothes as much as we could and climbed up from the cabin. It was a beautiful, sunny day. The boat stopped next to an area that appeared to be an abandoned boat dock. The captain gave us cards with information showing the name of our location. We walked for a few hundred yards and found a public telephone. From here, we called my parents' friends and informed them that we had arrived. They then called a taxi company that sent a car to pick us up and bring us to their house in Miami.

It was already October 27. My parents were again by the phone, waiting for the call from their friends. At approximately ten in the morning, they received the best news of their lives. They heard from their friends that we had arrived and we were safe. They were already arranging for us to travel to New York that night. After a thirty-minute car ride, we arrived at the house of our friends. They welcomed us with open arms. They took us into their home as if we were their own kids. We were able to get some rest, take a shower, and change into a new set of clothes. They went out and bought us the plane tickets for our trip into New York. They brought us to the airport in Miami where we boarded a flight destined for the city of our dreams.

TWO BICYCLES

On the night of October 27, 1978, Byron and I boarded a plane from Miami to Newark International Airport. It was incredible to think how we had actually made it to America, after a two-week journey filled with tears, anxiety, suspense, adventure, and danger in the high seas. I had a great sense of relief and inner peace knowing that I would soon see my parents. It had not dawned on me yet that I was now within the borders of the greatest country in the world. Although the trip took about two and a half hours, it seemed an eternity. We had seen many pictures of New York, and now we would be there in a few hours. Byron and I spent the time talking about the life that we had left behind and speculating about what our new home would be like—the tall buildings we had seen in the pictures, the enormous bridges, the snow, and the beaches. We already had an image of America in our minds, and we were now confident that we would be part of it.

Despite the many amazing changes that were in store for us, and despite the fact that we were about to enter the capital of the world, we remained fixated on riding our new bicycles—the ones that our parents and grandmothers had promised so many times. We had seen the pictures and we could not wait to get our hands on them.

Every few minutes, Byron would interrupt our conversation by reminding me about them. "Can you imagine the bicycles that our parents have for us?" We also discussed our costumes for Halloween. I wanted to be Superman and Byron wanted to be Batman. Even before arriving at the airport, we were starting to regain our childhood innocence, contemplating a normal childhood with our parents by our sides. Most of all, we talked about how nice it would be to be back in the arms of the parents we had not seen for two years. We imagined hugging our little "American" brother that we had never met, except in pictures.

As the plane approached a night-shrouded New York, we were dazzled by the lights below us, the tall skyscrapers, the soaring bridges with their necklaces of lights, the infinite magnitude of the city that seemed to go on and on without an end. From up above, it seemed as a city of lights. Even before setting foot on ground, we knew we would be living in a remarkable place. As I looked down through the small window, my thoughts drifted back to my parents. I realized that, within the colossal magnitude of this city, there were two simple people waiting for us—two dedicated, hard-working Colombians who had no documents in America, who had taken an enormous risk to be together with the kids they loved dearly, and who were dreaming of becoming part of the American dream.

Once the plane was on the ground, I could not wait to exit. I felt like a young boy who is being kept away from his toys at Christmas Eve. We were excited that within minutes—although it felt like infinity—we would see our parents. Despite our exhausting journey, we did not feel tired as we walked down the corridor towards a cluster of greeters waiting for their vacationing relatives. We did not even pay attention to the signs and posters advertising New York and the bounties of American commerce. As we approached, I was able to glimpse the faces of my parents, hand-in-hand, waving their arms and calling our names. As we approached closer and closer, tears started pouring from my eyes.

We tried very hard not to show any emotion. We had been instructed in Medellín not to make a dramatic scene until we reached our parents' apartment. We had practiced being cool. We had heard stories of people who had, in fact, been caught at the airport as they met their families.

Until this moment, we had followed all instructions religiously. But as we came closer to our parents, we could tell that they were both crying uncontrollably—their faces lush with tears and a mix of happiness and the remnants of the pain they had suffered from being so far from us for so long. They seemed like a pair of little kids who had lost their favorite toys and just found them. We forgot our instructions and started to weep as well, my lips tingling, my breathing rapid with excitement. We all embraced for what seemed like minutes, kissing one another and not saying a word. With the intense rush of emotion, we were not able to speak. The theatrical scene that we had been warned to avoid was on display right within the crowded airport, and had there been an immigration officer nearby, we probably would have been forced to join the group of unmasked travelers who end up getting deported. Can you imagine how ironic this would have been, having just risked our lives to come here, to be caught at the finish line?

There was another pleasant surprise about that reunion. In my mother's arms was a dark-haired baby, our little brother Marlon. He was our American brother, and although we had received the news in Medellín, we did not know quite what to make of it. For a time, it appeared that Marlon had become the center of my grandmothers' universe. They talked about him all the time and spent hours looking at pictures of him sent by my parents. We even daydreamed about being in his fortunate shoes, enclosed in my mother's arms and the luxuries of America. In all the pictures that my parents sent to Colombia, he was always surrounded by a multitude of toys. With some envy, we started to call him *el favorito*—the favorite. In fact, this nickname has persisted even until today. In my parents' arms at the airport, he appeared to be a cute boy, with black silky hair, dark eyes, dimples, and a sidelong, beguiling smile.

When we regained our composure, we headed to the taxi line to take the car that would bring us to our new home. As we walked, we were holding my mother's arms firmly; I was on one side and Byron on the other side. On the way to our house, my father pointed in the direction of the New York skyline, filled with a multitude of lights and huge skyscrapers. I realized for the first time why in Medellín we would also call them *rascacielos*. They really did appear to touch and scrape the sky. He pointed out each bridge we crossed or passed, so tall and arching compared to Colombia's smaller bridges.

Another thing that caught my immediate attention was the numerous traffic lights at each intersection and the large number of cars parked on the street. This was different from the streets of my town, where there were no cars parked on the street and where we spent all day playing soccer.

At about two in the morning, we arrived at a five-story, brick apartment building on 61st street, and my father gave us an animated presentation about the front door. "You see, my sons, these doors are automatic," he said. "They close on their own. Always hold that door for the next person. It's part of good manners here."

The vestibule and stairs were filthy, and near the staircase was an overflowing garbage can that had not been emptied in days. It was not what I had expected in America. We had heard that the sidewalks were full of televisions and other products that people no longer needed but that still worked well. We even imagined ourselves walking around the streets picking up some of these items so that we could send them back to Colombia.

We climbed to the second floor and entered apartment 3B. My mother took us on a tour. The place was clean and tidy, but very small. There was a cramped living room, a bedroom for my parents, and our room, which was next to the kitchen and contained a closet, a chest of drawers, and bunk beds.

More impressive than anything else were two brand-new bicycles parked along the wall that practically filled our room. We both owned bicycles in Colombia but not like these. These were *American* bicycles. The same bicycles that had consumed our thoughts for much of our plane ride from Miami. I knew how good they were because I happened to be an expert in bicycles, both riding them and building them. In Medellín, I had even put together a racing bike from scratch by buying individual parts with the one-dollar stipend my parents sent along every month. So, although this apartment was so small and we barely fit in this room, the excitement of being able to touch these bicycles made everything else insignificant. I told myself, "I can't wait to ride this beauty."

The kitchen was even smaller, with a table along the wall that could seat four people. I was particularly awestruck with how much food there was inside the refrigerator—apples, oranges, sodas, ice cream, and a gallon of milk. My grandmothers always had plenty of food in the house, but our refrigerator in Colombia was never packed like this. As I looked inside, the first object that caught my attention were the apples. In Medellín, apples were an expensive fruit. I had never eaten a whole apple before. Sometimes my grandmothers would buy a few at the supermarket. At home, we would then split them into quarters and share the pieces amongst the family. My father noticed our wide-eyed astonishment and, as was his habit, used the moment to teach us a lesson on how we might earn such a bounty.

"Here in America, both parents work, so you have to do your part in the house," he said. "Help with washing the dishes and cleaning the bathroom. Be considerate to your mother." This was the first of many lessons from our parents where they would compare our new life in America to the life that we had just left behind in Medellín. They would constantly remind us that with our newfound opportunity and privileges came responsibility and changes. In Medellín, the mother often stayed at home. Here, my mother worked full time and therefore we would have to help around the house.

By the next day, he had set up a schedule for washing the dishes. "This is how America works," he said. "We are a team and everyone has a part." He also warned us about another peculiarity of America. "You have to be careful not to make too much noise because everyone can hear what you say in the next apartment," he said. "And if you make too much noise, they'll even call the police."

After getting into bed that first night, Byron and I were overwhelmed by the images of our new country and the emotions of having reunited with our parents after so long. We could not fall asleep and talked into the early hours of the morning. We were having a hard time believing that we were actually in the United States, sleeping in the same house with both our parents for the first time in many years. And now, sleeping in their bedroom, we had a new intruder in our family, Marlon. We talked about our voyage, about how nauseated the other people smuggled in with us had become, about how scared we had been as the boat maneuvered across the rough seas in pitch darkness.

Soon we felt hungry and wanted to take an apple from the refrigerator. But we felt that in this strange house, with all its American rules, we could not do so without permission. So we woke my mother. She laughed, and then tears streamed down her cheeks.

"Of course you can have apples," she said. "You can eat anything you want. This is your house." Almost with a sense of anger, she commanded us not to ever ask her again if we could have anything from that refrigerator. "This is your house," she kept saying. She rose and stumbled into the kitchen and cut two apples in quarters, stripping away the core. As we enjoyed ourselves in the comfort of our tiny kitchen, we joked about how much better this was then our favorite snack in Barrio Antiqouia, *aguapanela,* or sugar-water, a sugar cane mixture we drank daily from a big bucket on the kitchen table.

- - - - - - - - -

The next few days were exciting and challenging. We visited a local park, Hudson County Park, and spent a day riding our American bicycles. We were surprised that we couldn't just walk outside and ride our bikes, as we would do in Medellín. Our new town was much different. The traffic on the streets of West New York is heavy and our parents felt that it was not safe for us to ride outside. So we went on a little trip to the park. I loved it. We had parks in Colombia and many beautiful natural resources, but our simple visit to Hudson County Park felt different. We felt very safe.

There was nothing like this in Barrio Antioquia—the generous expanse of manicured greenery, the lake in the middle, the little paths designed especially for bikers and skaters. It was a place where you could feel free to behave like a kid.

With all the excitement, we barely noticed how much colder the climate was than in Medellín, and over the next few days our mother had to remind us to wear a jacket before heading outside. As we strolled, we passed on gossip to our parents about their friends back home. Our parents, meanwhile, took every opportunity to show us how people in America lived and set the rules of this new road for us. Aware that we had been flirting with poor discipline before we left Medellin, my father wasted no time indicating that behavior like that would not be acceptable. The first, most important rule was that we had to do well in school. The second was that we had to respect and obey them. He made it clear that there would be no exceptions and there would be serious consequences. "These rules are not complicated, but you can be sure I'll enforce them," he said. "As long as you live under my roof, I am in charge."

It did not take me long, looking around the neighborhood and getting familiar with our building's residents, to realize we had not moved very far in the world by emigrating. There were many features of our new home that were no different from Barrio Antioquia and that echoed its spirit as well as its squalor. The building we lived in, 328 61st street, was low-income, rent-controlled, and heavily congested. It had five stories with five apartments on each floor, but many of the apartments were packed with two and sometimes three families living together. Spanish was the building's official language, and most residents didn't speak English. Neighbors were always hanging out on the corner or at our building's entrance and the stairs leading up to the entrance were always littered with cigarette butts, broken glass, and crumpled candy wrappers. Often, especially in the summer, kids would idle on the sidewalk into the late night hours, sometimes drinking or smoking. The block felt just like my street in Barrio Antioquia.

My mother was meticulous about keeping our apartment clean. However, she could not do anything about the little invaders that had set up camp within the confines of the building's walls: mice and roaches. At night, while I was studying at the dinner table, they would come alive and congregate in the kitchen, especially if the lights were out. We learned that leaving the light on in the kitchen would reduce the number of mice and roaches. If we fumigated our apartment, they would creep in from other apartments. It was a losing war, though my mother refused to give up and spent many hours cleaning our kitchen and bathroom to discourage the rodents from invading.

The floors and walls were thin and we could hear our neighbors pacing in the apartment above, and our neighbors underneath could hear us as well, especially the clumping of my little brother, Marlon, who for a time needed heavy, metallic-lined orthopedic shoes. The neighbors would make their displeasure known by banging a broomstick on their ceiling and the noise would come through our floor like a stern reprimand.

The sounds of Salsa were everywhere in our building, coming through the windows of the building that shared a courtyard with ours or up from a boom box on the sidewalk. It was the same music about prisons, drugs, gangs, and families split apart that I heard coming from the La Oasis bar in Barrio Antioquia. The music was by the same artists—Hector Lavoe, Celia Cruz, Willie Colon, Ruben Blades—and the songs were eclectic Latin American, as particular to Puerto Rico, Cuba, or Spanish Harlem as Colombia. It was not uncommon, especially on weekends, to have to fall asleep while such music blasted from other apartments.

Our building was filled with undocumented immigrants. A common joke during Colombia's April Fools'day—December 28, also known as the "Day of the Innocents"—was to knock on a neighbor's door and say that you were from *inmigracion*. We pulled this prank on our very first December 28th, knocking on the door of Josefina, the undocumented co-worker who had advised my mother about smuggling us into the country by boat. She lived in the next building and we knocked on her door, "*Somos agentes de inmigracion, por favor habra la puerta,*" we said. She apparently believed we were immigration agents, and hid silently inside her apartment for an entire day until she was certain that whoever had knocked had gone away. When my parents found out about our stunt, they were furious.

"This is not funny, guys," my mother said. "Mrs. Josefina was very nervous and became sick because she thought that immigration was looking for her." She and my father explained how devastating it could be to have a parent deported. "Just imagine what would happen if one of us was deported," my mother said. "That is why the thought of a visit from the immigration service can be terrifying," she said. We understood. We had experienced our parents' absence. Our parents also warned us to stay away from areas where it appeared that people were being questioned, and if we saw any activity like that to return to the apartment immediately.

"If they get us, we can all end up in Barrio Antioquia again, even Marlon," my father said. "Never speak to anyone about visas, or immigration, or answer any questions from strangers." I understood the idea of us getting sent back to Colombia, since America was not our native country after all. However, the idea of my little American brother having to go to Colombia seemed unjustified. He was born here in America. I wondered about how it could be his fault that his parents did not have documents.

I realized then that this was not a joking matter. This was a serious situation. This was one of our first lessons on a long process of becoming an expert at avoiding the immigration service and learning how to stay out of trouble and keep a low profile. I now understood that although I was calling America my new home, that my existence here was far from definite. I started to realize that my family and I were dwelling in the shadows of the real America.

A NEW LANGUAGE

The first Monday after we arrived in America, my mother woke me up early in the morning. Our first few days had been exhausting. We had been busy all weekend learning about the rules in America and riding our new bicycles. Sunday night, I had slept like a baby—until I suddenly felt my mother pull the blankets away and in a firm voice say, "Get up, kids, the vacation is over; you need to start school." As I slowly opened my eyes to the bright lights that she had just turned on, I felt like asking my mother to let us sleep a little bit more. My grandmother Rosa in Colombia would definitely have given us a few more minutes in the comfort of the warm bed and the blankets. Almost as if by instinct, I realized that this was not a good idea, and that I should just get up out of bed. I realized that things were about to change and our life was about to take a different direction.

I silently turned to face my mom and slowly dragged my body out of bed and proceeded to the bathroom. As I passed the kitchen, I noticed that it was still dark outside. I didn't know what time it was, but I had a feeling that it was still in the middle of the night. I asked my mom, "Where is Dad?" She responded, "He is already at work, and I need to bring you guys to school so that I can also get to my job." As Byron followed me out of bed, my mother was there with us, rushing us along in a calm but deliberate manner. "Hurry up, guys, we have a lot to do."

That first morning was the start of a well-orchestrated plan that my parents had for us. The fact is that immigrant parents already have a plan for their kids—it is called "an education." All immigrant groups see this as the vehicle to a better life. My parents were not any different. They had agonized over the decision to smuggle us into America so that we could get a better education. So, my mother took Byron and me to school to register us for the new school year, which had begun a few weeks before.

That morning, as we dressed up and got ready, I looked at my mother and I could sense urgency in her actions. She was determined to incorporate us into the American way of life immediately.

Public School #1 in West New York was a typical four-story brick public school building, no different than other American schools in major metropolitan cities. When I first saw the school, I was astounded by its great size, much bigger than my old school in Medellín. Once inside the building, I was impressed by how shiny the floors were, which almost reflected our faces as we walked. Everything seemed so organized. We strode into the main office early in the morning, and with the help of an interpreter, my mother filled out the necessary forms. She then hugged us farewell before heading for work.

"*Se tienen que comportar bien* (you need to behave well)," she said as she embraced us and left. Yes, it was that quick. My mother trusted the school system and left us in its care. She had confidence that we would thrive in it.

I wanted to ask my mother to stay longer, but I did not. I felt the need to be strong, to give my mother peace of mind, and to set an example for my younger brother. Byron and I were now alone with people we did not know and whom we did not understand. We sat silently on a bench outside the principal's office, waiting to meet with him and observing the different people coming in and out of the office. We did not know what to expect. We were frightened and wanted to cry, but we didn't because we were determined to do as our parents had instructed us.

I heard people all around speaking a flood of incomprehensible words, and harsh foreign sounds boomed from the school's loudspeakers. Just a few days before, we were wondering if we would survive the rolling, furtive journey across the Bermuda Triangle, and now we had a journey almost as formidable: learning to grow comfortable in a new land where people spoke a frightening tongue. I knew I would have to master it if I were to find new friends and take advantage of all the opportunities my parents had spoken so glowingly about.

When we were called into his office, the principal, Mr. Grasso, with an interpreter at his side, welcomed us. He was concise and sober and I found his words, as translated somberly by his female assistant, quite intimidating. "Welcome to your new home," he said. "We have many things to offer, but you have to behave and follow the rules. Otherwise, you will be suspended."

There was no hint of warmth in his face. He was all business. One of his assistants then escorted us through the wide halls to our classroom on the second floor. Everything was so different and intimidating that we felt like prisoners being escorted to their cells. I was just in a daze as we walked past the classrooms with students learning their lessons. Byron and I were sent to the same teacher and his name was Mr. Cardenas. He was a white man from Cuba who spoke Spanish with an accent that was different than what I was accustomed to, but which I could easily understand. He spoke in a firm, humorless, commanding voice, signaling to the students that he was in charge and we were his subjects.

Mr. Cardenas was giving a history lesson in Spanish to a room filled to the brim and asked us to be seated in the back, but there weren't any empty desks. So my brother and I shared a table at the back of the room, which we did for several weeks. Mr. Cardenas leafed through our school documents and briefly introduced us to the class. He also took a couple of minutes to explain his rules. This was an English as a Second Language class. Half the time we learned English, and the rest of the time we studied subjects like math and social studies in Spanish. Many of the kids in this class were extremely rowdy, and Mr. Cardenas had no choice but to be tough.

All around me, I heard students speaking foreign sounds. I felt as an outcast much of the day. I had learned a few English words in a sixth-grade course in Colombia, but these hardly made a difference. Learning a new language seemed overwhelming. My parents did not speak English, having always lived in the United States in communities where daily life was conducted in Spanish. In West New York, most of the residents were Cuban, Mexican, and South American; almost all were immigrants or children of immigrants.

My parents often lamented not having taken the time to learn English, blaming their fatiguing jobs. But they also did not need the language because they could survive very well with Spanish. Their friends spoke Spanish. There were Spanish newspapers and radio and television shows galore. They could shop along Bergenline Avenue in food, clothing, and furniture stores where all the salespeople spoke Spanish and where the products—like rice, beans, plantains, and tortillas—were often imported from their home countries. They could even conduct government business with Spanish-speaking bureaucrats.

In contrast to my parents, and many immigrants from Latin America, the European immigrants of the twentieth century were forced to adapt more quickly to their new language. These immigrants realized that being able to communicate in English would be essential if they wanted to thrive. My parents, even if they did not feel any desperation to do so themselves, realized that it would be essential for their children to master the language quickly.

As I looked around the ESL classroom, I noticed there were kids of different ages from a number of Spanish-speaking cultures—from Puerto Rico, the Dominican Republic, Mexico, and Colombia—all lumped together in the same room. Although this was an idea with good intentions, there were many practical problems. First of all, the classroom was crowded with over forty students and Mr. Cardenas did not have an assistant. Then the academic levels were different. My brother and I were placed in the same classroom even though we were two grades apart. We were learning the same subjects at a level that was often much too low for me and too advanced for him. In class, we fell comfortably into Spanish, just as our parents had found it easy to speak Spanish in the neighborhood. This did not help our acquisition of English.

The students in the class enjoyed spending time with one another because we all had similar backgrounds and interests. However, the rest of the school looked at us as outsiders and referred to us as the "refugees." Indeed, our class was known as the "refugee class." We became the target of ridicule and of practical jokes based on our ignorance of English. As you may imagine, for a teenager this was incredibly stressful.

On some occasions, my brother and I lost our tempers and ended up in fistfights with other students. One time, an older Puerto Rican boy taunted Byron and me about our refugee accents. When the teacher, Mr. Cardenas, slipped outside the classroom, Byron, who had a short temper, jumped on the boy and started punching him. I ran over to help, and the boy's friends joined to help him. The teacher walked in, stopped the brawl, and sent us all to the principal, Mr. Grasso, who informed my parents. My mother was the unlucky one who had to come to school to hear about her unruly son. My father's boss was so rigid that he would have fired him if he took a few hours off.

There was constant pressure from my parents to learn the language. "This is the only way that you will ever get ahead in life and be able to get into a university," they told us. At times, we thought their demands unfair because they really had not made the effort to learn the language themselves. They would only allow us to see the English television channels while they would watch the soap operas on the Spanish networks. But my mother used her own ordeal as a cautionary tale of what could happen if we didn't learn English. "You will end up working in a factory for twelve hours a day just like us," she said.

Soon, I began picking up the formalities of the new language and did well on the written exams, both in spelling and reading comprehension. But I struggled with conversations and with the pronunciation of words we were learning. I would often shy away from asking questions in class and speaking in English. If I knew that someone spoke Spanish, it was much easier to resort to it.

One of the first sentences that I learned in English was a defense mechanism: "No speak English." I found this phrase very useful. People would react sympathetically, be more forgiving of my clumsiness, and make a more concerted effort to communicate, at times speaking in Spanish or slowing down. Then, just as I was gaining confidence, someone would ask me to repeat something with an unsympathetic "what?" It felt like someone had thrown a bucket of cold water on my head.

In the days after we arrived, there was what seemed like a honeymoon period with my parents, a harmony that seemed to envelop our re-acquaintance in America. But news of our conflicts or failures in school kept making their way home and that honeymoon shattered.

Kind and gentle as she was, my mother was determined to keep our conduct in check, and over the next few months we gave her many chances. Our teachers sent home many notes informing them that we were not doing well. One time, my mother was warned that if we were involved in one more fight, we would be suspended for ten days. She was so shaken that she started crying. I was deeply moved by the sight of my mother in tears and promised her and the principal that I would change, but change did not come quickly.

As the poor grades and warning notes from school piled-up, the stress and the tension in my house increased. My mother displayed the vision, leadership, and strength that even then gave us optimism. Although she only went to school until the third grade, she had a gift for communication and understanding that many of us don't acquire even with a college education. She wouldn't withhold information from my father regarding some disciplinary or academic problem, but she presented it in a constructive way so that my father would see the problem as an issue to be solved rather than one requiring punishment. My mother realized that I was sincere and that I was trying to adapt and do well in school. She made my father understand this, instead of having him concentrate on the ultimatum that the principal had given us.

My father reminded us of some obvious facts. We had been given the chance of a lifetime by coming to the United States, and if we squandered it, we would end up exactly where he was— working in a factory twelve hours a day for the minimum wage. We, of course, had heard this line of wisdom before and knew its source. Although this was a rather simple message, it was a very powerful one. We witnessed firsthand how hard our parents worked, and we wanted to do better.

In time, my parents' drawn-out lectures seemed to have an effect. I found myself thinking long and hard about how I could turn things around. Education, I knew, was my only ticket out of my parents' vulnerable lives as undocumented immigrants.

The hurdles only grew taller when I made the transition into a regular seventh-grade class. The ESL class was growing too large for one teacher, so the school placed the students making the most progress into regular English-speaking classes. I was one of those chosen for the switch. My first American teacher was a hero and a savior. Mr. Sullivan was a tall, sturdily-built man with brown hair, green eyes, and a well-trimmed beard. He had a lovely sense of humor. He instinctively appreciated my troubles. At times, he would slow the lesson and repeat an idea or passage and that would give me enough time to write down what he said or take some notes. It was subtle, but I felt he was taking the trouble just for me. I was sure that this was the case because I could see him glancing in my direction as he was giving the lesson. Through him, I started to experience the greatness of individual American humanity, compassion, and generosity that make America the greatest country on earth.

Nevertheless, I felt in a world of solitude. After so much discipline, fear, and threats, I became one of the silent kids who seldom spoke up in class and rarely spoke to other students. I had very few friends, kept to the sidelines, and avoided situations that I feared would be trials for me.

To do better on tests, I learned to memorize long paragraphs of information, even if I really didn't understand the material. I also decided that I would concentrate on the subjects that I found the easiest. I did particularly well in mathematics where the language of numbers and symbols was universal and where English instructions mattered less. Two of the brightest and more respected students in the class, James Albright and Steve Piccini, were often helpful. I think they liked the fact that I was quiet, did not threaten them, and was starting to show that I was a good athlete in gym. They left me alone and teased or picked on other students; they took a shine to me and made me feel more at home. I really wanted to learn, but I also wanted to fit in, to share in my classmates' conversations, and to be part of the crowd. Incidentally, James Albright later became Madonna's famous bodyguard and lover in the early 1990s.

Slowly, my work and discipline began to improve. The only dissenting voice was my English teacher. She was concerned that my level was too far below that of my grade. She often threatened my mother that I would not be able to make it to the next level. I felt helpless. I had been able to solve the problem with my discipline, but I thought that acquiring full command of the language would take more time. In some ways, I thought that it was unjust to expect someone to become proficient in English at an eighth-grade level in just one year after coming here from a foreign country. But I didn't have a choice, so I studied long into the night. At the end of my first academic year, I only managed to get a conditional promotion. I had to attend summer school, and my parents had to pay for it.

For most people, this would not have been a large expense, but for my parents it was enormous. We were scarcely getting by with what they earned in their factories. They were still paying off the expenses of our stealthy voyage to Florida. But my parents understood how important it was that I succeed. We skipped some of our weekend outings and withdrew money from their savings. I made a promise to myself that I would master the new language, and the summer turned out to be very productive. I made some strides and was ready for eighth grade. But I was still far from being a fluent speaker.

One weekend during our first summer, we went to the Jersey shore town of Seaside Heights. We had a splendid day at the beach, followed by carnival rides and amusement games that lasted too far into the night. We needed to find an inexpensive hotel room and searched around. My parents sent me into each hotel to ask about their rates for the night. In one, I came back to tell my parents, "Dad this is great. The night at this hotel only costs sixteen dollars." My father was thrilled, and we all rushed into this hotel. We spent the night there, but in the morning it turned out that the night had cost us sixty dollars, not sixteen. I misunderstood the clerk at the hotel. My father was very upset to have to pay sixty dollars, half of his weekly salary. He did not understand how I had been here for several months and still confused these two simple words. It would not be the last time that my parents depended on me as their translator and facilitator in the English-speaking world and I disappointed them.

SMOKING IN A ROOM

I remembered exactly the way my room had looked in Medellín. At night it was dark and silent. Everyone in the house asleep, and I on my bed with a cigarette between my fingers. I was only thirteen years old and had wanted to learn how to smoke so that I could fit in with my group of friends, who were smoking cigarettes already. I wanted to be "cool."

As a new teen growing up in Barrio Antioquia and separated from my parents by thousands of miles, I felt free to look for new adventures. Many of my friends had already learned to smoke cigarettes, and had started drinking alcohol. I felt intense pressure to fit in and learn. To accomplish this, I would steal my grandmother Alicia's cigarettes from her room and, in the quiet of the night, when everyone was asleep and the doors were closed, I would light up a cigarette and smoke. I would pretend that I was there with my friends, getting compliments about my ability to smoke. I did the same with my friends during the festive holidays in December, taking sips of alcohol with friends.

One night, in bed lighting up a cigarette, my mind drifted to thinking of my humble parents, and I felt terrible that I was doing this. My parents would have been devastated if they had seen me. What a tragedy! They were killing themselves working in the factories of America as undocumented immigrants so that

I could have a better life, and I was more concerned about fitting in with my so-called friends. I had tears in my eyes, but I continued. I really wanted to fit in and be part of the group.

Now in America, I was still drawn to the lively, cheerful camaraderie of friends, even if that landed me into mischief that would anger my parents. Those feelings only grew more intense as a newcomer to this country, especially in my case because I felt different from the kids who were here already. It was important for me to stop being an outcast on the American scene. It was important for me to be part of the group, and on the streets of West New York, I found other Latino immigrants or children of immigrants who felt as I did, who wanted to be accepted and noticed in a country where they felt so marginal and insignificant.

So, of course, we went about it the wrong way. It took time for my rebellion to take shape. I came here in the fall and had to cope with weather I had never experienced before. Medellín has a very stable spring-like climate all year long. It is warm, but not humid, the ideal climate to enjoy sports and the outdoors.

The first winter here, of 1978-1979, was extraordinarily cold. Although I was dazzled by the first snowfall and enjoyed playing with it, its charm soon dimmed. Having to spend precious minutes putting on thick, heavy jackets and boots, I found myself wishing for the times when I could simply walk outside my house and meet my friends for a game of soccer. In the United States, we had to stay indoors much of the time. Our apartment complex was overcrowded, and our own apartment was cramped. Even the streets were far more congested than back home in Barrio Antioquia. Here, streets were lined with automobiles parked on both sides of the roadway. Traffic was heavy all day and into the night. The snow seemed to slow everything down and make every activity more burdensome. So, when the days started to lengthen and grow warmer, I found my spirits bursting out, and not always in rewarding ways.

The summer afforded us the time and the freedom to spend time outdoors and to be alone for long periods. I was fourteen and my brother was twelve, and we were spared the duty of taking care of our younger brother, Marlon. So both my parents could work, he was taken each day to a Colombian neighbor, Mrs. Fanny. She was an older Colombian woman who lived across the street in a fourth-floor apartment facing ours. She took care of two or three children at a time for little money. Marlon hated going there and would cry each time we left him. Mrs. Fanny not only enabled my parents to work, but through the front window of her apartment she could look across the street and keep an eye on us, too.

During this first summer in America, I would wake up early for my course in English. It would be over by the afternoon and I would have the rest of the day to wander the town of West New York with my friends. We were basically decent kids with working parents, and we simply had no outlet for funneling our high spirits and energy into something worthwhile. My parents could not afford day camps or other educational programs. We were young, we did not have video games, our parents were working, and we wanted excitement.

One summer day, we decided—for no sensible reason—that we would throw glass bottles at the entrances of different shops and run away. We dared one another to take turns doing so. The idea was to leave a pile of shattered glass that the owner would have to clean up. Who came up with this brilliant scheme I no longer remember. The idea worked smoothly at the first few stores, and we dashed away, laughing merrily at our feat. However, the owner of the grocery on the corner of 57th Street and Hudson Avenue was young and fast enough to catch my brother. Byron was adventurous and fearless and usually protected me in street fights in Barrio Antioquia, even fighting against bigger kids. But this man was stronger—seized him by the collar, and dragged him back to the store, threatening to call the police.

When we realized that he had been left behind, we returned to the store to plead with the owner. The owner realized that we were not budding lawbreakers and after several minutes of discussion with us, agreed to release my brother. Before we left, we had to clean up the glass, and promise that we would never do this again. We had a great sense of relief, and we abandoned this activity forever. My father would have seriously punished us if this man had called the police on us. I doubt that I would be telling you this story if my father had discovered what we had done at that time.

As if things could not get any worse, I also wanted to drink alcohol. One afternoon during that long summer, a group of us went to visit Marta and Maria, the two Colombian school-mates our age. Their parents were working and news soon spread among our crowd of an empty apartment. Around twenty teen-agers gathered there to dance to disco music. The sisters were expert dancers and had mastered all the steps from *Grease* and *Saturday Night Fever*. They taught us some of those steps, and soon, we were dancing away. In the fevered excitement, someone suggested we drink hard liquor—our native brew, *aguardiente*. It is a very strong, mint-flavored drink that produces an immediate burning sensation in the esophagus and fortifies the sense of doing something daring. One kid had a drink and then another and I started drinking, also. After three to four hours, I had drunk myself into near unconsciousness. Several friends had to help me stagger home and they put me to bed.

My mother came home from work two hours later to find me in bed. "Why are you sleeping so early?" she asked, shaking me awake. As she drew closer, she smelled the answer. The alcohol on my breath also explained the pool of vomit she had seen at the front door of the building, which she had blamed on some unknown neighbor. No, it was her own son who was responsible, and she was very upset. She got a leather belt and lashed me several times, crying and telling me how disappointed she was. "You will not get anywhere like this," she screamed. "This is not the reason that we worked so hard to bring you to America."

She gave me a good beating with a thick leather belt and made me take a shower. When I came out and dressed, she handed me a broom and made me sweep not only the front steps but all the building's hallways. As I did so, I worried about the next phase. What would happen when my father learned about my escapade? That night, while we were in the living room, she told him. This time he took a different approach. He did not beat me, but grounded Byron and me for the summer. We had to come home every day after our English course and remain at home through bedtime.

In general, my mother informed my father of our misbehavior at night before he fell asleep. She figured that at this time, my father would have less energy to wake us to discuss our actions. During the night, he would also have some time to reflect and let his anger cool. In those days and in our culture, it was customary for parents to give you a firm whipping with a belt if they wanted to teach you a lesson. My father would come into our room, tell us to find a belt and bring it to him, and then he would start belting us. Fortunately, this only happened a few times in my life. Each time that he did, he felt guilty. He felt worse than we did. He also realized, with time and experience, that he was more effective when he took the time to speak to us and teach us a lesson. Unfortunately, I gave him many opportunities.

Life in America seemed to be getting more complicated by the day. The carefree days playing soccer in the streets of Barrio Antioquia seemed so far in the past. Although I was now with my parents and I felt safe from violence in the streets, I felt the weight of my parents' demands on my shoulders. My parents wanted me to learn English and do well in school. My teachers expected my reading level to be on par with that of my classmates. Americans expected the rule of law. It seemed as if everything I did was inadequate. I was getting into trouble in school, drinking with friends, and getting into mischief in the street. Life in America was not simple after all.

Their sons' first summer in America had been hard for my parents. There had been vandalism, shoplifting, and fistfights. Almost on a daily basis, my father would return home from a hard day of work only to hear about some trouble we had gotten into. Sometimes, he wondered if he had waited too long to bring us to America, if we had been permanently ruined by the street life of Barrio Antioquia. However, he was not yet ready to give up on us.

My clever father had other powerful methods of teaching us how to mend our ways. He would have me visit his embroidery factory and take a few minutes to show me his working conditions—the dark, airless building, crammed with clanging embroidery machines, a tomb without air conditioning that sweltered in summer. I knew he spent twelve to fourteen hours there every day and that made me sad. He would caution me that if I didn't take advantage of America's opportunities, I would end up in a factory like that.

These conversations slowly began to have an impact. This did not happen on a single day, but it slowly evolved over the course of several months through many trials and tribulations. However, by eighth grade, my second year of school in America, I had started to correct my behavior. For the next five years, through my senior year of high school, I never missed a day of school. Even when I was sick, I would show up in class. My parents never got a note home again. We had worked our problems out as a family.

My parents understood, through their own hard-won experience, that growing up for most children is a winding road with rises and dips, triumphs and setbacks. They immersed themselves in their children's lives even if it meant sleepless nights and painful confrontations. They treated us with infinite affection and love similar to that shown the prodigal, squandering son in my favorite parable from the New Testament. The father explains the significance of atonement to the resentful older brother who had never disobeyed his father's orders. "This brother of yours was dead and is alive again; he was lost and is found" (Luke 15: 11-32).

My parents' methods worked with my brother Byron, too. For a period of several months during his junior year in high school, he dropped out of school and left the house to be with friends. For several months that felt like an eternity to my mother, we were not sure where he was living. But he came to realize that he had made a mistake, and when he returned home, he was welcomed with open arms. He finished his high school education and was able to straighten up his life.

A FRIEND

Our first Memorial Day weekend celebration in America was special. After a long, cold winter, this day turned out to be unusually warm and sunny, and Byron and I walked to Bergenline Avenue, West New York's main street, to see our first American parade. As we watched the veterans and military groups march by, marveling at their stately uniforms and clockwork pacing, we were approached by a skinny, bright-eyed, brown-haired boy whose name was William Posada. He was standing behind us, watching the parade, and overheard us speaking in Spanish. When he noticed the subtle distinctions of tone and rhythm that are characteristic of the Colombian accent, he approached us and asked, "Are you guys from Colombia?"

I answered, "Yes," and added, "we lived in Medellín and just moved to West New York a few months ago." William proceeded to tell us all about himself. We connected as friends immediately. Byron and I loved this kid right from the start. Although we had been instructed many times by our parents not to give any information to strangers, especially about our immigration here, we recognized instantly that William was someone that we could trust. He was warm, friendly, and sincere. If he didn't like something, he would tell you. He was an only child who lived with his mother after his parents' divorce. He had come to America as a toddler—legally—with a visa that his mother had secured. He seemed well educated for his age and unusually courteous, always greeting my parents with a brisk, "Hi Mr. and Mrs. Fernández! How are you doing today?" However, he was also full of fun, dashing about and speaking very quickly as if he were in a perpetual hurry. He was always coming up with some novel way that we could amuse ourselves. One week, his enthusiasm was boxing, another, it was weight lifting or roller-skating or gymnastics.

His mother worked two or three jobs at a time to make ends meet, including the night shift as a cleaner in an office, and so was seldom at home. Nevertheless, she was entirely devoted to him. One time, William and I were practicing some karate moves and he decided we should haul his mother's mattress to the park so we could practice falls.

"William, you must be crazy!" I said as we were dragging the mattress to the park. "Your mother is going to kill you."

"No, she loves me too much to do that," he said.

Over the next few months, he would become a best friend to Byron and me. The three of us became inseparable. If William thought other boys were poking fun at our accent, he would tell them, "Hey, give them a break! They just got here from Colombia." William found in us a larger family, and we found in him someone who could guide us through the social delicacies of life in a new country.

One of the groups marching in the parade was Boy Scouts Troop #129, West New York's troop. We watched with fascination and envy as these boys in decorated light green uniforms marched in near-perfect formation, proudly bearing the flags of the United States, the Boy Scouts, and Troop #129. We tagged closely behind the troop until their march ended at the town hall on 60th Street and soon found ourselves chatting with the Scouts and the Scoutmaster, William Harris. He gave us a lively picture of what the troop did and what was required of its members, and on the spur of the moment, the three of us decided to sign up.

We met on Friday nights at the American veteran's hall on 57th Street and Boulevard East with a captivating view of the nighttime Manhattan skyline. Mr. Harris was a tall, strong man who had fought in the Vietnam War, and he ran our troop like a real-life army unit. He was a strict disciplinarian and, at the same time, a gentle and sensitive leader who was always available to listen to our problems and offer advice. He often brought along some of his veteran friends to give us instructions in drill, camping, hiking, and emergency preparedness. I often thought that Mr. Harris believed that the war was not really over and that he was training a group of young soldiers to survive in battle.

We would start each meeting by reciting, in unison, the Scout oath and law, then split into four patrols, each with about five or six Scouts and a patrol leader, to practice our Scout skills like tying knots and first aid. I showed an early talent for both. At the end, we would put everything back in place, always leaving the place so spotless that no one would guess that a group of kids had just spent two to three hours there.

I loved knots. My English was already strong enough to read the Scout handbook, and I would envision the steps needed for a particular knot and repeat in my mind, "The square knot—right over left, and left over right." I might practice tying that knot hundreds of times for hours, soon becoming one of the speediest knotters in my troop.

The fastest was actually Byron, who represented our troop at the regional competitions. Now, knot tying is a big part of both of our lives—for me in suturing and other fine surgical procedures; for him, in fastening together the scaffolds that allow workers to climb the walls of tall buildings. I also became an expert in first aid, memorizing the passages from the Scout handbook for treating a broken bone or snakebite. I would sharpen my skills in contests we would have among the patrols, and soon I represented my troop at the first aid competitions.

I took special pleasure in wearing the Scout uniform. I would spend hours looking at the handbook, with its illustrations by Norman Rockwell, to make sure that my uniform was crisply pressed and neatly arranged. Mr. Harris demanded nothing less. I loved wearing the uniform during parades. I was very proud of wearing the sash displaying all the merit badges I had earned. I felt a deep pleasure in belonging to this select group.

I cherished the chances for weekend hikes and camping trips. Once a month, we would leave West New York on a Friday night and spend the weekend at campsites in Alpine, New Jersey, the Delaware River Water Gap, or the Poconos in Pennsylvania. I especially looked forward to canoeing for fifteen miles or more along the Delaware, relishing gliding through the white waters with the spray of cool water in my face or weaving through rocks and sandbanks. How different this was from the gritty clamor of West New York. What a wonderful escape into wilderness and beauty. And how nice it was to feel we kids could run our own lives—under the watchful eye of Mr. Harris, of course—with reliance on our own judgment. Here we could put into practice all the skills we were learning—putting up tents, tying knots, starting campfires, cutting wood, cooking, swimming, fishing, and hiking. We became experts at orienting ourselves in the woods with our compasses and figuring out how to get to different points. We learned how to work in groups, to trust our companions, and to work hard to gain their trust.

We cooked our own food and that allowed us to give our troop a taste of traditional Spanish flavor. My brother and I made *tostones* by peeling plantains, cutting them into one-inch pieces, frying them in oil until they were golden brown, and crushing them into a tortilla-like shape.

"I don't think that those bananas will taste good in that oil," Mr. Harris demurred. But we sprinkled a little salt on top and gave them to him and he loved them. He had a hearty appetite.

I enjoyed the long nights by the fire, singing Scout songs and telling stories past midnight, like the tale of "Indian Joe"—an ancient Scoutmaster whose son had disappeared in the wilderness and whose ghost still materializes at night searching for the lost boy. Several times, we camped out in winter. This was especially tough for my brother and me because our sleeping bags were the cheapest available at the local camping store—all that my parents could afford—and the cold would seep through the thin fabric. We didn't have clothing made of space-age fabrics to keep out the cold. We had to wear our own everyday winter coats and sweaters. At one point, I even put together my own backpack, following the detailed Scout handbook instructions and assembling it from scratch from materials I bought. During many of our meetings, Mr. Harris would say, "You have to be prepared for the worst—you never know when you will be out there in battle." He acted at times as if we were actually in a battle, getting ready to face the enemy.

Over time, I felt that I was not just part of the group, but a significant player. It didn't matter that I had a heavy accent, that I was South American, or—though the other boys didn't know it—that I was undocumented. I was good at tying knots and first aid. The campsites did not feel like a foreign country; the Scouts did not feel like foreign friends. Here, they did not call us "refugees." At school, many of my friends did not think that it was cool to be a Scout, and I did not go around announcing my membership or parading in my uniform. But if other students found out, I was not embarrassed. In our troop, we all followed the example of our great junior Scoutmaster, Jorge Moya, one of the high school's best baseball players. He was a well-built six-footer, so strong that a group of other Scouts could not pull him to the floor in our wrestling games. He was proud to be a Scout, he was popular in school, and his excitement about the Scouts was contagious.

During our meetings, we would recite the Scout Oath, which made me promise the following:

> On my honor I will do my best to do my duty to God and my country and to obey the Scout law, to help other people at all times, to keep myself physically strong, mentally awake, and morally straight.

At first, the oath did not seem that meaningful. Slowly, the program itself put these principles into action. I was learning to model the qualities the Scout law demanded—to be trustworthy, loyal, helpful, friendly, courteous, kind, obedient, cheerful, thrifty, brave, clean, and reverent. Subtly, without my realizing it, Scouting was tinkering with my character and strengthening my desire to make something of myself and become a better person. It was enhancing the code I was picking up at the dinner table from my parents and that I had absorbed from my grandmothers. After many setbacks, I was coming to the conclusion that at the end of the day, it was my life and my well being that were at stake. I was the one who was responsible for my actions.

My parents were pleased that Byron and I were Scouts, not just because we were developing strong self-discipline, but because we were immersed in a pursuit that American society valued and that left us with a strong work ethic and a solid moral foundation. Our membership enhanced whatever sense they had of belonging. I even began dreaming of a future at West Point, even researching what it took to gain admission. I soon found out that American citizenship was a fundamental requirement for getting into West Point. I wrote President Ronald Reagan to ask what he could do to help me, and after several months I received an answer from the State Department telling me that I absolutely had to be a citizen to qualify.

Scouting became a passion. I worked diligently and steadily at earning all the possible merit badges. With hard work, I could easily progress up the ranks: Scout, Tenderfoot, Second Class,

First Class, Star, Life, and finally Eagle Scout. I did not accomplish this by myself, but did it with other Scouts who shared the same zeal; we pushed one another along. The work and commitment bore fruit. We became, by far, the best troop in the region, routinely garnering the top awards in Scouting skills. Four members of my troop made Eagle at the same time, an almost unprecedented feat for our region.

The Eagle Scout graduation ceremony on May 27, 1983, was a special event for me. I was proud to join in the celebration with the three young men who had led my troop for several years, Jorge Moya, Hector Moya, and Bill Harris, the son of the Scoutmaster. As I was up on stage, receiving my award, I could not help but think of my dear friend William, who was not there with us but should have been. He had been there with us from the start when I first felt that rush of excitement as Troop 129 marched down Bergenline Avenue carrying its colorful flags. But something terrible had happened along the way.

_____

On an early December evening in 1980, William, my brother, and I were walking home after our weekly Scouts meeting as we usually did, heading from Boulevard East, up 57th Street, towards Bergenline Avenue in the center of town, then going our separate ways. This particular night we stopped at the corner and talked for over an hour. William had just started his freshman year at Memorial High. With his bright, dark, hopeful eyes framed by his curly dark hair, he spoke vividly about plans for the year. He seemed to dawdle, probably not wanting to go home to that empty house. His mother was not home; she was at her second job. He invited us to come over for a sleepover. We would have been glad to go, but our father had given us strict orders to return home after the meeting, so we waved William farewell.

At four in the morning, my mother woke us. "Where is William?" she wanted to know. William's mother could not find him. After working late, William's mother had arrived home to see the two-story house consumed by flames, my mother told us. We told her we did not know where William was, dreading what that meant. There was no answer to William's whereabouts for another two hours because the fire had been so intense that it was difficult to search. When the building had cooled down and the smoke diminished, the firemen did make a painstaking search. William's body was found in his bedroom closet. He probably had been awakened by the smoke, sought an escape route, and could only make it to a closet. I was deeply, deeply shaken and I don't think I ever felt so much pain. My brother and I cried for days. I felt a sense of profound emptiness that this calamity could happen to someone so young. For years, I felt guilty that Byron and I had not slept over at William's house. Perhaps we could have saved him. He was a great friend and would have surely been with us at that final ceremony, graduating as another Eagle Scout.

A year after that, there was another fire, and this time the Scouting lessons that Byron and I learned probably saved our lives and that of our then unborn brother. My parents had decided that they were not going to have any more children. We were not only in this country without documents but were living in a small two-bedroom apartment that required Marlon to sleep in my parents' bedroom. But my mother, who was almost 35, missed a period, and a doctor's visit confirmed that she was, indeed, pregnant. "Fine, my love, we must pray that the baby is healthy and things go well," my father said.

In time, they were excited about the idea of a new baby—they felt that this was a gift from God, and hoped that after three boys it would be a girl. Byron and I were also excited. We didn't have the same worries as our parents and welcomed an opportunity to have another little person around the house to play with. After the squalor of Colombia, I always thought that I had more than I could have imagined. Our living space was cramped, but we had shoes, toys, and plenty of food.

Then, that summer, when my mother was seven months pregnant, Byron and I were sleeping when my father rushed into the room in a panic. "Wake up, guys, we need to get out!" he shouted. "There is a fire." In fact, the entire apartment was already dark and filling with smoke. When we tried to open the front door, we realized that the corridor was thick with smoke, as well, and so black that we couldn't see our way there. We slammed the door shut. Trying to keep calm, Byron and I managed to remember some of the Boy Scout maneuvers we had learned. We dampened towels and packed them underneath the front door to prevent the smoke from seeping in. We put wet cloths over our mouths and nose to act as a filter, and gave wet cloths to my parents and Marlon. We put wet towels under the bedroom door, and my family clustered in that room, which faced the street. We opened the windows and breathed fresh air. Byron and I prepared for the prospect that all of us would have to repel from our second-floor apartment down to the street. We tied several sheets together with the knots that we had learned in the Scouts, until our makeshift rope ladder reached the sidewalk. Luckily, the fire engines arrived, set up a real ladder, and the firefighters helped us all climb down to safety.

The experience was frightening. We thought about William and how much he must have suffered during that terrible fire that took his life. We also worried for some days that my mother might lose the baby. My mother went to see her doctor and he confirmed that my mother and the baby were doing well. Our brother Alex was born September 23, 1981, a plump baby with gigantic cheeks and a disposition so peaceful that he would sleep through the night and day without crying.

GOING FOR THE GOLD

As I heard the bell signifying the last lap of the race, my body and legs felt heavy, almost as if I had bricks attached to my legs and arms. My breathing was heavy. I wanted to stop. But deep within me, I could hear my track and field coach, Sal Vega, screaming, "You've got to stay close; you have to push your body." And so I did.

I was in third place at the Hudson County half-mile race, two laps around the track at a blazing pace. I was exactly in the position that Coach Vega wanted me to be. He did not want me to be in first place or in last place. He just wanted me to be close to the leader. It was a tight race with three much taller, African-American kids leading the pace. Next, I had to make a move, and I did. I pushed my body, brought in my elbows close to my sides, and lifted up my knees, keeping pace with the leaders. As the last 100 yards of the race approached, I gathered enough momentum to overtake the leaders all the way until the finish line, crossing in a time of just under two minutes. Not a great time, but good enough to have won the half-mile championship for Hudson County.

I felt great. I had so much energy. I could see my coach was just as excited as he was jumping up and down, celebrating as much as I was. I had finally listened to my coach. I had followed his instructions, and it was worth it. I had shown myself that with passion and hard work, anything is possible. I had earned a gold medal.

In addition to the scouting program, I was developing a passion for activities other than mischief. As a child, I had never had an interest in running as a sport. My only interest was soccer. I had lived my life playing soccer most of the day on the paved streets of Barrio Antioquia. I continued with this sport here in America, and then I discovered the joy and the thrill of competitive running. In fact, this started in a rather surprising fashion.

One rainy day, while I was kicking around a soccer ball near our apartment building, Oscar, a Colombian-born teenager, wandered over and introduced himself. He lived across the street, but he and I had never really talked much. He told me he was a senior who played soccer for the local high school and he was on his way to a game in Hudson County Park, two miles away. He was going to jog there. That was his routine each day. He said, "Listen, Harold, this is how I get to be better than all the other kids; I work harder." He explained that daily running allowed him to strengthen his muscles, giving him an advantage over other players. I picked up my soccer ball and joined him on the run. Although I huffed and puffed, I was able to keep up with his pace and discovered how much I enjoyed the simple act of running. From then on, I started running long distances every day, and in the eighth grade, I joined my grammar school's track team.

When I entered Memorial High School in ninth grade, both soccer and running would become part of my life. In the fall, I played on the soccer team and ran cross-country. In the winter, I ran for the indoor track team, and in the spring, I ran for the outdoor track team. There was probably not one day during my high school career that I was not either practicing soccer or running. I felt for the first time that my life was changing in a positive direction. Instead of wanting to learn how to smoke or drink or throw bottles at storefronts, I now wanted to spend my days running.

It just happened that I met the right person. His name was Silverio (Sal) Vega. At Memorial High School, he was known as Coach Vega. He was a legendary person there, both as a star runner during his time as a student and as a coach of a very successful team that had won several county and state titles. Moreover, Coach Vega had been a standout long-distance runner at Tennessee University. He was currently in his prime as a runner. He had been named New Jersey runner of the year and had recently completed the New York City Marathon in two hours and twelve minutes. He had numerous endorsements for running, and he worked part time as a coach at the high school.

I met Coach Vega the winter of my freshman year in high school. I had just finished the soccer season, rested for a week, and decided that I was also going to run. On a cold, breezy November day, we met for the first day of practice for the indoor track team. We met at the high school, changed into running clothes, and started our practice by running two miles to the track field at the Hudson County Park. After resting for a few minutes, our coach, Sal Vega, appeared with a group of six to seven of the elite runners on the team. They had just completed a six-mile run. These guys looked great. They were dressed in what appeared to me like professional running clothes and were sporting brand-new Adidas and Nike running shoes. This group of runners had just won the Hudson County Cross Country Championship. Coach Vega gave us a pep talk and then divided us into two groups: freshman and the rest. He wanted to know what he was working with. We would have a practice mile race.

I was blown away by the speed of the race. The upperclassmen were coming in at around 4:40. I remember being nervous. I had not been running for several months, except for what I had done in soccer practice. I was already tired from the run to the park, and several of the other runners had been part of the cross-country team during the summer and fall. My fear of coming in last was realized, as I trailed the pack with a time of 5:30. As I approached the last turn of the race, I pushed as hard as I could, but it wasn't good enough. I was in last place.

Not a great start, I thought. I was devastated. I was developing a competitive mind, and I was very upset at this result. My only consolation was that I had worked hard and managed to stay close to the pack. I was depressed at my performance and at the thought of having to run another two miles back to the high school.

After I had changed and was walking out of the locker room, disheartened and with my head down, I was called in to see Coach Vega. As I approached him, he looked at me and said, "Harold, great job. I loved the way you hung in there." I could not believe what he had said. I thought, *Is he confusing me with someone else?* He was actually complimenting me on being last. In reality, he was complimenting me on having pushed myself and not given up. He saw that I was a fighter and that, with the right training, I could do well.

I was relieved that this important coach was taking the time to speak to me—an undocumented immigrant and a freshman who had just finished last in the tryout race. He must have seen something that I did not see, because he told me that he was very happy with my performance. He then explained how his team worked. He told me his basic rules. In an excited tone, he said, "First rule is to listen to me; second rule is not to forget rule number one." He promised me that he would make me a champion if I followed these basic rules.

In a very short period of time, I realized that Coach Vega was a special person. We had to call him by his first name, "Sal." He practiced with us every day. He took an interest in our families and in our performance in school. His team of runners was not just average, they were all superb competitors. The Memorial High School track and field team was one of the top programs in the state of New Jersey for many years. Our team was a family with a high amount of respect for our coach, a great person who led by example. I have always wondered how many kids in the barrios and ghettoes of America would benefit from meeting a coach like this. I was ready to learn how to run and compete.

Over the next few years, I improved significantly. I became one of the top runners in the county, both as a freshman and then as an upperclassman. As a sophomore, I made it to the indoor state championships, which were always held in the majestic Jadwin Gym at Princeton University. Until then, I knew very little about this place, except that this was the place selected by Albert Einstein when he had escaped Nazi control. Little did I suspect then that this would be my home for my four years of college.

The day of the meet was cold. We had just been through a huge snowstorm. The trip to Princeton from West New York took around three hours. We left early in the morning and arrived there at nine thirty. Upon exiting the bus, we were all moved at the sight of this huge domed complex. The inside was even more impressive. It was clean, dry, spacious, and the track was beautifully maintained. This was in sharp contrast to our usual indoor track for the local county competition, which was held at the armory in Jersey City. It was much smaller, always humid, foggy, and had a wooden track floor. At times, it was so cloudy that you could not see the entire field from the stands. At the armory, we had to stay indoors the entire day because of concerns about the safety of some of the surrounding streets. At Jadwin Gym, it was different. After the race, we would go for a short three-mile run on campus. This was the first time that I had seen such an incredible place. I was overwhelmed by such magnificent gothic structures, the appearance of the students walking across campus, and the well-maintained fields.

As we continued our run in a small group, we looked with fascination and envy inside the different buildings across the university. Since my friends knew that I was the top student at the high school, they often made comments about the possibility of me being admitted there. However, this was meant to be more of a humorous statement than an actual thought. We all knew how difficult it would be for any of us to get into a place like this. For many years, my high school had not had a student who had been admitted there.

My first race here was a good one. I was a sophomore, and my time for the half-mile run was two minutes and two seconds. I did not make it to the final heat of the state championship, but our team qualified for competition in the Penn State Relays for the two-mile relay race with a time of around eight minutes and eight seconds. This same year, I continued to improve my times, both in the half-mile run and in the mile run to 2:01 and 4:41, respectively.

On the bus ride from Princeton, I sat quietly in the back of the bus. I was not happy with the results. I wanted to do better. I figured that the only way to do better was to run more. So I decided that I would also run in the morning as I delivered the newspaper to my clients.

So, the next morning, I woke up at 4:45 a.m., I stumbled out of bed, dressed, and picked up the empty bag to deliver papers for my route. I came out of my building and started jogging lightly to get to the building on 57th and Boulevard East. There, I picked up the pack of papers, put it into the bag, and proceeded to complete my paper route. I was a paper delivery boy for a few years. I never missed a day, and after two years on the job, was selected as the paper carrier of the year by the *Hudson Dispatch*. My route consisted of about 115 papers. I would finish at about six in the morning. I had just enough time to take a shower, change, have a quick breakfast, and leave for school.

Since I wanted to train more, I decided that I wanted to use this time to get physically stronger and run even more. So much running probably did not help me as much as I thought. Coach Vega warned me about this. One day, as I was running and dropping one of the papers at an apartment, someone opened the door to one of the units. I was surprised to see Coach Vega at this door. This happened to be his parents' apartment, and he had been visiting. He witnessed what I was doing and thought that I was pushing myself too hard. He encouraged me to deliver the papers at a regular pace so as not to get hurt and save more energy for races and for the workouts.

I did not listen. I had always felt that the more I trained, the better I would be. In my simple mind, this was a simple concept. I felt that there must be a direct correlation between the amount of training you do and your performance. I did not voice my disagreement to Coach Vega, but I quietly continued to do what I felt was best. To make things worse, I also did an extra three-mile run at night and sometimes in the morning, in addition to the routine practice with the team. I did not listen to the expert. This probably contributed to a sense of burning out that I would feel at the end of each season at around the time of the important meets. As a result, I probably suffered from premature burnout syndrome, which occasionally happens to runners. My best time in the mile did not improve, and my time in the half-mile improved only slightly to just under two minutes. In hindsight, I strongly believe that I could have done better had I followed both of his simple rules.

My overall performance on the running track during my sophomore year was outstanding. Coach Vega was so happy, that he advised I dedicate myself to running. He convinced me to join the high school cross-country team for my junior year. I did— much to the displeasure of my soccer team coach, Frank Sabetta, and my friends on the soccer team. Unfortunately, I missed soccer dearly. This was, and still is, my favorite sport, the sport of my childhood that I carried deeply in my heart. Complicating matters, I did not enjoy cross-country running. I did well enough to make it to the all-county team at the end of the season, but the entire season had been a struggle. At the end of the season, I decided that I would return to the soccer team for my senior year.

I am glad that I did. My teammates were supportive and appreciative that I was back in the lineup. They overlooked that I had abandoned the team the previous season, and they named me co-captain of the varsity team. I was humbled by this opportunity and ready to lead the team. Our team was truly an immigrant group, made up of kids who had come to America from several Central and South American countries. Most of them did not speak English fluently. At times, our Italian coach Frank Sabetta would speak to us in broken Spanish or even Italian to explain the game plan. Many of the players looked up to me as not just the captain of the team, but as the player in the group who had made the transition into the mainstream of the student body. In addition, I was the top academic student in the entire school and a star athlete in track and field. They felt that I brought credibility and status to the team. This was evident at the annual school homecoming pep rally, when they asked me to lead the team as the captain to the cheers of a packed gymnasium of students. As in most high schools, soccer was not the most popular sport; but with our high school's increasingly immigrant student body, our team was gaining popularity, and they had high expectations for our team. We delivered.

On a cold afternoon in Jersey City, our team entered the field to play against the favored team from Hudson County, Bergen Catholic High School. Although we were the underdogs, we had done well and were confident. The contrast between the two teams could not have been greater. They were an almost all-white, Anglo-Saxon group of kids from a private Catholic school who had learned to play soccer in organized leagues and camps. They were much taller and stronger. Our team was made up of all immigrant kids, speaking mostly in Spanish to each other, who had learned to play soccer on the paved-streets of very poor and humble towns in our native countries. We had much better ball control and skills; they were stronger and had a better understanding of playing in the big fields. On this particular day, however, we wanted to win more than they did, and we won the game two to zero, becoming Hudson County Champions.

Although I really enjoyed playing forward, at Memorial, I had to play defense because I was one of the bigger kids on the team and could provide a sense of security each time we faced the stronger American teams. I was a solid player in defense, along with Byron, who also played defense with me. I was a good leader as a captain, but most of the credit for our great season should go to an incredibly talented 5'5" soccer player who had just immigrated to America from Honduras. His name was Julio Licona. This kid was an amazing soccer player as a sophomore. He was unstoppable. The only way he lost the ball was when the other team fouled him. Our game plan was simple: "Get the ball to Julio and he will score." Upon graduation, Julio got a scholarship to play at Fairleigh Dickinson University. His career as a soccer player was cut short by multiple knee injuries.

This was a great victory for the soccer program, and I am proud to have been part of it. The town had just finished a new soccer field, which was located just across from the high school. It was a beautiful field with a brand-new, soft, green lawn. This was our home field. During that year, the team would be undefeated at home. Overall, we had the best season in the history of Memorial High School. Our overall record was of seventeen wins and four losses. Two of the losses would come against Kearny High School, which would become the state champion. We won the county championship, the state sectionals, and made it to the next stage, where we were defeated by Kearny.

I was feeling more confident about myself. The taste of victory was invigorating. However, the sense of hard work, passion, and teamwork was even more powerful. This was true even when I lost or did not win a gold medal. As long as I felt that I had truly given my best effort, I was at peace.

STUDYING WITH MICE

As I sat at the small, round table in the corner of our tiny kitchen, I could hear the silence of the night. Looking outside the window that faced the next apartment building just a few feet away, I could only see darkness. It was two in the morning, and, finally, everyone in our building and the one next to us was sleeping. There was no music blasting from any of the surrounding apartments. There were no arguments to be heard, just the silence of the night, and yes, the mice and the roaches in our kitchen.

The roaches were scary. The mice were playful and charming. These were not ordinary mice, by the way; they were educated mice that had learned the art of survival in the overcrowded apartment complex where I lived. They would come out from hiding in the night and roam around the floor of the kitchen, searching for leftover food. At times, they would not come out because there was someone in the kitchen or because we would keep the lights on to keep them away. However, I think that they had now realized that I would be in the kitchen and I would not disturb them; it was not worth it. This was a battle that I could not win. I just had to ignore them. Sometimes, they would come into the kitchen and almost make visual contact with me. Upon realizing that it was me sitting by the table concentrating on my textbooks, they would go about their business.

My mother was tormented by the sound of the mice scurrying up the walls and the roaches sidling along the floor. She kept our own apartment sparkling clean. We told her many times, "Mom, we cannot win this battle; they are everywhere." However, I could not be distracted; I had to study for my classes, and I discovered that in my apartment complex the quietest time was after midnight. I created my own zone of solitude to contemplate and concentrate on the task at hand. This ability to focus amid everyday chaos was to prove useful as a surgical trainee, when I had to perform procedures on a critically ill patient in the loud conditions of an emergency room.

The truth is that it was not always convenient to study in my home. In our narrow bedroom, Byron and I shared one desk. When my mother was cooking in the kitchen or cleaning up after Marlon, the noise would echo into our bedroom. Our room faced an apartment about ten feet away, and one could clearly see and hear everything going on in that home. Our window shades were kept drawn, but I could hear the music blasting outside my window—not Vivaldi or Beethoven, but salsa, merengue, and tango songs of the common folks that I had heard streaming from the Oasis bar in Barrio Antioquia. All day I could hear neighbors quarrelling.

Many nights, before falling asleep, I would fantasize about ways to make our apartment physically larger to have a place where I could study without so many distractions. I imagined dividing our bedroom into two stories, almost like having a small crawl space close to the ceiling where I could just climb in and read without ever having to come out. When I asked my father about the practicality of that, he gave it some thought but said the landlord would never allow us to do it. I really think that he started to wonder if I was going a little crazy.

My mother definitely thought that I was losing my senses. After being one of the most social and friendly kids around, I was now becoming anti-social. When their friends would come to visit or there were people in the kitchen, I would quietly go inside my tiny bedroom. I was determined that I would use all of my energy on academics; nothing and no one would distract me from my commitment to school, athletics, and the Boy Scouts, in that order. I no longer had time for outside influences, and even shrugged off romances with pretty girls who had shown interest in my friendship. I did not need my parents to tell me to work hard. Indeed, my mother would often feel pity for me and implore me to stop working and take a break. Knocking on the door to my bedroom, she would call in a low, sweet voice, "My love, please come out and have something to eat." Sometimes I would say, "No, I don't want anything," or I would just ignore her. A few minutes later, she would then say, "Can I bring you a cup of coffee?"

At other times, she would ask me to come out of the room to speak to friends that were visiting or watch an engaging movie. I would refuse, sometimes rudely. I was too preoccupied with my work. I found an escape in studying. I could immerse myself in a particular subject and discover that I would become more passionate about it the more that I learned. In my small room in our small apartment, with the mice going by, I could escape inside the books I was reading and find tremendous pleasure figuring out ideas and concepts. I was also driven because I had been assured by all the important people in my life—my grandmothers and my parents—that hard work in school would lead to a better life. Perhaps it would also enable me to help my struggling parents and my grandmothers. This thought added a level of urgency to what I was doing. Given our precarious situation in America as undocumented immigrants, I also dreamed that somehow, in some way I could not foresee, my achievements would help us become legal residents.

In the days leading up to the start of high school, I had become preoccupied with how I might fit in. I no longer wanted to be an outsider. I was excited at the idea of a new beginning at a school where the other students didn't know that I had recently come from another country. I was beginning to feel more comfortable with the English language and I was hoping that in the new school I would be recognized simply as a freshman and not as a "refugee." I still had a long way to go until I could read, speak, and write with a sense of mastery, though. I was especially conscious of my heavy accent. Each time that I spoke in public, I worried that I was not being understood. At the same time, I had fears of not doing well. The academic work would be much more demanding, the competition more intense.

Memorial High School was a vibrant place. Many of the kids were sons and daughters of recent immigrants. The rest had parents who had immigrated here many years previously. It was a teeming place in the heart of West New York with over four hundred students in every grade. Each of us heard many times from our parents that the only way to get ahead in life was with an education. So, Memorial was a school that seemed to bristle with immigrant-striving, hunger, and determination. There was no shortage of talented students and athletes. Memorial's baseball team was often ranked as one of the top in the country, and its soccer, football, and track and field programs were also highly regarded.

The school principal was Joseph N. Coviello. Tall, silver-haired, and sturdily built, he was an honorable man and embodied all the qualities of a commanding general. To keep in shape, he walked to school every morning from his house in neighboring North Bergen. I would sometimes pass him on Palisades Avenue during my early-morning training sessions. In the winter months, he always wore a hat and a long coat. When I glimpsed him during my morning workouts, I marveled at his physical resemblance to the pictures I had seen of the legendary Alabama football coach, Paul "Bear" Bryant. In fact, Principal Coviello was Memorial's head football coach for many years and led the school to seven state championships. In 1994, he would be elected to the New Jersey Athletic Hall of Fame.

With that same drive and hard work, he assembled a faculty at Memorial that many other high schools in New Jersey could not match. The most important to me was my homeroom and English teacher, Geraldine Schmidt. She was firm, yet kind and understanding, and treated each student with a sense of his or her individuality. During my high school years, she became my second mother. She was an energetic woman who enjoyed having discussions in class and getting students to participate. I was quiet and reserved, and preferred to be brief in any of my comments. Although I was often criticized by teachers and family for being concise, I found consolation in Shakespeare's epigram that "brevity is the soul of wit." Mrs. Schmidt was patient and slowly lured me into her circle of trust. In due course, she became a dear friend. She always seemed to have the inside scoop in everything that went on in my life at Memorial, even when I tried to keep it a secret. Somehow, she knew who my friends were, who I was flirting with, or who I had a crush on. She seemed to look out for me. At the start of each year, I felt as if my new teachers already knew who I was because Mrs. Schmidt had spoken to them. "Oh, I have heard so many wonderful things about you," a teacher would come up and tell me. In this way, I started each class with an advantage, like a head start in a race. I had found an American teacher who had great affection for me. I am confident that she would have felt that way even if she discovered my immigration secret.

Early in my high school years, I adopted an unconventional method of studying. The impetus probably came from the Boy Scouts and its motto of "Be Prepared." I decided that in each subject I would actually try to teach myself the material before it was presented in class. I was not always successful in grasping the lesson, but I was familiar with the concepts before the teacher introduced them. This method also kept me one or two lessons

ahead of the class. When the teacher talked about slopes in algebra, I had already learned about them. I did so well in Algebra
that the math department allowed me to take both Geometry
and Algebra 2 during tenth grade, so that I could catch up to
the other students in the college prep group. Sometimes I felt
as if I were cheating because I could easily grasp the ideas being
taught in class. I knew, though, that I could display mastery of
the day's material not because I was smarter than the other kids,
but because I had already learned it on my own.

One afternoon, after the end of the first marking-period, I
was leaving biology class and heading to algebra when I saw a
large cluster of students gathered around a list that had been
posted near the principal's office. Curious, I edged into the commotion. When I was close enough, I noticed the list was titled
"Honor Roll" and ranked the top one hundred students in each
grade. I wasn't aware that I would be ranked against the other
students. I knew that there was an honor roll but not that there
would actually be an ordered list of the top numerical grade point
averages listed in a way that everyone could see it as they passed
in front of the principal's office. As I glanced at the list, I noticed
that in the freshman class listing, Lourdes Leal, a very intelligent Cuban girl, ranked first. Then as I looked down the list, I
noticed that my name was in the third position, tied for second
with a close friend, Yazid Ebeid. I knew that I had done well but
was speechless that I had done *that* well. The other students in
the top twenty were my classmates in the college prep courses.
These were very talented kids, and I could not quite believe that
I had surpassed so many. I was strangely moved at this affirma-
tion of my work. However, I was not deceived into thinking that
this made me superior to anyone else. I was honest with myself.
I knew in my heart that many of these students were more talented than I was, but I also knew that each day I was among the
best prepared.

My parents—despite their own lack of schooling or possibly because of it—always drummed home the paramount importance of education. They were too busy with their fatiguing factory jobs to get very involved in the content of what we were actually learning, and by high school, of course, they could no longer help us. But they provided a vivid and powerful model of persistent discipline and dedication to a goal. Their hard work insured that we had a roof over our heads and food on the table so we could concentrate on studying. Their day-by-day attention to how we were doing in school showed us how much they cared about our progress. Their seriousness about meeting the obligations of life seemed to filter into my own outlook.

- - - - - - - - -

Just as I was starting to do really well in school, our lives suddenly came to a standstill on a cold day on December 5, 1982. My parents received a phone call telling them that my grandmother Alicia had died. My father's mother had been sick for months from heart failure brought on by her diabetes. In the last weeks, there were calls every few days from Aunt Gilma in Colombia telling us how much pain my grandmother was in and how much discomfort she was feeling.

"You must come back," she told my father. "Mother is very sick and she keeps losing weight. She doesn't have long to live. You should be at her bedside. She has not seen you in so many years, and this may be the last opportunity." My father felt very guilty and said to my mother, "I need to go back." Then he would talk on the phone with his mother and she would leave no doubt about what he must do.

"You stay put in the United States," she insisted. "Make sure you don't come back. Think about your family. That is most important. I'll be fine. My son, I beg you that you stay. I know that in spirit you will always be with me, even when I die. You must promise me that you will stay there."

My father knew he would risk everything if he returned—his family's well being, his children's education, his job. The problem of undocumented immigrants was front-page news, and the United States government was clamping down. If he flew back, he might find it impossible to return unless he smuggled himself across the Mexican border by foot or in the trunk of a car—both were dangerous options given what he heard about the treacherous crossing from Mexico. The journey could be very expensive and possibly fatal. Besides, there was always the chance that if he remained patient, the American government might shift gears and legalize those people who could prove they had been in this country and working for a fixed amount of time. Indeed, under the leadership of a republican president, the Immigration Act of 1986 granted amnesty to undocumented immigrants who entered the United States before January 1, 1982 and had resided and worked there without leaving. Although he was in great pain and anguish, he decided not to visit his ailing mother. My grandmother Alicia would have been very sad if she saw him return to Colombia just to see her die.

Then the phone call came that he had been dreading. We were sitting in the living room and we heard my father on the phone with Gilma and we knew from his face that Grandmother Alicia was gone. My father was so overcome that he gave the phone to my mother while he wrestled with the news, tears gathering in his eyes. "I have to go back now, for the funeral," he said, his voice very solemn. He sat on the sofa, crying, my mother trying to console him. My brother and I remained standing in a corner, quietly watching my parents, and feeling pained that my father could not be with his mother when she passed on. We felt that we had abandoned my grandmother in her last few days.

A dark cloud seemed to descend on our small apartment. However, we were confident that my father knew that he could not go back. He soon rose to his feet and lit a candle next to a faded photograph of his mother. Over the next nine days, he went to church every day to say his *novenas*, lighting candles at another photograph of her that was adorned with flowers and a cross. It was the only way he could mark his mother's death.

In an ironic twist of fates, that same night, my parents had been called to come to Memorial High for their first parent-teacher conference that year. It would have been an anxious time for them at any time, since they didn't know what to expect about their once-unruly firstborn who was so unfamiliar with this new land. Somehow, my father was able to calm down and muster the courage to attend parents' night at the high school.

My father appeared like a beaten man. Despite all his successes so far, now he could not return to Colombia to see his mother one last time. Fortunately, the deep sadness and anguish was slightly diminished by his discussion with my teachers. On this sad night, my parents received uplifting evaluations from my teachers. One of them in particular, was an important role model for me. This was my biology teacher, Mr. Kirchmer. He was a young and energetic man who first introduced me to the beauty of living organisms in an elegant and colorful way. He spoke to my parents through a Spanish interpreter. Fortunately, the evaluations were all excellent.

With great excitement, Mr. Kirchmer said, "I wish my own son was as good as Harold." At some point, he even tried speaking some Spanish, telling my parents, "*Hijo excellente.*"

My mother tried to restrain herself, to maintain her dignity and poise, but I could see tears begin to run down her face. She rose and gave Mr. Kirchmer a warm hug. All the sacrifice they had made, the years separated from their sons, the long days in the factories, the stern lectures every time we strayed into mischief, the sacrifice they made to abstain from visiting family when my grandmother Alicia passed away, were paying off. Their son was thriving in this new world. For my father, how painful for him it must have been that his mother could not be with him to share in his pride. How painful it must have been that the inhuman, unjust logic of immigration laws had kept his dying mother apart from him.

Nevertheless, my father took comfort in knowing that I was responding to his pleas that I work hard. When he returned from the conference, he knelt by his bed and thanked the Lord. He also thanked my grandmother Alicia for her sacrifice and compassionate understanding. He made copies of my report card, with the glowing teacher comments, and taped it to the inside of his locker at work. He was proud of my work, and would often call over his colleagues and show them. Eventually, the door of his locker was filled with report cards, newspaper clippings, and other mementoes of my accomplishments.

THE YOUNG SCIENTIST

On a cold winter morning, as I kneeled down to pick up the bundle of newspapers to start my daily delivery route, my attention was captivated by a front-page photograph of students posing with medals around their necks and celebrating their scientific accomplishments at the annual science fair sponsored by the Stevens Institute of Technology. The small print under the picture listed the names of the students and referenced the page in the paper where one could find the article. With a rush of excitement, I ripped one of the papers out of the bundle and flipped to that page. I was filled with a spark of energy, fascination, and envy at the accomplishments of these kids. "Wow," I kept saying to myself. Little did I know that this rush of excitement that I felt would be a catalyst for my own personal journey into the art of investigation and scientific discovery.

The journey, however, was long and arduous, and it all started with little baby steps. By then, my daily routine throughout high school had become physically punishing. Even before my regular school classes, I'd already had a grueling morning. I would wake up every day at 4:45 a.m., change into my street clothes, and distribute newspapers for the *Hudson Dispatch*. My parents did not want me to do the paper route because they felt that it would distract me from my studies. However, there were things I wanted to buy but didn't have the money for—equipment for the Boy Scouts, more stylish clothes, and a computer, which I knew I could not ask them to pay for. I could use the forty dollars a week the paper route paid. In addition, I liked the idea of delivering a service and getting compensated for it.

I delivered newspapers to 115 homes a day, picking up the heavy bundle in the lobby of a modern apartment complex on 57th Street and Boulevard East. Then, I would stuff the newspapers into a bag that I slung from my shoulder. The bag was heavy, so I would change it to the other side after ten to fifteen minutes. I started at the 26th floor and dropped papers on almost every floor of that building, forty in all, dashing down the stairs as quickly as I could so I could strengthen my legs and knees for track competitions. Next, I would sprint over to a smaller building, deliver papers there, and then take on the neighborhood's stand-alone houses. The bag would grow lighter and I was able to sprint the last stretch of the route, figuring this would make me stronger for soccer and track.

On Thursdays, I would collect the home delivery fees, knocking on each door and asking for payment. My English was still clumsy. One time I knocked on the door and the lady inside asked, "Who is it?" I replied, "Boy paper!" I heard her laughing as I waited for her to open the door. Byron, who often accompanied me on Thursdays, also realized my error and started laughing. Even to this day, he reminds me of how awkward I sounded when I said this. Despite my insecurities, however, I decided at the outset that I would be a great paperboy. My plan was to never skip a delivery day—whether it rained or snowed or I was sick—and always deliver the paper on time. After a few months, the word got around that the service was excellent, and I was able to quickly increase my number of clients. This may not have been a great start, but as a young kid, I began to understand the concept of working hard and doing my best to accomplish a job.

I would finish my route at about six in the morning, have just enough time to take a shower, change, skip breakfast, and leave for school. In addition to the exercise, I also used this time for reflection and for reviewing some of my school lessons in my mind. I would review aloud formulas for my geometry class or algebra; other times, I would daydream. My mind would drift into thinking of one day being able to help my parents or even become a doctor. On this ordinary morning, as I delivered the papers, after briefly reading the article about the students in the science fair, I got this idea into my head that I would develop a project for a science fair. I was a stubborn kid. Whenever I had an idea, I had to make it happen. I stopped and read the article again. I was mesmerized that students my own age could do such sophisticated work. I sat down on the bundle of papers and started thinking about what I could possibly do. I started asking myself how I could do something like that so that I could be on the paper instead of delivering the paper.

The article said, "Stevens Institute in Hoboken, one of the top engineering schools in the Northeast, holds this contest each year, to encourage high school students to pursue their interests in technological research and engineering." I was in the early months of my second year of high school and right there and then I decided that I needed to do a project like the students in the photograph had done.

I knew that it would be difficult but not impossible. I was already immersed in sports and scouting and was trying to sustain an A average. I wasn't very inventive and didn't have anyone that I could come to for advice on planning this kind of research. My parents would not be of much practical help, since neither spoke English or had a scientific background. I could have asked for the help of one of my science teachers, all of whom were excellent, but as a relative newcomer to American society, I still didn't feel comfortable sharing my thoughts with them.

I only needed to find a project. For the next few months this became my foremost concern. I would repeatedly tell myself, "I need to do something!" This is what I was thinking one December night in 1982 while I was walking down Bergenline Avenue. During the holidays, Bergenline Avenue, West New York's main north-south shopping street, is packed with crowds doing their holiday shopping. The dominant language in the shops was Spanish. Even the Chinese and Arab merchants speak Spanish fluently. As I walked, shivering from the cold with my hands in my coat pocket, I tried to rush home so that I could finish my work.

I briefly glanced at a window with computers. I had never had a computer. I had never seen or used a computer before, but I had seen all the commercials about using computers for playing video games. As I stood at the glass window, staring at these computers, I overheard a couple discussing the virtues of a Commodore computer in the window. With great excitement, the wife explained to the husband how useful this machine could be for their kids' schoolwork. I don't know if the husband was really listening, but I was. She then proceeded to explain how their kids could even use this computer for school assignments and projects. When I heard the word "projects," I was in a daze. I instantly made the connection of my desire to enter a science fair competition. I thought that maybe, just maybe, I could use a computer, too, and I began to play with the thought that I could use a computer to develop a project for the Stevens Institute contest.

I rushed home thinking about computers. But I really did not know what they did or how they worked. I didn't even know how expensive they were. I wondered in my head if my parents could even afford to buy one? The next time that I passed by the store, I gathered the courage to go inside and ask for information. The store clerk explained that the most popular computers were the Texas Instruments TI-94/A, the Commodore 64, and the IBM. He also explained that although all of them could be used to play games, they could also be used for schoolwork and for developing projects. Computers, I learned were expensive. As I left the store, I realized my parents would be skeptical of spending so much on something that might be used for games that would distract me from my studies. So I had to come up with a plan.

I first mentioned the idea to my mother; I knew that she would be more receptive. I explained to her that I could use this computer for school. I also told her that I would save all my earnings from the paper route to help with the expense. My mother could sense the excitement that I had, because she said yes immediately. "Of course, my son, let me talk it over with your father and we will come up with the money." Upon hearing that I could use this for my education, my father also said yes, they would help me. My parents said that they would provide half the money for the least expensive of the three, the TI-94. I had saved enough from my earnings on the newspaper route to provide the remainder.

I got the TI-94/A computer on Christmas Eve of 1982, and it was love at first sight. By tradition in Colombia, we celebrate on Christmas Eve, usually with Colombian food, dancing, and celebrating into the next morning. At midnight, we pause to open up the gifts by the Christmas tree. I couldn't wait to get my hands on the computer. As my mother distributed the gifts, she handed this one to me and said, "Enjoy it, my son. You deserve this and more." I took the box into my room with Byron and we ripped out the paper. I slid the computer out of the box and set it up on top of the television set in my room.

The computer came with a detailed instruction manual and a book on BASIC computer language so that I could, if I read it meticulously, learn how to write programs. That first night, as everyone was partying and celebrating into the late morning—and as Byron was playing with other toys—I started teaching myself how to work this computer.

For the next several weeks, I became addicted to these books, memorizing every detail and teaching myself computer language.

I could not believe the idea that one could talk to these machines and instruct them to do tasks. I started writing simple programs and within a few weeks progressed to more complex ones. To the frustration of Byron, I rarely used the computer for playing games. I had a project to develop. Even to this day, he playfully reminds me that I stole part of his childhood.

The next steps, of course, were to actually design and develop an idea. As I taught myself the language of computers, my mind was also consumed with trying to figure out a project. Every morning I would wake up, and each night I would go to bed thinking of what I could do. The answer came to me suddenly one day while I was sitting quietly on my chair, trying to copy the notes that my general chemistry teacher was writing on the board.

Mr. Thomas Simione had been a teacher of general chemistry at Memorial for many years, and I could sense that he had lost some of his understanding of the material. He was a good teacher, but over the years had lost some of the interest. He could copy the lesson from his well-kept notes onto the chalkboard but he could not explain it to the students. One lesson that sparked my interest was his explanation of the "electron cloud." He would get up in front of the board, pick an element from the periodic table, and copy from his notes the electronic configuration of the electrons on the board. However, he could not explain it to us in a way that we could actually understand. As I looked at the board, I got the idea that this would be my project. I said to myself, *I will teach myself everything there is to know about the electron cloud and I will write a program that teaches other students how to do it.* I thought then—and I know now after many years of education— that anyone can learn anything if it is presented in the right manner by someone who really understands the material.

Most students fear general chemistry because there are too few teachers who can explain the subject well. Even in my honors chemistry class, there were smart students who could not understand what the teacher was trying to convey about basic principles. I was filled with youthful presumptuousness and decided for my science project I would explain an essential principle to such students—the electronic configuration of each element in the periodic table.

Each element has a specific number of electrons surrounding the nucleus, and theories by Niels Bohr and Max Planck use mathematical formulas to pinpoint the configuration of the electrons—the precise positions and pattern of the electrons that orbit the central nucleus. I wrote a program to teach students how to make calculations to figure out the electronic configuration for themselves. The title of my project was "Application of Computers to Chemistry," and it had two other sections that also aimed to illustrate how a computer could be used to get across concepts in chemistry. There was a complex graphics program that simulated an experiment showing how the organic compound chloral hydrate is produced. There was also a tool that was designed to teach students how to calculate nuclear binding energy of several atoms by using the concept of mass defect and Einstein's equation of $E=MC^2$.

It took me several months of intensive labor to write this program. Because I didn't have any formal training in computers, I am sure that some of the algorithms I used were not optimal. Nevertheless, I finished the entire project on my own. I didn't ask anyone for help or advice. One hundred percent of the work was derived from my ideas and my own labor. Although it was not perfect, I was very proud of the final result. I entered my project in the Stevens Institute Science Fair for 1984, my junior year. After preliminary rounds that took a few weeks, I received a letter telling me that my project had been selected as a finalist and would be displayed to the judges. I was ecstatic.

On the day of the final competition, I had the opportunity to see the other projects and meet the other competitors. There were ten finalists, students from Indian and Chinese immigrant homes, as well as those from longer-rooted American homes. I could not help noticing that I was the only Hispanic student. I also could not help noticing that parents accompanied each student, with many of the fathers in jackets and ties and the mothers in elegant dresses. My parents were not able to make it to the contest. They needed to work. Yet, my parents' faces glowed with pride at what I was doing. "Oh my son, we are so proud of you, of all this wonderful work that you are doing because you work so hard," my mother told me.

My father, in particular, knew that I was doing something special because it was related to the work Albert Einstein had done. My father esteemed that name, even if he had no understanding of relativity or quantum physics. Unfortunately, he, as well as my mother, could not take a day off to attend a science fair. Their factories didn't even allow them any sick days. My parents did not have any legal documents to be here in America. They realized that they could be fired from their jobs even if they missed one day of work.

So on the day of the competition I was alone with my TI-94/A computer. Most of the other finalists were dressed in suits and ties. I was more casually dressed, in jeans and a neat and comfortable shirt. The other students used the more advanced and expensive computers IBM or Commodore-64 models that allowed storage on floppy disks. My project was saved on an ordinary cassette tape and to play it I had to attach a tape recorder to my computer. I imagined the other students and their parents thinking, "How can this kid possibly be competing with his toy computer?" Each time that I loaded my program, it would take ten to fifteen minutes to start. A judge would come by and ask to see my project and I would have to ask him or her to look at another project first and return in ten minutes. At other times, I would try to distract the judge with an expanded verbal explanation of my project to allow time for the program to boot. Still, by the afternoon, I felt that the judges understood that my project was an original idea and, just as important, that I had done the work on my own, without any assistance from teachers or parents. At the end of the day, the judges met and announced the top three finishers in each category. I finished in third place in my category.

A few weeks later, I received a letter from Rensselaer Polytechnic Institute (RPI) that invited me to apply to their annual summer program for high school students in math and science. The school had been told that I had participated in the Stevens science fair and placed well. RPI in Troy in upstate New York is one of the country's top engineering schools. The eight-week summer program offered two college-level courses in computer science: Introduction to Minicomputers and Computer Fundamentals 101. Each course covered an entire semester's work in a four-week period

I was not only intrigued by the program but felt that it would allow me to demonstrate that I had the skills and the determination to handle academic work at the best colleges. I was hesitant to apply because of the expense—$6,000 for the two sessions with tuition, room, and board. There was no way that my family could afford this. Six thousand dollars was one third of my father's annual salary. However, I applied anyway and attached a letter, telling the school how eager I was to take part in the program and requesting financial help. I explained that my father made about $18,000 a year working in an embroidery factory and that my mother made $6,000 in a clothing factory, and this income was barely enough for a family of six. I also informed them that no one in my family had ever studied beyond the third grade of grammar school, and acceptance to the summer program would be a dream come true for my entire family.

A few weeks later, I was surprised to receive a letter admitting me and granting me a full financial aid package. I showed the letter to my parents and they were astonished. My father could not believe that this was possible. He thought that I was not reading the letter correctly. I, too, had doubts that this could be true and wondered if someone had made an error. However, I soon understood that I was the beneficiary of American generosity at its best. I had received the trust of the admissions committee. Now I would need to show the school that I deserved the opportunity.

The summer of 1984, the summer after my junior year of high school, would be the first time that I would leave my home for anything longer than a weekend Scout hike. We planned the trip to RPI carefully. I bought a map of New York State at the local gas station and sat with my father around the kitchen table, planning the route to Troy. My father had recently learned how to drive. He was able to do this because in those days you didn't need a green card to get a license. We celebrated the day when he came home after taking the written test and then an actual driver's test and announced, "I passed the test!" This is probably an insignificant accomplishment for many American fathers. However, given the hurdles—his weak English, his undocumented status, and his lack of a car—it was an important milestone for our family and we were all very proud of him. He went out and bought himself an old gray Ford Zephyr. It was in terrible shape but it could take us out of West New York to some of our favorite places, like Bear Mountain State Park and the Jersey shore. Until he owned that car, we had to take a bus from the Port Authority terminal in midtown Manhattan if we wanted to go anywhere.

Still, my father was very uncomfortable driving long distances on a highway, especially since road signs might be perplexing, and we decided that my mother's brother, Hector, who had taught my father to drive, would lead us to Troy. He took his family along and he led us up the New York State Thruway, with my father and our family following in the Ford Zephyr.

In total, about ten people accompanied me to Troy. After all, my spending a summer at RPI was a monumental event for my extended family, and everyone wanted to witness it. None of them had ever spent any time on a college campus, but they understood that a university was a place of distinction. The idea that a young member of our humble family had been given the opportunity to travel and study at a university was a change in their perception of themselves. For weeks before we left, my RPI summer became the talk of the town within my parents' circle of friends. The idea that now I was going to spend an entire summer at a university outside of West New York gave all of us hope that things could be better. Someone just like them was going to study with some of the country's best students. They all wanted to be part of the journey; they didn't want to be left out.

We made it to the campus without any breakdowns. That day at the dorm, there was a luncheon for the program's students and their families. Most students had come with their parents. I had come with my entire family—parents, brothers, uncle, cousins, and dog. It was obvious at the gathering which one was the immigrant Hispanic family. My brothers were running around, yammering in Spanish, and my mother was silently sobbing because I would be away from home for a whole summer. Being more practical, my father was preoccupied with making sure that we had not misunderstood the financial aid letter and that I would actually be able to afford to stay at the school. Otherwise, he might have to return to fetch me. He urged me to inquire about the letter at the registrar's office.

There was a line of students and their parents, who we could see were signing forms and then going over to the cashier's desk and taking out checkbooks to pay the bill. My father, standing alongside me, was nervous because he didn't have a checkbook and had no idea how he was going to pay any fees that might be required. I registered and then moved to the cashier's desk, but instead of having to write a check, I was handed a check by the clerk, a stipend for books and supplies. My father was relieved and we returned to the luncheon to enjoy a few moments together as a family before my family would have to leave me on my own and drive back to West New York. My father was anxious about driving at night and so could only stay a couple of hours.

RPI was my first immersion in a solidly American environment. The program's forty students hailed from as far away as California, but there was only one other Hispanic, a student from a wealthy Puerto Rican family who had attended a private school in his homeland. I shared a room with David, a tall, slim blond student from Kansas. During one of our first conversations, he asked me, "Do you play anything?"

"Yes, I play soccer," I replied.

"Oh, no, I mean do you play any musical instruments?" I didn't and had never had music lessons. His pastime, the trumpet, was more refined. Although we were friendly, we had very different interests and most of our conversations centered on our coursework. With the computer courses he had already taken in his high school, he did not have to work as hard and could spend more time watching television, practicing the trumpet, and socializing.

Each of the courses was designed around a project using a different computer language—BASIC, ForTran, or Pascal. The material was far more advanced than the programs I had used just a few months before at the science fair. We spent about six hours a day in the classroom, and each day, we had programming assignments that were due the next day.

The other students attending that summer also seemed much further along in their computer skills than me, but I also understood that I shared something very fundamental with all of them. All these students wanted to score well in the courses—you could see it in their eyes—and I, too, was there to do well. In fact, I probably wanted to do better than most of them because it was more important for me. Coming from a relatively unknown high school, a positive effort at RPI would improve my chances of getting noticed by a good college. Because I was far behind in computer skills, I had to work even harder and learn from my classmates. The school made sure that we had access to several teaching assistants, and I was not embarrassed to show up at the cafeteria after dinner for daily tutoring sessions. I knew that at the end of the course, my transcript would only show my grade; it wouldn't have an asterisk indicating that I had obtained special tutoring. I was never ashamed to ask my roommate or other students for help. I was grateful that the students, even if they viewed me as a rival, were willing to explain difficult concepts.

I realized early on that I was different from the other students—my accent, my culture, my interests, even my preferences in food made me stand out. The dorm cafeteria served American food: burgers, pizza, macaroni and cheese, and roast beef. Initially, it was exciting to be eating such popular meals. But after a few weeks, I longed for my mother's cooking—the rice, beans, *tostones*, and *arepas*. While Michael Jordan and the American basketball team's feats in the 1984 Summer Olympics captivated other students, I was perfecting my computer projects. I took only a few breaks, mostly to run a few miles each day or kick around a soccer ball to keep in shape for the fall season. Still, I found this taste of college and the freedom to be on my own liberating and exhilarating. I could study in a richly stocked library on a table of my own with no salsa or merengue blasting from across the alley.

During this summer, I managed to really concentrate on my schoolwork. I avoided any romantic friendships. There was a pretty, blue-eyed, blonde from New Jersey who flirted with me, smiling and sometimes chatting in a friendly way. However, I was very shy and fixated on my schoolwork. A few times during that summer, we went into town on weekends, mostly to a Friendly's restaurant. But my budget was very tight and I couldn't afford even those meals. So when my friends asked me to go, I would make up an excuse and say I had to study. Most days the real reason was I did not have the money.

After a while, the other students considered me something of a loner. Undoubtedly, at times I felt that I did not quite belong in this program. I was an undocumented immigrant and I was taking scholarship money that would otherwise have been given to an American citizen. I tried to tell myself that the scholarship was entirely based on academics and did not take into account my immigration status. I told myself that one day I would become a lawful citizen, and, by sacrificing many extra hours to become the best professional, I would make up for any undeserved awards I received along the way. On good days, I believed this, on bad days, questions gnawed at me.

In any case, I accomplished what I had set out to do. I earned A's for both of my courses. My experience would no doubt impress a college admissions committee. Even if my high school was not well known to them, I had shown that I could do well in a rigorous, competitive environment. When I returned home from Troy, I rode a bus into the Port Authority terminal in Manhattan. As I was sitting on this bus, I thought about the sequence of events that had started with a simple idea as I picked up the bundle of newspapers to deliver, and it was facilitated by the money that I earned with a humble job of delivering newspapers and by the generosity of an academic institution like RPI. "This is great, I love America," I whispered to myself.

PHOTOS

My father, and my mother carrying me
when I was just a few months old.

Me, grandmother Rosa, my brother Byron, and grandmother Alicia.
My parents were living in America as undocumented immigrants.

My brother Byron, grandmother Rosa carrying my infant
cousin Erika, Me with a cowboy hat, and my best friend
in Colombia, Marlon. Both Erika and Marlon were killed
at a very young age as a result of senseless violence.

Our first picture in America. Me, my mother carrying
my young brother Marlon, and my brother Byron.

Me and Byron. Our first outing in America
was to see the Statue of Liberty.

Our first picture as a family in America.

Me and Byron after going to the airport to pick up our youngest brother
Marlon, in the middle. Because our family was undocumented, my
parents made us wear the complete Boy Scout uniform to the airport so
that we were less liable to arouse suspicion of the immigration service.

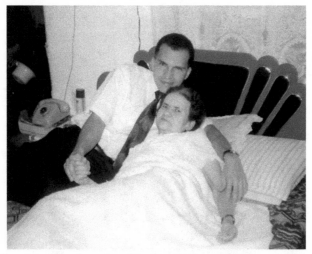

Me with grandmother Rosa a few days before she died.

Me and my sweetheart.

My kids, Brandon and Jasmine.

The moments in life that I enjoy the most. Receiving love from my kids.

Brandon and Me

My parents

My hero. My little cousin Hector serving on his second
tour in Afghanistan defending our country.

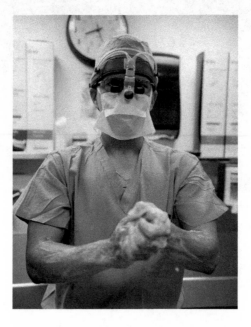

Me, getting ready for open-heart surgery.

DWELLING IN THE SHADOWS

On a cold winter morning, my father had just finished working the night shift at his embroidery factory on 64th and Broadway and got off at 7:30 a.m. A heavy snowstorm was coming down, and a friend who owned a small car offered him and two friends a lift to their apartments. Since his apartment was only a few blocks away, my father usually preferred to walk, but because it was so cold, he and one of his friends got into the car. Unfortunately, the other colleague—a man named Santiago who also lived close by—decided to walk. At the corner, about forty yards from the factory, the immigration van was waiting.

People in the community learned to recognize the cars that prowled the streets of West New York looking for undocumented immigrants, but Santiago may not have had the time to see the van that was waiting at the corner. As he reached the corner, an immigration officer stopped him. It was too late for him to run or hide. They wanted to see his "green card." Santiago did not have this document. He was an undocumented immigrant. He was quickly loaded into the van and taken into custody. The immigration officers had to hurry. They had a feeling that this would be a good day. It was very early and they already had one in the van. Santiago was soon on a plane back to Colombia. His wife and two young kids remained behind in America.

My father did not see what occurred because he had accepted the offer to ride in the car of his friend. Otherwise, he may have had the same misfortune as Santiago. At around ten that morning, my father received a call from Santiago's wife, Nuvia, describing the events of the morning. She also said that the van was still making its rounds in the neighborhood.

My father immediately called my mother at her clothing factory on 64th Street and Palisade Avenue and warned her that the immigration service was in the vicinity and that its officers might raid her factory. He urged her to return home. She hurried out, and as she was scurrying south on Palisade Avenue, she saw the van slowly making its way toward another factory. My mother managed to keep her composure and keep walking, pretending that the sight of the van did not disturb her. That same car would soon catch a friend of my mother's, Naomi. My mother came home, and together she and my father knelt down in prayer, thanking the Lord and the Virgin Mary for helping them elude the INS for another day. My father understood how close he had come to being deported. Had he decided to walk with Santiago, he would have certainly had the same misfortune.

On another occasion, my father was working when officers strode into his factory unannounced and started asking workers for green cards. My father and another friend managed to dash upstairs and hide under the large embroidery sheets resting against the wall. As the immigration officers passed by, my father and his friend could hear their footsteps and the questions they were asking the workers. However, the officers never spotted them. When the officers left, my father resumed working. Visits like these explained why my father preferred to work the night shift; he felt that it was less likely that immigration agents would randomly show up during the middle of the night.

Although each visit from immigration brought enormous stress, our community learned to live with the knowledge that we were being pursued. Some even saved up to pay for the smugglers' fees, bribes, and other expenses needed to return to America if they were caught. This is what both Santiago and Naomi did. After Santiago and Naomi were deported, they both made their way back to the United States through Mexico.

This was the reality of life for all of us as undocumented immigrants. We lived in the shadows of American society with the ever-present fear of some day being discovered. Whatever glories I was achieving at Memorial High, whatever attention teachers, students, or athletics rooters would give me, I was constantly aware that I carried a secret that I could never acknowledge. I was an undocumented immigrant—a person in this country without authorization, without any documents. No victory on the track, no trips to the gym at Princeton, no county championship, nor any Eagle Scout award could erase that.

When I was growing up in Colombia, "Pedro Navaja" (Peter the Knife) was the title of a popular song played at *La Oasis.* It is a masterpiece of the salsa genre by the famed Panamanian artist Rubén Blades. In the lyrics, a killer drifts through the dark streets of El Barrio searching for a victim. As he wanders around, an ordinary-looking automobile roams the streets.

> Un carro pasa muy despacito por la avenida.
>
> (A car passes slowly through the street.)
>
> No tiene marcas pero todos saben que es policía.
>
> (It is not marked, but everyone knows it is a police car.)

The person without documents is both like the song's unmarked police car and the shadowed criminal. Like the police car, everyone around knows that you are in disguise, hiding in plain sight, pretending to be something you are not. And like the criminal, you always feel you are being hunted. Even though you are in this country to work honestly, you understand that many will shy away because they may feel there is something vaguely sinister about you.

At certain moments, I felt this way as I walked through the halls of Memorial, through the downtown of West New York, and in quintessential American places like the Princeton campus when we went for our track meets. As I took in the beauty of that imposing campus, I felt that I did not belong—like I was an intruder, marginal, different, displaced.

As such, the undocumented immigrant keeps a low profile, makes every attempt to live within the letter of the law. This was what my family did for many years. We and other undocumented immigrants lived an underground existence with the ever-present fear of being uncovered. We learned to maneuver through a labyrinth of obstacles and not be detected by the Immigration and Naturalization Service, as the agency was known until recent years. Nonetheless, the great majority of the undocumented community had developed deep roots and intimate bonds to our American society. Many had children who were born here, and were legitimate American citizens. Millions worked in the kitchens of thousands of restaurants or on thousands of construction sites; they trimmed lawns, swabbed floors, and cleaned toilets, picked fruits and vegetables on the nation's farms, baby-sat children for women trying to make a career for themselves.

Such qualms did not stop the immigration service from raiding Hispanic communities in search of people who could not produce legal documents. There were many such visits in West New York while I was growing up. My parents, Byron, and I lived with the fear that one day an immigration officer would come knocking on our door demanding to inspect our papers, and we would be deported back to Colombia.

The immigration service knows well the cities and towns where immigrants live and work. West New York was the "Embroidery

Capital of the World," and it also had a robust clothing industry, so its factories attracted immigrants willing to take low-paying jobs. The factories would be open day and night in two, twelve-hour shifts. Immigration officers could randomly show up and find many undocumented workers.

More than anything, of course, my parents wanted to become legal residents. They listened to the news constantly, hoping that politicians would pass an amnesty law to fix their status here. They also sought advice on many occasions from lawyers. But all the lawyers seemed glad to take their money and inform them that they did not qualify in any way for a green card. The lawyers' most creative advice was that my parents get a divorce and then marry American citizens for at least a few years. On one of these sessions, one at which my brothers and I came along, a lawyer warned us in very clear terms that we could all end up in jail. He was very harsh in his choice of words and my mother came out of the meeting with tears in her eyes.

Young as we were, the anxiety of being discovered was something we children adjusted to. We prepared mentally for the day when one of our parents might not return home after a day's work. We had seen this happen to some of the parents of our schoolmates and friends, had seen families broken up. And we were sometimes embroiled in our parents' schemes to avoid capture.

Airports were well known as places swarming with immigration officers because they were also swarming with undocumented immigrants meeting arriving or departing relatives. So when my parents needed to go to Newark International Airport to pick up Marlon after he took a trip to Colombia, they came up with a clever scheme to trick the officers. Marlon was our true American citizen, had obtained a passport with his New Jersey birth certificate, and so could be sent away for the summer to visit his grandmothers in Colombia. My mother's uncle was bringing him back on the plane, but my parents were concerned that as they waited for Marlon's arrival, immigration officers might spot them. So they made Byron and I dress up in our Boy Scout uniforms. They figured that the parents of two Scouts would less likely arouse suspicions. My parents also believed that in the event they were caught, the officers would show them compassion; after all, they were so hungry to become American that they raised two Boy Scouts. We picked Marlon up without any incident.

As a teenager, I was less frightened than my parents about the notion of being discovered by the INS, since the agents never made their rounds in the schools. At times, I would even forget that I was undocumented, reminded only when an American kid would tease me about my accent. Still, as the time to apply to college approached, I realized I would need two essential documents: a green card and a social security card. I needed a social security card to fill out the single line on college applications that asked for my social security number. To get a social security number, I would need a green card—proof of legal residency. Many college applications also require non-citizens to submit a Xerox copy of their green cards. Without legal residency, I had to secure a counterfeit green card. Through a series of contacts, we found a person who sold them for $250. The document, my parents were told, would be an exact replica of a real one and it would have my picture on it. The only way to know that it wasn't real was to check the number against the central INS database— but who would go through that trouble?

When the green card was delivered two weeks later, I examined it carefully. Although I had never seen a real one before, I persuaded myself that the card in my possession did not look real. Nonetheless, I didn't have much of a choice. I would need to use it for college applications, and also to obtain a genuine social security number at a social security office. We were advised not to visit the local office in West New York. With so many immigrants in town, the clerks there were quite familiar with forged green cards. Instead, we were urged to visit an office in a smaller New Jersey town without a large immigrant population.

One of the places recommended was the town of Long Branch on the central New Jersey coast. So, I decided to make my way to that town.

On a boiling, humid, August day in 1983, between my junior and senior years of high school, I took a bus by myself from the Port Authority terminal in Manhattan to Long Branch. The Long Branch bus station was two miles from the local Social Security office and I had to walk the entire way. When I reached the office, I was sweating profusely. It was not just from the heat, but also from anxiety and desperation about what I was about to do. I was now in an office of the United States government and about to present the officials there with a forged document.

When the lady at the desk saw that I was drenched, she offered me a glass of water. I gladly took it and informed her that I was there to apply for a Social Security card. I told her that I lived in West New York, but that I had a summer job in the Long Branch area. She took some of my information and then asked me to come inside where a second clerk would finish processing the application. She then asked me for my green card. Trembling, I reached into my wallet and put the card on her desk. She glanced at it briefly, put it back on the desk, and then left for an office nearby.

From where I was sitting, I could see that she was making telephone calls. I was too far away to figure out the nature of her calls, but after a few minutes of waiting, I became convinced that she was calling the Immigration and Naturalization Service to check on the green card's authenticity. I was growing more anxious by the second. I could no longer tolerate the tension and decided that I would make an escape. When it appeared that she was not looking in my direction, I went over to her desk, picked up my green card and all the other documents that I had filled out, and I walked out of the office. No one saw me and I made an uneventful exit. Once outside, I didn't run, but I strode as fast as I could to the bus station and returned home two hours later.

I was disheartened that I still didn't have a social security card, but happy that I had been able to escape without any major problems. I realized then that I did not have the strength to present this forged document to anyone in person.

Over the next few weeks, the deadlines for submitting college applications approached. We asked friends for other means of getting a social security number and learned of a worker at one of the federal offices who, for a small fee, would process an application for a valid number. I would be getting a card actually printed by the Social Security Administration, and the worker would not ask to see a residency card. This worker let me obtain a social security card with an apparently legitimate number. In fact, for many years after college, I thought that it was a valid document. However, I discovered that it wasn't when I was about to start medical school and tried to open a bank account in Boston. A bank officer informed me that the number belonged to a dead person.

SPIRES AND GARGOYLES

In the fall of 1985, I entered Princeton as a freshman. The university had offered me the opportunity to attend a special two-week orientation program, and I gladly accepted. I had been waiting for this moment for years, and I could not wait any longer. I wanted to be part of the Princeton family. On my first day on campus, after I had unpacked my luggage in my dorm room at Brown Hall, I stepped outside for a stroll around the university to enjoy the beauty and serenity of its grounds. As I made my way around, exuberant at the thought of being an official Princeton student, I glanced at the different buildings and found myself enchanted by the spires, the gargoyles adorning hidden corners and hideaways, the castle-like dormitories, the teeming libraries, and the hoary traditions associated with each structure. In the gritty factory town of West New York, I had often fallen asleep while gazing at these dreamy campus scenes in the student handbook. When I actually saw the campus, I reacted no differently than F. Scott Fitzgerald had three generations before when, as a boy from an upper-middle-class, if provincial, Midwestern home he came to Princeton. He depicted his reaction lyrically through the eyes of his awed young protagonist, Amory Blaine, in the 1920 classic, This Side of Paradise.

Princeton of the daytime filtered slowly into his consciousness—West and Reunion, redolent of the sixties, Seventy-
nine Hall, brick-red and arrogant, Upper and Lower Pyne,
aristocratic Elizabethan ladies not quite content to live
among shopkeepers, and topping all, climbing with clear
blue aspiration, the great dreaming spires of Holder and
Cleveland towers.

From the first he loved Princeton—its lazy beauty, its
half-grasped significance, the wild moonlight revel of the
rushes, the handsome, prosperous big-game crowds, and
under it all the air of struggle that pervaded his class.

However, I came to the school with a very different background
than the standard Princeton student or from the one that Amory
brought with him. Although she was not from the privileged class,
Amory's mother sent him to a prep school and raised him on
the high points of Western culture. "She fed him sections of the
'Fêtes Galantes' before he was ten; at eleven he could talk glibly,
if rather reminiscently, of Brahms and Mozart and Beethoven."
By contrast, I had been raised in the streets of Barrio Antioquia
in Medellín, Colombia, listening to the lyrics of tango and salsa
songs that spoke of violence and rebellion, the harsh realities of
drugs, death, and prison. My schools had been the rough-and-
tumble corridors of Memorial High.

Nevertheless, I too was required to thrive on "this side of
paradise." In addition, as a Hispanic student, I saw myself as rep-
resenting the hopes and struggles of new immigrants, of minori-
ties, and of working-class kids—three groups whose ranks had
greatly increased at Princeton since Fitzgerald's days.

On my return from my walk around campus, as I climbed
up the hill that leads to Brown Hall, a car pulled up alongside
me. The driver asked me for directions to Brown Hall. As I
showed them the way, I was struck by the beauty of the attractive African-American young lady sitting in the passenger seat

next to her father. We did not make eye contact, but I could sense that we both looked at each other with intrigue. I later learned that her name was Tina Marie Harris. She and her parents arrived in a station wagon loaded with all the clothes and gear she would need for college. They had traveled by car all the way from Indianapolis.

The next time that I saw her was at the Third World Center, a shabby old house a half-mile from the main campus on Prospect Avenue. It served as a cultural center for Hispanic and African-American students. This was a place where we could spend time with students with similar social, economic, and cultural backgrounds. There was a welcome lecture that first Saturday, and afterward we lingered in a large common room that had a grand piano in the corner.

When I entered, I heard a soothing, bell-like voice singing a gospel song and some masterful piano playing. As I got closer, I noticed that it was the girl in the station wagon who was performing. Her long-nailed fingers moved effortlessly across the keys and her face exuded the fervor the song made her feel. In the crowd that gathered around, it was obvious that her songs of struggle and faith touched and inspired all of us.

A few nights later, we gathered for a dance at Forbes, a former golf resort for wealthy people that was now one of the residential colleges. The hotel's ballroom, its elegance accentuated by waxed wooden floors, Oriental carpets, and opulent chandeliers, was swarming with upper classmen from the athletic clubs that were starting to return for their two-week, pre-school, training camps. These juniors and seniors would be trying to impress the new freshman girls. I thought Tina would not want to dance with me. I was just an insignificant freshman from a small town and, even further back, from a third world country. During our few conversations, there were things I said that she didn't quite make out, and she forced me to repeat myself. Somehow one of my new friends, Steve Watkins, and I wandered over to where

Tina was talking with friends and I learned she was planning to go back to the dorm because she was not having a good time. It was after one in the morning and dark and deserted outside, and when some of the guys expressed concern for Tina's returning by herself, I offered my company.

"I don't feel well, either, so I'll walk back with her," I said. She picked up her light coat—it was a cool, late-summer night—and we started on our way to Brown Hall. I had my hands in my jacket pockets. At some point, she put her arm inside my elbow. I was not sure what this meant, whether it was romantic or just friendly. I felt anxious, but luckily, Tina did most of the talking. She seemed well-informed about a wide spectrum of subjects and felt free voicing her thoughts about each one. She asked me several questions about soccer, even though she didn't like the sport.

As we approached Brown Hall, I didn't know how to end the evening, so I asked Tina if she wanted to see the Prospect Gardens behind the president's home. We sat on a small bench hidden within the trees and, in this isolated, dimly lit setting, quiet except for the footsteps of an occasional student, I somehow managed to summon the courage to put my arm around Tina and then kiss her on the lips. I was scared that she might push me away, but she responded tenderly. We spent several minutes kissing and embracing. Our conversation became more intimate; she told me about her family, I told her about mine. Then, she said it was getting late and explained that she had to go to church in the morning. So we walked back to Brown Hall. That night, I slept restlessly, thinking about Tina, about having kissed this dazzling girl. I also felt guilty. I was at Princeton to study, and all I could think about was Tina.

I had already had a taste of intense college life. There was not only the summer at Rensselaer Polytechnic Institute, but just before entering Princeton, I took two college-level courses in calculus and chemistry at the College of Mount St. Vincent in Riverdale, New York, that were sponsored by an organization, Prep for Prep, that aimed to help college-bound minority students. Still, once at Princeton, I quickly found myself feeling anxious to be sitting in the same classes with students who were clearly better prepared than I was. I was determined, however, that I would match them and kept telling myself that to do so I would study until I dropped. This was my only chance at evening the playing field, even if it meant giving up the distinctive social activities that Princeton had to offer.

The real reason that I arrived on campus two weeks before the rest of the entering class was that the university realized that there were students like me who might need special atten-tion and instruction—athletes, students from poor and minority backgrounds, students from families where no one had attended college. This was a time for orientation and guidance, so that we could be introduced to life at Princeton and its academic demands with a taste of courses in calculus, chemistry, and writing. The first two were not difficult, but I realized that writing would be a challenge and my clumsy accent—my mangling of everyday English, my unfamiliarity with American idioms—would haunt me throughout my four years. My one consolation was that I had already acquired the study habits they were urging us to adopt.

My roommate for the program was Shawn, a white student from Kansas whose father was a physician. He was the state champion in chess. He took great pleasure in asking me to play and showing how much better he was. Losing didn't dishearten me; I was just an occasional chess player and was intent on prov-ing my merits in the classroom, not on the chessboard. However, the most striking part of our time as roommates was Shawn's wardrobe— his expensive shoes, pants, and sweaters. Once, he went shopping with his parents on Nassau Street and came back with a pair of $200 shoes. I had never spent more than twenty dollars on a pair. So I promptly sensed there was a great cultural and economic divide between us, and after the two-week pro-gram was over we seldom saw each other.

One of the great benefits of attending this program was the opportunity to meet and interact with other students with diverse backgrounds and interests. Although we all had our own unique set of circumstances, we discovered that, despite our differences, we shared many experiences. Nonetheless, as I discovered early in my Princeton education, I had much to learn from my fellow students.

One close friend, whom I met my first week, was Steve Watkins. He was a strong, good-looking, six-foot-four-inch student from a prosperous black family in Washington, D.C. who hoped to play both football and basketball for Princeton. His father was a doctor and had been a strict disciplinarian all of Steve's life, having great expectations for him. We felt at ease with each other and quickly became friends despite our different backgrounds. We both enjoyed sports. He was a born athlete and even played soccer well, though not as well as I did. I took some pleasure in showing off my soccer footwork on the Princeton field. He greatly overshadowed me on the basketball court.

One warm afternoon at the outdoor basketball courts behind Dillon gym, he was patiently dribbling the ball toward the basket waiting for an opening, and I provoked him to make his move, shouting, "Come on, boy!" He was startled. He didn't say much, but I could see in his face that something was not right. I had no idea what I had said or done to cause this sudden change. We finished off the game as if nothing had happened and went our separate ways.

That night, as we walked together to our dormitory at Brown Hall, Steve told me that he had felt insulted by what I said during the game. He explained that "boy" was a term slave owners used toward the people that served them and that it had remained a term of belittlement long into the twentieth century. My heart sank. Even today, I blame myself for having been so ignorant. Steve had waited several hours to calmly tell me something that had deeply troubled him.

Throughout high school, I had learned only superficially of the struggles of black Americans and had never discussed the topic with my parents or teachers. I did not have any black friends. I wondered how I could have offended my friend this way. I certainly did not mean for my statement to be taken in the context Steve took it. I felt terrible. There was no excuse for this; I should have known better. I was upset that Steve had been hurt and I apologized. He accepted my apology, and he sensed that I was genuinely troubled by what I had done. I was just starting to learn some of the subtleties of the great struggle of the African-American people.

Race and social status were discussed as gingerly at Princeton as anywhere else during those years. However, in intimate circles, we would confide episodes where we experienced insults or subtle signs of intolerance. More than one black student told me of times when they had walked on the main drag, Nassau Street, at night and a white couple walking ahead would glance nervously back at them as they drew closer. Sometimes, the couple would speed up or change direction and look for an open shop. At first, I thought these newfound friends were just being paranoid. But over several years, I would hear white students, apparently thinking of me as one of their own, make subtly disparaging comments, suggesting they didn't think highly of blacks or found them intimidating. I am sure that similar insults were probably said of Hispanics when I was not present.

For my first year, I was assigned to Hamilton Hall in Mathey College, one of Princeton's five residential colleges. I shared a small room, with a window overlooking a stately gothic courtyard, with a Mexican immigrant, Juan Almaguer. Juan had grown up in East Los Angeles and had been part of the original class taught by Jaime Escalante, who had left a lucrative science career to teach calculus to poor, troubled students, and whose experiences were documented in the inspirational Hollywood film *Stand and Deliver*. Juan was slender, tall, with a thick mustache, and he carried himself as if he came from an aristocratic European family. However, Juan and I shared many social and economic experiences. Juan was paying his way through Princeton by washing dishes in Mathey's cafeteria.

The students that I grew to know in the Hamilton dorm included the sons of doctors, lawyers, and businessmen, and even a Rockefeller grandson. I was surrounded by the very type of talented, self-confident young people that Amory described in *This Side of Paradise*. For him, they stirred up feelings of his own inferiority, making him wonder if there was something vulgar about his clothes or his baggage and feel unnecessarily "stiff and awkward among these white flannelled, bareheaded youths" and "the savoir-faire with which they strolled."

At night, as I tried to fall asleep, I often wondered if I deserved to be at Princeton. For starters, I had used a counterfeit green card and social security number in my application. Scholastically, I had doubts about whether my education in West New York could possibly match that of students who had gone to prestigious prep schools and selective public schools. In my classes or in social circles, I had a tendency to hold back because I was embarrassed of my foreign accent when speaking in English.

I moved around campus as if I was on stage and other students were evaluating my performance and finding it deficient. Although I dressed neatly, I was glaringly aware that my clothes were less expensive. I ate all my meals at the cafeteria, whose food I considered gourmet quality, though most students knew better. Unlike the wealthier students, I worked shifts washing dishes in the cafeteria and added to my spending money by tutoring the daughter of Arcadio Díaz-Quiñones, my Spanish literature professor, in calculus and helping him with his research projects. My parents and grandmothers had hammered manners into me, urging me always to be cordial in conversations and to respect my elders. Still, I was very self-conscious about my accent and was never as articulate or expressive as other students. Each time that I spun out an awkward sentence, I was sure other students wondered what I was doing at Princeton.

I wondered myself if I belonged. I would look at the caliber—and outright celebrity—of some students and feel like I had been thrown in a dream world that I could not possibly merit. One night, as I was getting my food on my tray in the cafeteria, placing peanut butter and jelly on bread for my dinner sandwich, I noticed a strikingly tall, shapely girl waiting for me to finish. It was Brooke Shields, *the* Brooke Shields, who had starred in movies like *Pretty Baby* and *Blue Lagoon*. She was a junior when I was a freshman and had returned that day to Mathey to have dinner with freshman friends. I anxiously hurried patching together the sandwich, and moved along to get some drinks, pretending that I did not care who she was. Of course I did.

Yet whatever insecurities I had, I came to see Mathey as a protective cocoon, a home away from my West New York home. During one of the dorm meetings with our residential assistant, the students revealed a little about their backgrounds. Most told of parents who were physicians, lawyers, and owners of companies. I simply said that my parents worked in textile factories. I felt proud of the hard work my grandmothers, as solitary women, had done raising Byron and me, and proud of how hard my father and mother had labored to send money back to Colombia so we could eat. Yet, in this talented group of students, I felt I was different. I could not summon the same prestigious family résumé. I tried to persuade myself that my background was distinctive but not necessarily worse. For the most part, I succeeded. In fact, there were times I felt an inner strength knowing that I was now going to be in the same classes with these elite students and that, by working tirelessly, I could show them I was as good as they were.

The laurels of excellence belonged to those who were hungry, and I was hungry. In the classroom, I was still very quiet, but I could demonstrate my grasp of the material when it came time to answer questions on a written test. More than a few students relied on their stellar high school records to carry them through, but I could match them by being well prepared.

I devised a scheme for studying that would carry me even through my days in medical school. I kept two notebooks for every course. In one, I took notes on what the professor said in the classroom. At night, I would copy the notes onto another notebook. Here, I would rewrite all the professor's remarks in a comprehensible and organized fashion, supplementing the summaries with explanations from the textbook or with my own interpretations, as well as with diagrams and pictures. If I did not understand something, I made it a point to hunt down the professor later that day to secure an explanation. I would read a required chapter so many times that I would end up memorizing much of it. I was always ahead of the reading list by two or three weeks, which allowed me to ask the appropriate questions.

I often took my commitment to an extreme, even if the rest of my life suffered. I decided, for example, that I could not have any distractions—no music, no conversations. Therefore, I could not study in my room or in the library. I had to find private places that I could call my own. Princeton had many such niches that one could claim at night and on weekends. I was particularly attached to the large rooms in Palmer Hall that once housed the physics classrooms, where, nearly half a century before, Einstein had given some of his famous lectures. The idea of sitting in the same rooms where one of the greatest minds had taught inspired me. On Saturday, I often disappeared after breakfast and would not be seen again until Sunday dinner. I would only stop to eat or go to the bathroom. I was fiercely selfish with my study habits and never revealed my secret locations to anyone, not even to Tina.

I had another eccentric but highly effective system of study. Each of the classrooms that I selected had to have a large blackboard. I would read about a problem, solve it, and then step up to the board and pretend that I was teaching it to a class. I would do so in a loud voice. I am sure that if anyone ever saw me, he or she would have probably thought that I was in need of psychiatric help. However, this routine worked well for me. I found that if I could teach a concept to someone else, then I probably understood it. This system was also effective because it prevented me from falling asleep on top of my book as I was studying. At the first sign of dozing off, I would get up and go to the chalkboard. I discovered that the physical act of getting up was refreshing, re-energizing, and very effective in preventing moments of snooze that tend to occur during reading. Although Tina never understood why I had to study unaccompanied, I always figured that no one would really want to share a room with someone who was studying in such an unorthodox fashion. Notwithstanding the intricacies of my background, my social inadequacies, my peculiar study habits, and all my struggles, the system that I designed worked flawlessly. To my own surprise, I got all A's in my first semester.

A DAY OF GLOOM

On an ordinary evening during my second semester at Princeton, I finished my dinner, took my dirty plates to the kitchen sink, and said good-bye to my friends. After dinner, we usually went our separate ways around campus. I had fallen behind in some of my work, so I rushed out of the dining hall and crossed the narrow alley into the ground floor of Hamilton Hall to pick up my mail before making my way to the library for a long night of intense studying.

The dining hall at Mathey College, one of Princeton's five residential colleges, resembled an enormous gothic sanctuary from the Renaissance. I loved having dinner there with my friends at the end of the day. This was a time to relax, enjoy the company of friends, and forget about the work. The conversations, the camaraderie, and the stories we shared as students I still cherish today. As the evening approached, the last remaining rays of light would make their way through the large windows into the center of the walkway, creating an ambience of a place of worship or meditation. At times, I would stop and enjoy the grandiosity and beauty of the architectural details. My thoughts would typically conclude with some feeling of guilt and thoughts that I didn't belong in this historic institution, thoughts that my stay here would only be brief. I did not have legal immigration documents to be in America. I thought that it was just a matter of time before this dream would end.

As I picked up the mail, I noticed that one of the letters was from the assistant Dean of Mathey College, Nancy Kanach. For some reason, this letter got my attention and I stopped briefly to open it up. The letter said, "Dear Harold, having looked at your first-semester grades, I have noticed that you are one of the top students in the university." She congratulated me and encouraged me to keep up the good work. Reading this letter brought tears of joy to my eyes. I read it many times. The letter was more important to me than any trophy, diploma, or certificate I had ever received. It erased all the doubts I'd had about whether I deserved to occupy a place at this incredible institution. The fact that I had not graduated from one of the elite private high schools in the country was no longer important. Princeton University had trusted in me, and I had responded. In one semester, I had proved wrong those who rejected the principles of affirmative action.

A university admissions committee has a daunting task. I am currently a volunteer for the Princeton admissions committee, so I understand the difficulties. In my opinion, every applicant I have interviewed in the last five years has deserved to be admitted. I know for sure that all these kids would have been able to do the work required of them by my alma mater. Unfortunately, only a very small percentage of these very qualified students could be accepted.

The process by which a committee tries to decipher which students are more deserving or more qualified is complicated. All students have had their own formative experiences. Trying to compare a student from a poor neighborhood in Trenton to a student from a private school on the north shore of Long Island with total objectivity may prove an impossible task. Yet, the decision process needs to be fair to both students.

I strongly feel that it is important to examine the obstacles that an applicant has had to overcome. This is what affirmative action is. It should clearly be differentiated from the concept of quotas. Affirmative action means that a company or university should have the flexibility in its decision-making process to evaluate each candidate fully. Our accomplishments do not occur in a vacuum—they occur in settings with degrees of difficulty attached. The level of difficulty is different for each of us, and this is what affirmative action attempts to take into account. I do not think that Affirmative action is designed to elevate an under-qualified or undeserving applicant above one who is better qualified on the basis of race. It means evaluating each applicant individually on his or her own merits, taking into account the barriers that each person has needed to overcome to accomplish those results.

The reality is that affirmative action happens in our society every day. For example, the great financial companies of Manhattan show favoritism toward applicants based on many different criteria, many of them not related to an applicant's ability or qualifications. In my case, the Princeton University admissions team took a close look at my life. They examined my application beyond my good but not perfect SAT results and beyond the fact that I had graduated from a relatively unknown public high school in a mostly Hispanic neighborhood. They probably also noticed that my application consisted of accomplishments I had achieved *after* learning English as a second language. Whatever the discussions that may have gone on within the admissions committee about me, the letter from Dean Kanach identifying me as one of the top students proved that I belonged at Princeton. And because of what it meant to me, I kept that letter to myself. I never shared it with my parents or with any of my close friends. I tucked the letter behind some books in one of my desk drawers, hidden away but easily retrieved during moments when I would doubt myself. Beneficiary of affirmative action or not, I was pleased with my achievements so far, and I was determined that I would work just as hard or harder in my second semester.

One of the highlights of my second semester was my Spanish literature course, taught by Professor Arcadio Díaz-Quiñones. His lectures were vivid, informative, and colorful. His analysis of the major works of Spanish literature was unique and thought provoking. One of his principles for deriving meaning from literature was that each book or poem should evoke and stimulate one's own personal interpretation in the context of one's own experience. It opened my mind to thoughts and possibilities about the meaning of Latin American literature that I had never entertained before. Nevertheless, as I sat in Professor Díaz's class, with a view through the window toward the beautiful Gothic sculptures in the courtyard of East Pyne, I never imagined the significance that this wonderful man and his words would have in my life.

In addition to the intellectual challenges, the second term also inspired me with the arrival of springtime and warmer days, which are so welcome in the Northeast. In fact, each time the springtime comes around even now, I reminisce about my days and evenings at Princeton. As early as March, many classes would begin to meet outside on the perfectly manicured lawns outside McCosh Hall. On sunny days, many students would lie on the grass wearing little clothing, trying to advance the color of their skin to a tanner complexion.

In the afternoons before dinner, other students would participate in outdoor activities such as playing Frisbee, having picnics, and enjoying outdoor parties. The energy of the other students was contagious.

I felt stronger and more self-assured at this point than I had at any time. Instead of being distracted by the pleasant surroundings, I was strengthened to concentrate and work even harder. Although I was participating in some of the social and leisurely activities, most of my time was still spent studying. The coursework was more difficult, but I was gaining confidence with each passing day. Everything appeared too perfect; I was sure something was about to change. I was sure that a day of gloom was approaching. I was correct, for one of my old secrets would come back to haunt me.

The progress that I had made toward feeling like a legitimate part of this cherished American house of education screeched to an abrupt halt one spring evening during my second semester. The year was almost over. We would soon be going home for the spring holiday and then returning for a month-long reading period that would be followed by final exams. I was eagerly looking forward to going home, to tasting my mother's Colombian cooking again and hearing my parents' Spanish wit and earthy insights. I followed my usual midweek routine. I had dinner with Tina and then returned to my dorm room. On the ground floor, I headed, as usual, toward the mailbox. There was a letter. I noticed that it was from the university's dean of foreign students, Janina Issawi. I assumed that it was probably an invitation to a social event for foreign students stuck at Princeton during the holiday break.

I tore the envelope open and read the letter. It was an official letter reminding foreign-born students who were not yet American citizens to set up an appointment with Mrs. Issawi and bring along their original legal residency documents so that they could be photocopied for inclusion in the student's file. The letter further explained that this was an official request to allow the federal government to keep track of students who were permanent residents and who were receiving government grants or loans, as I was. But this letter was not a routine matter for me. Princeton had already seen a copy of my green card in my application for admission, but now the dean needed to see the original and I knew that the original was a forgery purchased by my parents on the black market. Walking into a Princeton dean's office and handing her fake document would not be routine for me.

The abysmal hole in my stomach was the polar opposite of the joy I felt when I had received the letter from Dean Kanach congratulating me on my first semester grades. It was as if everything had been instantly overturned. I said to myself, "Oh, my God, my Princeton career is about to end." The dream of American success that had begun at an abandoned dock on the Florida coast was about to shatter.

Several students were standing around, opening mail, so I slipped the letter inside its envelope. I didn't want anyone to glimpse its contents. Tina, who had come to the mailboxes with me, was nearby. My feelings cascaded from nervousness, to sadness, to outright gloom, and my face, a contrast to the lighthearted faces of students receiving letters from their families, must have telegraphed my emotions. It is hard to hide bad news, and Tina, searching my face, noticed immediately that something was awry.

"What's wrong, Harold?" she asked.

"I can't tell you now," I said, turning away. I could not look her in the eye. "I need to go back to my room," I said. "I'll see you later."

Tina sensed that I had received bad news and insisted on accompanying me. When we got to my room, she forcefully reached into my coat pocket and grabbed the letter. I let her read it and when she looked up, she said she could not understand why it upset me so.

"It's just a routine letter; what is wrong?" she said.

Of course, we had never spoken about my residency status before, so how could she understand? Indeed, I had never spoken to anyone at Princeton about the subject. As far as Tina was concerned, I was as much a citizen of this country as she was.

I started to explain, but it still took several minutes for her to grasp the gravity of my dilemma. I told her bluntly that I was an undocumented immigrant and that I could be deported to

Colombia overnight if immigration officials discovered the truth. Princeton could throw me out and probably would, I told her. Although we had been together for just a few months, we had grown to love each other. So, when the full weight of my predicament sank in, I could tell that Tina felt my anguish. Tears welled in her eyes. Without offering any advice, Tina suggested that we pray. "God, give us your guidance," she murmured, and I repeated her simple appeal.

For the next few days, I was consumed with figuring out what I should do. I did not speak about the dean's request with anyone besides Tina, not even with my parents. I knew that it would tear them apart to learn that I might be expelled, that I might be barred from the American opportunities they had worked so hard to give me. They were so proud that I was a student at Princeton. I pictured my father's locker at work, plastered with newspaper articles—in English and Spanish—about my accomplishments in the classroom and on the field. He would often call his friends, bosses, or even random visitors, and show them the inside of his locker. His boss might earn more money, have a more prestigious job, but he did not have a son at Princeton. As I lay on my bed during those harrowing nights, I would think of how terrible it would be for my parents, how much they would cry, if I were to suddenly arrive at our apartment in West New York—luggage in hand—and tell them, "It is over—my career at Princeton is finished." I am not exaggerating when I say that my parents would have died of sadness.

My choices actually were quite simple. I could meet with the dean and show her my fake green card, and hope I might charm my way through. Or I could confess and tell her that I did not have any legal documents. I no longer had the heart for the first option. It was pure fear. I remembered how, a few years earlier, I had failed to follow all the way through with my plan to get a social security card in Long Branch, N.J. If a government clerk could frighten me so, how much more was I frightened by the prospect of having to fool a Princeton dean? So, I wanted to confess my actions to someone that I could trust.

Over the course of the semester, I had come to feel that my professor in Spanish literature, Arcadio Díaz-Quiñones, was not only a foremost scholar, but was also a kind, wise, and generous friend. So, a few days after I had opened the dean's letter, I waited after his class and asked if he could spare a few minutes. He put me at ease by telling me I could have as much time as I wanted. He closed the door, and we sat down next to each other at the end of the long rectangular table.

As I was about to speak, I sensed that I would not utter a single word without breaking down. In front of Tina, I had kept all my emotions in check, but I could no longer do that with Professor Díaz. The tension and anxiety that had built up inside of me exploded. Before I said any words, I dropped my head on the table and wept. Professor Díaz put his hand on my shoulder and held it there consolingly. After a few minutes, I collected myself and described all that I had had to do to get into this country and my efforts ever since to disguise my residency status. I told him how frightened I was that I would be discharged from Princeton and what that would do to my family.

Professor Díaz listened patiently. He was interested in every detail of my story, almost as if he were intently reading some vivid, picaresque novel. When I was done, he advised me not to tell anyone else about what had happened and to keep plugging along with my schoolwork. He assured me that he would speak to Mrs. Issawi, who was a close friend. He also said that he would discuss the problem with the dean of students, Eugene Lowe, and the president of the university, William G. Bowen. The thought that such authority figures would be analyzing my case terrified me, but Professor Díaz's confidence seemed to calm me down.

Over the next few weeks, he met with several administrators. At first, he told me later, he discussed the problem in the abstract, without mentioning my name, but eventually he presented the full facts to Mrs. Issawi and other deans, as well as the president of the university. The result was that I was summoned to meet with Nancy Weiss, the dean of Mathey College.

As we met in her office, I found Mrs. Weiss to be compassionate. I felt at ease in her presence, although I feared what she might say. She started by saying that Princeton was proud to have me in its student body. Nevertheless, she described two formidable issues that the university now had to confront. First, I had broken the students' honor code. This essential Princeton tradition affirms that you cannot cheat or lie, and I had lied. Then, she said, I had been receiving government grants intended for American citizens or permanent residents. Since I was neither, my taking the money violated the law. "But, Harold," she said, "both problems have solutions, and the university wants to help you."

Just as I was feeling crushed by the scope of the problems she had outlined, Mrs. Weiss gave me a glimmer of hope. I looked up with an invigorated concentration. To address the first issue, she said, I would have to write a substantial essay explaining my understanding of the school's honor code, how I had broken it, and why I wanted a pardon. To resolve the second problem, Princeton would change my status to that of a foreign student. With that change, the university would furnish all my grants and loans with its own funds, not with those of the federal government. This shift meant that Princeton would be contributing more than $16,000 a year so that I could study there. It was like having a full Princeton scholarship.

I left Mrs. Weiss's office feeling enormous relief; I had squared myself away with the university. However, it quickly occurred to me that I could not quite breathe a sigh of relief because solving this problem at Princeton had done nothing for my undocumented status and that of my family's. I was no longer an imposter at Princeton, but my family was still undocumented. I knew I would encounter this issue at other stages in my school and work career and I didn't want to endure the same agony I had just been through. While Princeton was willing to let me stay, there was still a real chance that the Immigration and Naturalization Service would send me back to Colombia.

When I finally told my parents of how Princeton learned that I was an undocumented immigrant, the peak of the drama had largely passed. I traveled home for a weekend and explained to them what had happened—but in reverse order. I told them that everything had been solved, that Princeton had arranged for us to meet with one of its lawyers that specializes in immigration, and that he would be trying to help us. Then I explained how Princeton came to put us in touch with its lawyer, and about my confession. As I told them the story, my mother sat next to me, gently weeping. She felt terrible that their decision to enter the country without documents had put me through such anguish and that they had been able to do little to help.

My mother said, "Harold, *mi amor*, you are a great person. Keep working hard and your dreams will become a reality." My father had been silent, fearing the worst, and he finally said, "Oh, my son, please forgive us for having put you through such torment, but keep working hard and America will keep on helping you."

AMERICAN COMPASSION

On a warm day in May of 1986, I woke up early, just before dawn. As I looked outside my small window facing the serenity of the Hamilton courtyard, I noticed that it was still dark outside. I climbed down from my bunk bed, quietly picked up a towel, soap, toothpaste, and toothbrush, and made my way down two stories to the bathroom in the basement of Hamilton Hall. I made sure that I was very quiet, since I did not want to wake up my roommate Juan who was sleeping in the bottom bed. The entire dorm was silent. All the students were sleeping and getting some rest so that they could proceed to their classes in the morning. The semester was quickly coming to an end, and finals would be coming soon. We were all concentrated and focused on getting ready for final exams. However, I had another concern and worry on my mind. Princeton had opened its doors, but I still had a catastrophic fear that on days like today would tear me up inside. Today, my family and I had an appointment with the Immigration and Naturalization Service (INS). Although this was just one of several routine visits, on each occasion, an immigration judge would be carefully reviewing our case. While my classmates were resting, I had to get up early so that I could go to the INS building in Newark. I was scared. I had been dreading this appointment all week.

On this day, we were scheduled to meet in person with the immigration judge. He would be deciding our fate. He could, in a moment, decide if we could stay in America or if we would be deported. As harsh as it may appear, there was a chance that I would not return to campus. After a quick shower, I got dressed, put several books in my backpack, and made my way down Alexander Street to get the train that would bring me to Newark. This was a solitary and solemn walk as I strolled down the street—just me, my books, and my fears that this could be the end.

As I made my way in the midst of the imposing gothic dorms of the upperclassmen, I was praying that I would someday be able to reside there as a junior and senior. Although I may have appeared calm on the outside, I was anxious and desperate inside. The uncertainty of my future and the thoughts that my wonderful dream could end were at times overwhelming and unbearable.

Nonetheless, despite the turmoil of my situation as an undocumented student, life would go on, and I had to move with it. So, I forced all negative thoughts away and prayed that the judge would be compassionate. I developed a routine that would accommodate my school schedule. On the days when I had an appointment, I would wake up early, take the New Jersey Transit commuter train to Newark, an hour-long ride, and then take a bus to the immigration office. I would come loaded with books to study while I was on the train or waiting in lines. I had decided that the stress and the time spent at the immigration proceedings would not distract me from my mission to do well in school.

After nearly half a dozen routine visits with the immigration service, I became an expert at knowing the general routine, which consisted of a line to get into the building, where we would then proceed to a large common area to begin an adventure through one of the densest, most intractable bureaucracies in America. Every visit involved at least half a day of waiting in lines. There was a line to get into the building, and then, once inside the building, a line to be assigned a waiting room. Once inside the waiting room, which was grimy and dusty, you had to sit on hard plastic seats or folding metal chairs or, if the seats were filled, squat on the floor, and wait for another number to be called. Then we would wait, and wait, and wait.

The waiting room was often filled to capacity with people from every corner of the globe. I could not help thinking that the ambiance was similar to that of the processing area at Ellis Island when the European immigrants arrived at the turn of the twentieth century. Now the countries of origin were different, immigrants hailed from Mexico, Central America, South America, China, India, Pakistan, and Africa. But our goals, I thought to myself, were the same as the goals of the earlier generation. I would often look around at the faces in the room and I could feel the anxiety and uncertainty of these supplicants. We all had dreams of been accepted into American society, and we all feared that this opportunity could be denied. We understood the reality of our situation and the threat that hung over us.

In the midst of so much fervor, anxiety, and emotion, I would quietly search for a corner where I could settle down and hide in my other world, my other existence—my studies at Princeton. I would open my bag and take out one of my books so that I could forget my surroundings. Other people around me also read, usually short novels or magazines, but I stood out with my thick textbooks for physics, calculus, and organic chemistry. While waiting in these lines, or sitting down in one of the corners of this waiting room, I solved many of the complex equations that were stumping me in class. Each time I did, I let out some expression of triumph or contentment, and I would draw strange looks from the others who must have thought I was talking to myself.

When we were finally called up to a window, an agent would speak to us harshly, letting us know who was in charge. On the other side, the immigrant always replied in a gentle voice with kindness, humility, and warmth, almost as if begging for compassion. "Good morning, officer, can you please tell me where I need to go for this letter?" Next, you would get a brusque answer, and follow-up questions were ignored or cut off with a firm and rude, "Next!"

This is how things worked at the INS, and no one could change it. Moreover, no one ever seemed to complain or argue or ask to see a supervisor. Everyone was afraid that complaining would somehow compromise his or her application. Everyone in this room was in a state of anguish and panic, including my family. Each time that we were called into the courtroom and appeared before the judge, we risked being deported. We would wait until our lawyer met briefly with the judge—we were just one of several clients the lawyer was handling that day—and listen to him exchange a few words. The judge would look over the documents, Colombian passports, birth certificates for Alex and Marlon, report cards, income tax returns, letters from my parents' employers, letters from Princeton, and ask our lawyer for additional documents. Very rarely would he address us directly, and even then through the interpreter,

"Mr. Fernandez, do you work in an embroidery factory?" the judge would ask.

"*Si, su majestad,*" my father replied after the translator had interpreted. "Yes, your honor."

"Mr. Fernandez, how long have you lived in this country? Mr. Fernandez, what university does your son attend?"

The judge appeared to be thinking aloud, as if he were trying to find some justification in the file to keep us in the country. Then he would utter a few words that we almost could not hear, but that our lawyer understood.

"Okay, Mr. Fernandez, no residency, we need to wait, but you can continue to live here," the judge said.

The lawyer would take us off to the side and explain the judge's statements. Each time that we heard such words, we were relieved. We were not being deported, at least for now. We had been placed in a category known as "suspension of deportation proceedings." Several times, friends or relatives advised us to forget the proceedings and not to return to Newark. They argued that it was likely the judge would rule against our petition and then we would be deported on the spot. They explained that we had an insurmountable barrier. My parents, Byron, and I had slipped into the country deliberately, knowing that what we were doing was an illegal immigration act. My parents had come here with forged or invalid documents and my brother and I had been smuggled on a small boat from the Bahamas.

We had been informed that we were facing a monumental obstacle. Our previous acts meant that we would have to exit the country, apply and get approved for a visa, re-enter the Unites States in a legal way, and then begin new proceedings with immigration. Doing so would have seriously compromised my studies at Princeton and my parents' jobs. We were in a complex predicament, one that seemed hopeless.

But God, it seemed, was on our side. The judge in charge of our case had a conscience that would not allow him to conclude the hearings and order the deportation of a decent, hard working family, similar to most of the undocumented families that today are struggling in America without documents. At each hearing, he kept saying he needed more time.

The bottom line is that for undocumented immigrants, the American dream is not a house or an automobile or a wide-screen television; it is obtaining a small piece of laminated paper that shows that you are a legal resident of the United States. One reason that the green card is so cherished is that the process to obtain one is daunting, even demoralizing.

Now that I was a student at Princeton, I became obsessed with finding out how my family could obtain a green card. At times, I even let my hunt supersede my studies. I researched every twist of the process, becoming an amateur expert. But the more that I learned, the more unrealistic my family's quest seemed.

I wrote multiple letters to every influential person that I could think of, including Governor Thomas Kean of New Jersey, Senator Bill Bradley, and even the president, who was then Ronald Reagan. Both Governor Kean and Senator Bradley happened to be Princeton alumni, so I was hoping that they would be more sympathetic to my dilemma. In each letter, I would list my accomplishments and express a fierce desire to live in this country. I received responses from both, with words of support and their personal recommendation that my family be granted legal residency.

At the time, there were a few well-defined categories under which the Immigration and Naturalization Service granted legal residency to people already living in the United States. My family did not qualify for any of these, but they came close in one: they had American-born children. My parents had two sons who were born here. Marlon was born on May 10, 1977, and, their fourth son, Alex, was born on September 23, 1981. Until 1977, parents would automatically become legal residents if they gave birth to a child on American soil. But this provision had been eliminated during the presidency of Jimmy Carter while my mother was pregnant with Marlon. Nevertheless, I learned that judges presiding at deportation proceedings tended to be sympathetic to people having American born children or siblings; after all, deporting the parents would have a great impact on the welfare of the American citizens.

Undocumented families live every day dreaming of ways to correct their immigration status in America. Even before my crisis at Princeton, my parents had consulted with many lawyers and the consensus was that they stay as far from the immigration authorities as possible. Most lawyers did not want to open a file on us, let alone submit an application to INS. But, as in medicine, if you speak to enough professionals you will eventually find one who will give you a differing opinion. We discovered a lawyer in

Manhattan's Chinatown who took our case and submitted our information to the INS.

This was a tremendous gamble. After years of our hiding from immigration authorities, this lawyer basically notified those authorities that there was a Fernandez family living without legal documents on 61st Street in West New York. He would be our representative at all our proceedings and persuaded us that there was a good possibility that we may be granted residency if we showed up in court. Although an amateur, I already knew there were few if any exceptions to the immigration laws, little room for sympathy on the part of the judge, and rare instances of liberal interpretation between the lines. You either met all their criteria or you didn't, and if you didn't, you would be deported to your native country. But even with this knowledge, I hoped and prayed for the best.

After a few meetings with our lawyer, I began losing confidence. He seemed to have very little interest in us. He would forget our names and other details of our case and misplace important documents. Often, I would need to correct him or remind him of some crucial facts that bolstered our case. I realized afterward that he was not eager to represent us in a long and drawn-out case. He had already received a flat $1,500 fee for his services, so he was seeking only a quick resolution. Perhaps I was too cynical and pessimistic because my family's future was riding on the outcome. It is also possible that we didn't have a strong case. Princeton had also scheduled an appointment for my family to consult with the Manhattan lawyer it used to obtain visas for visiting faculty and his advice was not reassuring. He told us what we already suspected: it would take a miracle for my family to remain in America.

As it turned out, our first meeting with the immigration judge went well. My family was not granted legal residency, but we were not deported either. Instead, we entered a gray area called "suspension of deportation proceedings." Essentially, the judge, a man named Nathan Gordon, had decided that he needed more time to study the case because there were many roots to our life in America. The main issue, he indicated, was that deporting my parents, Byron, and me would cause tremendous hardship to two American citizens, my little brothers. Judge Gordon seemed reasonable. He saw a hard-working family that had come to America in search of a better future and were contributing to the well-being of the country in the same way as did the European immigrants of a century before, the Irish, Italians, and Jews—perhaps even his own grandparents. He showed humanity. He was aware that the decisions that he made regarding the fate of undocumented people would affect many other lives as well, including those of long-established Americans. He realized that most of the undocumented are people who may not have entered the country according to the law, but who end up, through their hard work, making America a better place. After this first meeting he also informed us that we would need to return to this office regularly for periodic review of our case.

In retrospect, I feel that the compassion expressed in the letters of support from Governor Kean, Senator Bradley, and several Princeton officials may have helped. One person, in particular, did more than write me a letter. Senator Bradley had a distinguished life as a student at Princeton and was the star of an Ivy League basketball team that improbably made it to the Final Four of the NCAA tournament. He became a Rhodes Scholar and then a star basketball player for the New York Knicks in its heyday, leading them to a national championship. He was a public servant who had served several terms as a US senator and was regarded as a likely candidate for president. To my surprise, I received a follow-up letter from his office that asked me to please call and speak to his secretary. He wanted to know the name of the judge who was handling our case and the date and time for our next appointment. His letter stirred my hopes that this would be the missing piece needed to firm up our case. I understood that even the power of a United States senator was limited, but I was confident that a personal call would not hurt.

I was nervous about calling Bradley's office, but over the next two days, I collected the information the office wanted and rehearsed what I would say to his secretary. I was uncertain if I should call. I even wondered, why would a senator even have any interest in helping me, an undocumented immigrant? I was sure that his office must have been very busy. I was only a college student who could not even vote yet. There wasn't anything that I could possibly offer in return. I finally collected myself and made the call.

When I finally called his secretary, I introduced myself as a Princeton student and described the purpose of my call. She placed me on hold and after a few minutes, another woman picked up the phone. "I have been waiting for your call," she said.

I was ecstatic. I am not sure if it was her tone or the words themselves, but I was overflowing with new assurance and confidence when I heard the words: "I have been waiting for your call." I was not on the phone for long. The woman, an aide to the senator, then asked me the information that she had requested in the letter. When I was done, she thanked me and wished me good luck. That was the end of the only conversation that I ever had with the senator's office. I never saw him or spoke to him in person or on the phone, but I came away with a sense of optimism. I had feared the worst—expulsion—but now I had a sense that something good might happen on our next visit. My parents were not as confident. They had already witnessed the despair of families being split apart when relatives were deported back to their native countries.

Then on one ordinary occasion we all prepared for one of our seemingly routine visits to the immigration office. I vividly remember this warm, clear, August morning in 1986. We all followed our family routines for immigration service appointments. We dressed up in our finest clothes and drove to Newark, where my father, as was his habit, parked in the first empty spot he saw, blocks away from the immigration office. We walked the long distance but still arrived at the Newark office early and waited in line to gain entrance. Our entire family was there, including Marlon and Alex. It was always a good idea to show up as a family, especially if the smaller American-born kids were the basis of the appeal. When we finally made it to the courtroom, the judge moved quickly from case to case. We sat in the benches in the back, filled with fear, but hopeful that matters would go well. The best-case scenario, my parents believed, would involve having to exit the country, re-enter the country legally, and then go through the immigration court all over again.

As I heard the clerk call, "Fernandez, Case Number—" we all stood up and moved to the front of the room with our lawyer. There was silence as the judge quickly looked over our file and reviewed some of his previous notes. He then summoned our lawyer to come to his side. They had a brief conversation— our lawyer made a few statements summarizing the arguments in favor of our remaining and showed the judge the supportive letters that I had received. After a brief silence and another review of our file, the judge restated the arguments on our behalf. But this time, he made an unanticipated statement. He suddenly declared that our proceedings were at an end.

"You have all been granted legal permanent residency in the United States of America," he said. "Welcome to the United States." Without giving us time to absorb the magnitude of what he had just said, he promptly called the next case. I could not take in his exact words, but I knew with a dizzying rush of excitement that he had ruled in our favor. My parents did not understand English, so they did not immediately grasp the news. We rose and walked with our lawyer to the corridor outside the courtroom, where he congratulated us and told us in Spanish that we were now permanent residents and should receive our green cards in the mail in the next twelve to eighteen months. He asked us to call his office if any other issues came up and walked off.

We were stunned. Even when I informed my parents what had happened, they couldn't comprehend the significance of the ruling. But slowly, as I explained and re-explained in Spanish, they assimilated the good news. I knew they did because they began hugging my brothers and me and we hugged one another as well. Marlon and Alex could not understand what the big deal was; they, after all, had known nothing but American soil. "Harold, my love," my mother said, "now you can continue your studies and become a great doctor without any worries."

My parents understood that my quest to become a doctor could have been halted in a heartbeat if that judge ruled against us, and if he had, they would have been devastated, knowing how many years of hard work I had put in. My parents had prepared for the worst, believing that it was impossible for us to be awarded legal residency. As we walked down the corridor, our smiles radiated our jubilation. Usually, as we left the INS building, we would tease my father for parking so far away, but that day the walk felt like a short hop.

On the way home, doubts and suspicions started to surface. My father asked me a series of questions that I didn't have an answer for. Our Colombian passports, for example, should have been stamped with some indication that our deportation proceedings had been suspended.

"Why didn't they put a stamp on our passports?" he asked. "Why didn't they take another set of pictures for the green card? Why didn't they ask us for a recent medical exam? Why didn't they ask us to leave the country and return?" Caught up in the excitement of what had happened, we had forgotten to ask our lawyer such questions. We even started to wonder if there was an error. "There is no error," my mother said. "This is a good and compassionate judge and he liked our family."

Our doubts and worries intensified during the next few days as we shared our news with friends and others and they would raise the same questions. We became so concerned that two weeks later, the entire family returned to the INS building with our passports and weathered the long lines once more until we reached an immigration officer. He told us that we didn't need stamps, but if we were insistent, we could leave our passports and return two hours later. "Yes, officer," my father said, "please put the stamps on the passport."

We were so incredulous of our good fortune that we needed hard evidence. The final confirmation was obtained eight months later, when the green cards started arriving in the mail. Byron's came first, then my mother's two days later, then mine a couple of weeks after that, and finally my father's. We were now officially, legally, authentically in America.

I have never attempted to inquire from anyone if Senator Bradley did, in fact, personally call the judge and, if he did, what influence he might have had. It may have been a coincidence that we were being granted legal residency just a few weeks after my contact with his office. It may also be possible that the senator did have a brief conversation with the judge that sparked some additional reflection about our situation, particularly because the Senate at the time was pondering a general amnesty for undocumented immigrants who had been in the country longer than five years. Perhaps Senator Bradley had told the judge that the amnesty was likely to be passed, which it was later that year. Still, I'd like to think that Senator Bradley was willing to support a cause that he felt was righteous, despite the fact that there was no possibility of political gain. In 2003, Senator Bradley was awarded an honorary Doctor of Civil Law from Oxford University, and one of the stated reasons was that he was a "powerful advocate for the weak." I'd like to think that I learned firsthand how truthful this statement was. I also like to think that it is now the time for America to find a compassionate resolution to the great humanitarian tragedy affecting millions of undocumented families such as mine.

THIS SIDE OF PARADISE

On a late Friday night in the winter of 1987, I was intensely concentrating on a review of one of the organic chemistry chapters
in a room at Palmer Hall, presently the Frist Campus Center. I
had a test coming up and I wanted to get ahead in the reading.
As I was walking back and forth between the desk and the chalkboard, following my ordinary study routine, I caught a sight outside the window of a group of students walking through Prospect
Gardens and in the direction of Prospect Avenue. They were
headed to the eating clubs for a night of partying, camaraderie,
and drinking. This was not the first time that I caught sight of
students going towards the clubs, but I would just ignore it and
continue with my studies. Most nights, I was able to resist the
temptation of abandoning my studies to join the weekend celebration at the eating clubs. But tonight, as I turned to continue
with my work, I remembered that Tina had invited me to join
her at the arch sing at 1879 Hall, which faces the direction of
Prospect Avenue, at 11 p.m.

Earlier in the day, Tina had informed me that she would be
singing at the 1879 arch with her a cappella group, the Tigerlilies.
This is one of the traditional singing groups at Princeton with
the most coveted membership. Tina had been ecstatic because
she had gained a place in this group after a long and hard audi-

tion process that often favored acquaintances of the members. Although Tina did not have any inside connections, her singing was so astonishing that she was voted in.

As I looked at the clock on the wall, I realized that I was already a few minutes late. So I dropped all my books, put on my coat, and ran out of the building towards the 1879 Hall arch. I got there just in time. The Tigerlilies had not performed yet. They were next. A moment later, they lined up in a semicircle just underneath the imposing arch that faces Prospect Avenue. My eyes were focused on Tina. She looked so lively and beautiful standing there amongst a great group of talented singers. The group performed a few songs. During one of the songs, she stepped forward and performed a solo piece. I was simply fascinated by the adorable sound of her voice resonating and echoing within the walls of this great arch. After she finished, she was followed by big applause from the other students. I was in the crowd and could hear many students commenting on how gifted she was. I must admit that when I first saw her step forth to perform a solo, I was definitely more nervous than she was. Each time she did this, I would become very anxious and get chills down my body. For her, it was so natural. She would just take a step forward, take a look into the sky, and allow her voice to just flow out of her body in a sweet sound that was almost angelic.

Following her performance, she came over to my side, gave me a kiss, and said, "Thank you, Harold, it means a lot to me that you came tonight." I was so proud of her, and delighted in the joy as many students came over to congratulate her for her incredible voice. She then invited me to a party at the Third World Center, and although I really wanted to return to my books, I gladly accepted.

Holding hands, we made our way along Prospect Avenue, which is lined by stately mansions on either side that house the eating clubs, one of the oldest social traditions at Princeton and also the centerpiece of entertainment for students on the weekend. By spring of the second year, Princeton requires students to decide whether they wanted to join an eating club or dine on their own.

F. Scott Fitzgerald taught the world about these clubs, but their origins go back to the late nineteenth century, when Princeton's upper-class dorms, now known as "junior slums," either had no dining halls or mediocre ones, and so wealthier families set up dining clubs off campus. Each club has its own history, traditions, and unique composition. There were ten such clubs when I was there, with names like Cottage, Cap and Gown, Tower, Ivy, Tiger Inn, Cloister Inn, Quadrangle, and Terrace. They were housed in elegant mansions, primarily along Prospect Avenue. They hired their own chefs and maintained "taprooms" for drinking. Enthusiastic members tended to stop by several times a day, not just for a meal, but also for a game of pool or meeting with friends. Some of the clubs were exclusive and selected their members through a process of screening interviews known as "bicker," where members argued over which applicants to take. During the time I was there, the clubs had a diverse membership that included both genders and different ethnic groups, though three of them, Tiger Inn, Cottage, and Ivy, were still mounting a legal fight to keep women out.

Students who had developed strong friendships or connections with a particular club did all they could to become members, much like students at other colleges try to get chosen by certain exclusive fraternities and sororities. Those who didn't aim for one of these clubs or couldn't get in could dine independently or join one of the non-selective eating clubs through a lottery system. My friend, Alex Wagenberger, a compatriot from a wealthy family in Bogota, was on track to be selected for Cottage, one of the clubs with a rich aristocratic tradition. Alex was the first Jewish student I had ever met. He came from a family that had immigrated to Colombia to escape Hitler's persecution. Despite his cushioned background, Alex was a model of diligence. The same perseverance that helped his family reestablish themselves in a new country helped him become a top student at Princeton. Alex's entry into Cottage would mean that I could eventually get invitations to many of the social events hosted there.

My friend Mauricio, another private school alumnus whose parents were from a wealthy family in Mexico, also joined Cottage. My friend, Enrique Saez, a Spaniard raised in a small and humble town on the outskirts of Madrid and the valedictorian at the prestigious Hun School, a boarding school in Princeton, was selected to Cap and Gown (Brooke Shields's eating club).

But I mostly stayed out of the eating-club competition, first ending up in the lottery and getting assigned to the Elm Club. This was a low-key club located just across from the Third World Center with great food and a pleasant, unassuming ambience. The elite clubs were not places I particularly obsessed about. The mansions seemed too opulent for my comfort, and while the music at these clubs was appealing, there was very little dancing. Students would just break into small groups, drink beer, talk for hours, or, as it got later, sing along to the songs. I spent many wonderful hours in these clubs, chatting with friends like Alex and Enrique. But I always felt more at home with my friends at the Third World Center. This was my home away from my dorm room. There I would meet Tina, Steve Watkins, my roommate Juan, and my other Spanish and African-American friends.

The center was not in a mansion, but in an old run-down building that seemed more familiar to the students who had grown up in rundown buildings, and provided a needed, perhaps ironic, counterpoint to the formality of the Princeton campus. Here people danced to the music—hip-hop, disco, Salsa, and Merengue. I was used to dancing at my parents' gatherings, both in Barrio Antioquia and in West New York. Salsa and Merengue were always a part of my parents' social life, and here it was part of mine, as well.

The few times in my four years at Princeton that I made plans to spend the night at the eating clubs, I would start the evening with Juan and Enrique, meet up with Mauricio and Alex at their eating clubs, and then eventually split up and end up at the Third World Center with the people that I felt more at ease with—the people with whom I shared the same roots, struggles, and dreams. Not that this was what we discussed during those days. My best friend, Juan, for example, was someone I felt I had grown up with and had known for years, so similar were our immigrant backgrounds and ordeals.

Although Juan didn't have the physical appearance of being Hispanic, his mother had migrated from Mexico to Los Angeles. He was ivory-skinned, with blue eyes, light-brown hair, and a six-foot-four frame. Like me, he was passionate about soccer. Neither of us had any spending money, yet each time that we would go to a fast-food hangout, we would both quarrel over who would pay the bill. Most of the time, we spoke Spanish to each other; it just felt more natural, even in a large room where people were chattering cheerfully. At times, other students were not happy being excluded from the conversation; they felt that we might be gossiping about them. We didn't mean to exclude them; we would just forget that we were speaking Spanish.

After parties at the Third World Center or at an eating club, Juan, Enrique, Mauricio and I might finish the night by going to Hoagie Haven, a small, run-down, all-night joint on Nassau Street. It was famous on campus for its cheese steak sandwiches.

"I'll have a foot long with mayonnaise, lettuce, and tomato," I would tell the guy making the sandwich. I found myself often dwelling on this sandwich guy, realizing that he was a young Latino, probably an immigrant, working for his livelihood. I was also an immigrant, but I was on the other side of the counter, an official student at Princeton. I could not help thinking how narrow the distance between us was, that with a small turn or two in fortune I could have ended up making sandwiches for privileged students hungry after a night of music and dancing. Juan and I would often put in our orders in Spanish and the workers would be surprised and pleased. At times, they would prepare our sandwiches with more cheese and more steak.

Moments like these would make me realize how fragile my situation was. I was living in the bubble of a dream that could explode at any minute. I would feel guilty after one of these robust evenings, asking myself as I walked back to my dorm room, "Why am I spending this kind of time at parties?" I felt that I should be studying. In fact, sometimes I would return to my dorm after a party and force myself to open up a textbook and study until I dropped asleep. Sometimes, as I was nodding off, I would think that the place I more fittingly belonged to was on the streets and alleys of Barrio Antioquia or the sock factory at Medias Crystal, rather than Princeton's arches and halls.

Perhaps it was only in my mind, but throughout my years at Princeton, there were frequent reminders that I was not a mainstream student. Even once I was granted legitimate status in America, it was difficult to shake the foreignness I continued to feel. Although I had never spent much effort on the style of my clothes, I was aware that many other students did and often bought theirs in the decorous and expensive shops that lined the main drag of Nassau Street. My mother bought all my clothes in West New York's discount stores.

Another social disparity was evident during vacations. I couldn't afford trips to the Caribbean to relax on the beach or to Europe to take in the ancient art and history. I longed to take such trips, and I would look on with interest and more than a dash of envy as friends returned with photographs and tales of their exotic adventures. When I had breaks, I would visit my parents in West New York in Apartment 3B. I would take two buses—one from Nassau Street to the bus terminal in Manhattan, and then another bus from there to West New York—and be dropped off on 61st Street and Bergenline Avenue.

Each of my return trips reminded me how different my life in college was from my hometown. In Princeton, I was bathed in the tranquility of my dorm room and the imposing gothic archi-tectural masterpieces that surrounded this historic campus, and I was surrounded by students who had clear and ambitious goals. In my apartment, I would again be immersed in the struggles of my parents, who were living paycheck to paycheck, crammed in a small apartment with roaches and mice and the daylong clamor of music and arguments from other apartments.

However, there were two places at Princeton where I felt at ease, the classroom and the soccer field. I set myself two major goals: improving my performance in soccer and concentrating on my studies. During my sophomore year, I took classes in physics, advanced biology, linear algebra, and organic chemistry. There didn't seem to be any other course at Princeton with the history, expectations, hovering anxiety, and colorful lore of organic chem-istry. Among students considering careers in medicine, this was probably Princeton's most feared course. It was make or break for medicine. Whether it was true or not, we believed that no medi-cal school in the country would grant an interview to a student who scored lower than a B.

The professor for this course was the legendary Dr. Maitland Jones, Jr., who in physique and personality oddly resembled Hollywood's daringly adventurous professor, Indiana Jones. Slender and bearded, he had a discursive mind and published dozens of papers about many exotic and rare molecules. But he was also the kind of offbeat character who could be passionate about jazz and the Grateful Dead. He would make each lecture more animated than the previous one, and his enthusiasm for chemistry was contagious.

There were over two hundred students in his course, and it seemed that he hypnotized them all. Each morning, he lit up the board with rainbow-colored pictures of organic molecules inter-acting with their environment and with one another. All students had a special pen for this course that contained ink cartridges in several colors, so we could then imitate the same patterns that he used on his board drawings. When he changed chalks, you could hear, almost in unison, students clicking their pens to change the color of ink. By lecture's end, the board looked like something dazzling and flamboyant out of *Sesame Street*. Dr. Jones was not there to teach students the basic chemical nomenclature, the equations, or the simple properties that govern the behavior of carbon-based compounds. That, he figured, students could learn by reading the textbook. And the fact that many of us wanted to go to medical school was the farthest thing from his mind. Indeed, many students gave up their dreams of pursuing medicine because they could not handle the intensity of his course. He was exploiting all his powers to show us esoteric aspects of organic chemistry, to show us the behavior of molecules we had not considered, molecules that needed to be imagined in three-dimensions even if they had to be drawn on our two-dimensional notebooks.

In late October of 1986, we had our first midterm. Like many tests at Princeton, it was given at night, which gave the entire exercise a slightly eerie aura. I studied through the night, forgoing sleep, and spent all day getting ready for the test. It started at seven o'clock in the evening and would take three hours. Several of us met at the courtyard of Mathey College to take the long walk across the campus to the Frick Laboratory, where the test was being given.

The walk had the flavor of a religious pilgrimage. We even had to walk through the McCosh courtyard, which is next to the chapel, an imposing gothic monument that made me feel as if I were walking through St. Peter's Basilica in the Vatican. As we neared Frick, we could see students approaching from different directions around campus, all of us visibly nervous. By 6:45 p.m., the students were in their seats. An assistant came around and gave each student a small, twenty-page booklet in which to write answers. On the front was the Princeton name, and below it the Princeton honor code, which we had to acknowledge with a signature: "I pledge my honor that I have not violated the honor code during this examination." We all knew the honor code; it meant that you would not cheat and that you would tell the professor if you saw someone cheating. I had experienced its power before when I had to confess about my forged documents.

Then Dr. Jones strode in and announced that we could start. There was the mass flutter of opening exam booklets and the hush of students trying to decipher the complex set of questions. Each of us had so much riding on this test.

As I scanned the booklet, I realized that I could draw the three-dimensional images and molecules that Dr. Jones wanted. The room was silent, except for the occasional mutter of frustration or anxious shift of position in a chair. The silence was interrupted a few times by Dr. Jones, who stepped to the front and gave us an update on a World Series game being played that day between the Boston Red Sox and the New York Mets. We all took a few seconds to cheer each time he announced that the Mets were winning. After three hours of intense pressure and anxiety, I was relieved to complete the test. Two days later, I was ecstatic to discover that I scored an A plus on this exam.

I mastered organic chemistry so well that I would later become an official university tutor, and that success steered me into choosing as my major molecular biology. It was a relatively new department at Princeton with world-class scientists that had just moved to a new home at Lewis Thomas Laboratory. The chairman was Arnold Levine who would go on to become president of Rockefeller University. Another prominent staff member was Shirley M. Tilghman who would become the first woman president at Princeton. I went to their open house events aimed at luring prospective majors and felt their enthusiasm and love for learning. I wanted to be part of this department and to immerse myself in the field of DNA. I wanted to know everything about every aspect of the molecule that carries the information in our cells.

In my dorm room, I plastered pictures on the walls and ceiling of biological molecules, including all the components of DNA, just as other students had photographs of athletes or buxom women. I figured that I could study all these molecules and think about them even as I went to sleep at night. I was doing great with my academic work.

Many things at Princeton did not work out as well for me. Any notion I had about achieving glory on Princeton's soccer fields soon proved an illusion. I may have been a champion at West New York, but here I was competing with students recruited from some of the country's best high school teams. The coach, Bob Bradley, who went on to become the coach of the US national team, assigned me to the B team, the equivalent of the junior varsity. We practiced with the A team but we competed in less-prestigious tournaments, against some of the local colleges, and against the junior varsity teams from other Ivy League schools. I always felt that I had the skills to play with the A team, but I could never impress Coach Bradley. My style of play was very different from what he had in mind. In moments of desperation, I griped to myself that the coach didn't put me in because I was Hispanic. However, I came to realize Coach Bradley would never have done anything like that. He was a great coach and human being. The reality was that I just wasn't the right player at that particular time for what that coach needed for his team. Still, by junior year, I had become so frustrated I decided to drop competitive soccer. I told myself I had more important things to worry about, such as keeping up with my grades and concentrating on my independent research.

As I expected, another part of my social life also did not work out for me. My eating club, the Elm Club, was not to my liking. Its students seemed to spend a lot of time playing pool and drinking. I was not a drinker. So, after my junior year, I quit Elm and became an independent, which meant I ate where I wished. I felt I could save money this way, and since my closest companion, Tina, also did not join an eating club, we would cook simple meals together with other independent students or haunt the cheap restaurants. My friends like Alex, Enrique, and Mauricio—more accustomed to a world of privilege through either their families or the prep schools they had spent time in—thrived in their eating clubs and socialized more with the mainstream students, participating in the regular Princeton activities and social life of the eating clubs.

Consequently, I spent most of my free time with Tina. After social events on Friday or Saturday nights at the Third World Center, we would often conclude the night with an intimate chat and follow this with more tender moments, sometimes in her dorm room if her roommates were not around or sometimes in the infinite number of hideaways around the university. Although Tina had not had a Hispanic boyfriend before, she liked that I was different from other boys she had dated in the past. She happened to be taking courses in Spanish, so she enjoyed my speaking Spanish to her, especially if what I said had amorous connotations. One night, our conversation turned philosophical.

"Harold, do you pray at night?" she asked.

"Sometimes," I said.

"Do you believe in God?"

"Yes," I said.

"Then why don't you pray every night?" she asked.

As the conversation continued with deeper reflections on both our parts, she made me realize that if I really believed in a God, then it would be wise to take a few seconds to, as Tina would say, "talk to God." Tina had great inner strength and serenity and believed that you could have your own, personal, direct relationship with God through personal prayer. This was in sharp contrast to what I had learned in my religion classes about the need to have a priest or a saint as an intermediary between me and God. At each meal, she would pause for a few seconds and murmur a short, silent prayer to thank God for the food. Prayer was interspersed throughout her day.

Soon, I found myself going to a church she had been attending on Nassau Street, one that had a young, charismatic pastor who preached about the relationship with God in a rational way. This was a big step for me, because I had always worshiped at Roman Catholic churches. I was refreshed by the idea of going to a place that didn't make any distinctions among forms of Christianity, and just concentrated on Jesus' simple message of unconditional love and clemency.

We became a serious couple, and began to talk about possibly spending many years together. I visited her family in Indianapolis and stayed with her wonderful grandmother. She came up to West New York to meet my parents and stayed for a couple of days in our small apartment. Although our home was tidy and warm, I was apprehensive that she would step into the kitchen at night and see the mice and roaches roaming freely across the floor.

– – – – – – – –

During some of my lonely moments, when I was away from friends, I would lie in bed at night, looking up at the pictures of the DNA molecules and amino acids that I had posted on the slanted roof just above my bed. I would fall asleep dreaming of my plans for studying medicine, and distract myself from unhappy and unfounded thoughts or fears. Sometimes, I found myself recalling a song that I used to hear as a boy in Barrio Antioquia playing on the steps of La Oasis. The song, "El Preso" (The Prisoner), is about an imprisoned drug dealer in the worst jail in Colombia, la Gorgona, and describes the agony and despair of spending time locked up, closed in by four walls, without being able to see family and friends. This song would give me strength as I tried to master the elements of DNA and my other studies. After all, there was a metaphor in my mind: I, too, was locked up by four walls, far from family and familiar territory, but I was expanding my mind, doing something that someday would give me a career that would allow me to help others.

In my final semester at Princeton, I signed up for my last courses, determined to devote most of my free time to completing my senior thesis. It was a research project in molecular biology aimed at discovering the sequence of base pairs in a protein that might have an important role in how cancer cells migrate around the body. My advisor was Dr. Jean Shwarsbauer, one of the most intelligent and talented people I had met at the school. Although she was a strict disciplinarian, she knew when to be flexible and when to be tough. I was also waiting to hear from Harvard Medical School, where I had applied.

One day at the start of that semester, I ran into my roommate Juan while walking to my dorm and he told me that the dean of students, Eugene Lowe, was urgently looking for me. He said that his office had left two messages on the answering machine saying that they needed to see me right away. When I heard this, my heart dropped. My first thought was that I was in some kind of trouble. I was asking myself, "Why would a dean be looking for me?" I stopped off at the room to drop off my books, and my other roommate told me that the dean's office had called several times. I got even more anxious and began to worry that something had gone wrong with my immigration status, or that Princeton had concluded that because I was not completely truthful in my application I would be kicked out just as I was about to graduate. That fear must have propelled me because I found myself running to the dean's office, which was located on the second floor of West College next to Nassau Hall, the office of the president.

The secretary asked me to take a seat, and as I waited, I felt the same displacement and sense of being lost that I felt on my first day in an American school, about to meet the principal for the first time and hearing a foreign language over the intercom. I recalled that three years before, just a few offices away on this same floor, I had also waited anxiously to meet the dean for foreign students to talk about my immigration status.

Dean Lowe offered me a drink of water and a seat on the other side of his desk. He began describing a prize that the university presented every year during its two-day alumni weekend in February. I had vaguely heard about these weekends, but focusing on my studies, I paid them little mind. Dean Lowe said the weekend was an opportunity for the alumni to rediscover the university and its academic programs and reconnect with old friends. On Alumni Day of 1989, I would have an opportunity to be part of this tradition, Dean Lowe told me. I would be receiving a prize—actually sharing it with another student. It is called the Moses Taylor Pyne Prize and is the highest general distinction awarded by the university to a graduating senior. He told me it was named for Moses Taylor Pyne, Class of 1877, three-decade trustee who had devoted much of his energy to expanding Princeton into a first-rank university.

As I left his office and walked back to my dorm room, I was relieved that I was not in some sort of trouble and slowly I let feelings of excitement seep in. I knew that I had worked hard and done well, but I never expected this honor. With the exception of a single B, I had garnered straight A's. I had played near-varsity soccer, volunteered in the emergency room at the Princeton Medical Center, and was president of the minority medical student society—known as Imhotep, in honor of the first black physician from ancient Egypt. I had tutored kids in Trenton and volunteered at the local hospital. I wondered if the selection committee also took into account the circumstances that I had faced spiriting into the country in a boat, having to learn English only a few years before entering Princeton, and living here as an undocumented immigrant. In any case, I was grateful and humbled that a leading national university like Princeton recognized my hard work.

On alumni weekend, my parents came in to be part of the celebration. We entered the luncheon at Jadwin Gym, the same place where I had first been introduced to Princeton as a high school runner. The gym was draped in the Princeton colors of black and orange, and the hundreds of old Princetonians and their families who were there wore splashes of black and orange in their ties and scarves. My co-winner of the Pyne Prize was a gifted young lady named Suzanne Hagedorn. By her sophomore year, she had already discovered important original sources for ancient works of literature. She and I shared the stage with the other alumni winners and with the university's president, Dr. Harold T. Shapiro, an accomplished scholar who was Princeton's first Jewish president. He listened as I gave a one-minute acceptance speech. I had spent many hours preparing it. I wanted it to be simple and honest, but at the same time I wanted my words to call attention to the most important factor that allowed me to be present on that stage, the example of steady work set by my parents.

As part of the prize, Suzanne and I received a large check, splitting the equivalent of a full year's tuition. When I came down from the stage and I saw my parents, I could tell they were thrilled. My mother had tears in her eyes. We sat down and took pleasure in the different alumni who came to our table to offer their congratulations and words of support. I pulled out the check and then handed it to my parents. They were in the process of trying to buy their first home; they still lived in the same two-bedroom apartment as when I first came to West New York, and needed a few thousand dollars more for their closing expenses and down payment. They refused to take the money, saying it was mine. However, I persuaded them that this was not a gift, but a loan that they would pay back while I was in medical school. I was honored by the award, and grateful to receive this large sum of money. However, I was just as pleased to be able to help my parents buy their first home. The value of the immeasurable gifts that I had received from my parents was much greater than anything that I could ever give them in return.

THE GIRL IN THE SCHOOL UNIFORM

The summer prior to my senior year at Princeton I had the opportunity to return to my native country. This trip to Colombia in the summer of 1988 was my first after our teenage journey ten years before. The visit was my parents' idea. They hungered to see their relatives and their hometown, and they brought along Marlon and Alex. Byron was going through a rebellious period, and he decided not to partake in the emotional family reunion. My grandmother Alicia had passed away, but grandmother Rosa was still alive. Although many things had changed, the legendary spring-like climate of Medellín was still a welcomed reward, although the thought of crime and senseless violence that still lingered in the streets of Barrio Antioquia was of great concern to all of us.

Right after the jet landed at Medellín's modern, new airport in Rio Negro, all the passengers in the plane let out a big hand of applause. This actually still happens in many flights that return from America to Colombia. I think that at the moment of landing we all have a sense of gratitude to God for giving us this opportunity to once again see the home and the people that are so dear in our lives.

After disembarking, we then proceeded to the customs office and then to the baggage carousel. As we waited for our bags, I could make out the image of my grandmother Rosa through the glass wall that was separating the room where family members were anxiously waiting for their loved ones. All my emotions came to a climax, and I could not hold back the tears. She was the woman who had been my tender mother for so much of my childhood and had been so prudent about so many choices we had to make. I had not seen her for ten years, and because she had been ill, I had been afraid that I would not see her again. She was physically there, surrounded by many relatives that included my aunts Gilma and Christina and a multitude of cousins, some of whom I had never seen before, and all of whom were waving their arms and screaming.

After our bags were checked by customs, I ran first to Rosa, kissing and embracing her tenderly. She had aged so much in the ten years we had been apart. The pain of separation from her beloved daughter and grandchildren and the daily conflicts around her had taken an immense toll on her body and her health. I knew she was proud of all I had accomplished, but Rosa would have loved me even if I had dropped out of school and became a vagrant. Seeing grandmother Rosa, I could not help but think about grandmother Alicia, whose funeral we could not attend because we were undocumented.

The next morning I walked around the streets of Barrio Antioquia, aware that it remained a treacherous neighborhood. I was warned by my family not to walk the streets alone, that my American clothes and sneakers would single me out as a possible target. I was also told that some of the neighborhood residents resented arrogant expatriates, so I should never give the impression that I was looking down at anyone. I did not have any problems with this. I did not feel better than anyone around me. As I strolled the streets, I felt at home.

These were the streets where I had played countless hours of soccer, raced the go-carts known as *carros de rodillos*, and spent many hours with friends dreaming about life in America. These were the streets where I had learned to fight, even if I was not very good at it. I could not help remembering, though, that these were also the streets where childhood friends collected slips of papers from discarded cigarette packs and sold them to the young men on the corners—men armed with guns under their ponchos, who would roll them into marijuana joints.

Collecting cigarette papers was the first step my friends took to becoming drug dealers. I had been fortunate. My grandmothers threatened to kill me if I joined my friends in such mischief. Now, ten years later, my life had changed significantly and I cherished the opportunity to walk around these streets and reminisce of the old days with friends.

In the afternoon, I was talking to my little cousin Ericka on the balcony of our old house in Colombia. My grandmother had built a second story on top of our old ranch house. Because most of the other houses only had one story, one could see the entire block. Although Ericka was only twelve, she had already matured beyond her years, and she loved gossip. As she was telling me different stories about the neighborhood and bringing me up to date, she paused for a second and said, "Harold, there is my best friend, Sandra." She turned and pointed to a girl ambling down the street.

I looked over and saw a striking slender girl in a blue and white uniform just returning from her school day. Her long ebony hair seemed to cascade down to her waist. Ericka called to her, and Sandra looked up with her large brown eyes. She pretended not to notice, but she must have known who I was. There had been lots of excitement on the block when my family returned, just as there was every time a family came home from the United States. I waved, and this time she flashed a smile. I could not help noticing as she disappeared into her home that the checkered skirt of her uniform was slightly above her knees, a sign of some daring on her part, since school rules require skirts to fall below the knee. I thought she was simply gorgeous. Even from a distance, and before embarking on any conversation, I felt a connection. I am not sure if it was her smile, the exaggerated swivel of her hips as she walked down the street, her shapely figure, or her penetrating glance that caught my attention. I was instantly in awe. However, I felt a twinge of guilt. Although she had the physical appearance of a young, mature woman, Sandra was just sixteen. In addition, I was supposed to be in love with Tina, and we had been planning for our life together after Princeton.

As Sandra approached and then entered her house, which was just across the street, I thought about her childhood and her struggles. I had actually known Sandra since she was just a few years old. She was seven years younger, and while playing soccer in front of our Barrio Antioquia house, I would sometimes see her and her older sister Patricia watching our games through the metal window grates of their home. Her mother was overly protective of her daughters, seldom allowing them to play outside. They would stand at the window longingly watching the other kids play.

Sandra was the middle child of three adopted girls. Besides the older sister, Patricia, there was also a younger sister named Jennifer. The family was very poor. Her father, Nando, took jobs in construction and shoe-making, but spent months at a time out of work and had a reputation for drinking excessively and being a womanizer. The person who held the house together was her mother, Nena, short for Maria Elena. She seemed larger than her five-foot-one frame and achieved this impression by a boisterous personality. She was always yelling, giving orders, and cursing. The family survived on the earnings from raising pigs and chickens in the back yard. They would buy baby pigs, grow them to profitable adulthood, and sell them. Nando would walk the neighborhood with a bucket on his shoulders, asking people for leftover food to feed the pigs. As expected, their house smelled of pigs, and Sandra's family was often the subject of neighborhood laughter.

When I had made my way to Florida in 1978, Sandra was just six. I had no reason to think of her again until, in my early twenties, my uncle Hector returned from a vacation in Medellín and showed us photographs he had taken. I was captivated by those snapshots of friends and relatives I had not seen for years, and I felt a deep desire to return to my native country. One photograph was of Sandra sitting on a rock near the entrance to her house, and another of Sandra sweeping the street outside her house with a broom. Sandra had changed; she was now a beautiful young woman.

A few days after I arrived for my first return visit to Colombia, Ericka told me that Sandra had wished me *saludes*. In Colombia, this means that a girl has seen something in you she likes and wants to be your friend, and if you return the *saludes*, it means that you want to be her friend. I told Ericka to pass on my *saludes*. The next time I saw Sandra again was from our balcony. She was sitting on the sidewalk outside her house with three or four girlfriends. I decided I wanted to meet her, so I hopped downstairs and walked over to her house where she had been talking with her friends. I introduced myself.

Sandra was dressed in dark jeans and a white peasant blouse that left her shoulders bare. We began talking about life in America and, while she appeared timid initially, she soon grew more at ease. I could tell by a flicker in her dark eyes and the tone of her voice that she liked me, and her friends could as well, because they slipped away so we could chat by ourselves. Sandra, it was apparent, had fallen in love with American culture and had many questions. She wanted to know about the bridges, skyscrapers, and other sights she had seen on television. She wanted to know about American musicians, Guns 'n' Roses, Chicago, Michael Jackson, and Bon Jovi. She had an old tape player and told me she often listened to those artists even if she did not understand the lyrics. She had dreams of becoming a fashion model and traveling to America, but she also wondered how she could ever afford the expense of the trip or afford to go to college. The family could barely afford the medications her mother needed.

She was very pleasant and friendly, framing each comment with an engaging smile. She confided in a shy murmur that she had recently had a boyfriend, but he was very possessive and they had broken up after a couple of months. Sandra did not ask me about my girlfriend, but she knew I had one because Ericka had so informed her.

In the next few days, we spent many hours together on the sidewalk outside her house. For several days, she did not invite me inside, perhaps because she seemed sensitive about her family raising pigs at home. Nena, her mother, though, was not embarrassed and invited me inside more than once to show off the pigs.

"No, Mom, he doesn't have to see the pigs," Sandra protested.

Sandra, I was to learn, spent many hours caring for and feeding the pigs, even giving them vaccinations. She had to work to help her parents put food on the table. She also spent many hours cleaning her house so that it did not smell. Sandra did not reveal all this; her mother did, however, sometimes to Sandra's exasperation.

"Mom, he doesn't have to know this," she would interrupt.

In the three weeks I was in Colombia on that visit, I came to realize how much Sandra and I had in common—our culture, our spirituality, and our sensitivities. We even rooted for the same soccer team, El Nacional, the professional team from Medellín. We watched games together on her black and white television, which would stop working every half hour, requiring Sandra to stand and smack the set on the side.

As we spent more time together, I felt a great affection and attraction for this delightful sixteen year old girl, but I was also aware that there were what appeared to be insurmountable obstacles between us. Nonetheless, our flirtation remained only friendly, except on one occasion, the day before I returned to America, when I asked if I could kiss her. When she answered, "Yes, of course," I gave her a single kiss on her cheek. That was as romantic as our relationship became that visit.

Some of my relatives, however, felt that something was blooming and expressed some concern. They had heard that because Sandra was so pretty, some of the local drug-trafficking *mafiosos* had already expressed interest, and that Sandra, like other girls from poor families, might see this as an opportunity to escape out of her poverty. I told those relatives, because I believed it myself, that Sandra seemed different and would resist such temptations, that she had ambitious plans and wanted to stay in school. I pointed out that Sandra's mother would never allow her to marry a drug dealer or assassin. Indeed, the only reason Nena allowed me to see Sandra was that she saw me as a serious university student.

When I returned for my senior year at Princeton, Sandra's face, her voice, the memory of her aroma clung to me. But I tried to force myself to forget her. I was in love with Tina. I pulled back, writing only a few letters and keeping even those and Sandra's replies secret from Tina. Our letters indicated that we were resigned to the possibility that our relationship might not blossom any further because of differences in age, geography, and experience.

Along the way, I also learned that Sandra was dating someone else. So, I focused my emotions on Tina, who was doing everything she could to learn about my Colombian culture, taking Spanish classes, accompanying me to parties thrown by Latino groups, learning how to dance salsa and merengue. Our relationship, however, was not perfect, and as we grew closer, we became more possessive with each other. Often, I was irritated by her trips to New York to rehearse with Paul Simon's group, her trips with the university's gospel ensemble, and one of its a cappella groups, the Tigerlillies. I was jealous each time I would see her chatting amiably with other guys. This behavior and my possessive protests angered Tina.

As I entered my final year at Princeton, I had made a final decision to dedicate my life as a doctor. For me, this was not a spur-of-the-moment decision but one that evolved over the course of my early life. In large part, I was influenced—some might say manipulated—by the not-very-subtle signals emanating from my grandmothers. A doctor is what I should become, they let me know. When I was a small boy, they dressed me up as a doctor and gave me doctor toys to play with. This profession touched our lives dearly. A doctor treated my grandmother Alicia when she was ailing with cancer, and a doctor treated my grandmother Rosa through several illnesses. Though they could barely write, both of them appreciated the fact that doctors, unlike other professionals, saw it as their obligation to soothe and treat the sick, even if their customers were too poor to pay. They revered doctors for making this sacrifice, and so did the rest of their circle.

By the time I was an immigrant student in America, there were other forces as well. For one thing, wisely or not, I felt without consciously articulating it that only becoming a respected professional would vindicate the lonesome, depleting days that my parents endured to bring us over on that small boat. When my medical school applications or my interviewers asked me why I wanted to become a doctor, I also thought about the sense of satisfaction and fulfillment that I would feel helping others in need.

As someone who grew up poor, I appreciated the fact that doctors, particularly those in hospitals, treat people no matter how poor or abandoned they may be. Any patient who shows up at an emergency room in America will be evaluated and treated, despite the often-sizable costs the hospital may endure. This is, of course, very different from any other industry in a capitalist society. A hungry person cannot just walk into a restaurant and demand food, nor can a homeless person walk into a hotel and ask for a room. Despite all its glitzy gadgets and its fragmentation, medicine has remained a pursuit that places human dignity and survival above other values.

I applied for admission to ten different medical schools. In November of 1988, I was admitted to Johns Hopkins Medical School, my second choice, so I cancelled my applications to all other schools and waited for word from my first choice, Harvard. In March, I got it. Harvard accepted me into the program it runs jointly with the Massachusetts Institute of Technology in Health Sciences and Technology. I waited that summer with almost childish anticipation, imagining that I would soon be wearing an actual white coat, handling a real stethoscope.

No one seemed to exult more happiness and pride than my grandmother, Rosa. During my Princeton years, she had written several letters in Spanish from Colombia letting me know how proud she was that I had decided to become a doctor. This is what she wrote in a letter to me in March 1989, after I had been accepted in the Harvard-MIT program.

> The sacrifices that your parents have made will allow you to become a physician, serving society and saving many lives, even if they cannot pay. I am sure of this because you are a humble and honest person who treats his parents and family with respect. I pray to God that he gives you many years of good health so that you may enjoy your beautiful profession.

My grandmother was not a leading authority on any subject. She could barely write. Nonetheless, a hard life had given her the wisdom to discern that because we have received so much, we need to give back. My favorite thinker, Albert Einstein, said it only slightly better. "Every day I remind myself that my inner and outer life are based on the labors of other men, living and dead, and that I must exert myself in order to give in the same measure as I have received and I am still receiving."

When I graduated from Princeton in 1989, Sandra sent me a letter and a card. "I am so proud of you," the card said in a simple fashion. "I am happy to have met you, and I wish you the best. With all my love, Sandra." She was now seventeen and more beautiful and womanly. I kept thinking how implausible our relationship would be. I was on my way to Harvard Medical School and Sandra was a high school student in a remote corner of Colombia. Nevertheless, I held on to the letter and the card, burying them in a spot where only I could find them.

Following graduation, my relationship with Tina started to weaken. At the start of the next school year, we found ourselves in different medical schools, Harvard and Yale, and tried to go about our lives like a couple separated by their geographically distant jobs. A group of three students at Harvard who had girlfriends at Yale would make the drive from Boston to New Haven almost every weekend—a two-hour ride—and stay there from Friday night until Sunday night, or Monday morning. But that year proved a difficult one for our relationship. Perhaps it was the stress of the first year of medical school. Perhaps it was the distance. Inconsequential slights or disregards became the spark of angry fights. At times, we stopped talking to each other for weeks. It was clear we were drifting apart, tearing at each other emotionally.

ON MY WAY TO HARVARD

On a sunny day in September of 1989, we loaded up a car with all my belongings. I was headed up north to become a student at the best medical school in the world, Harvard Medical School. My trip to Boston was reminiscent of the trip five years before to RPI in Rensselaer, when I was a junior at Memorial High School. My whole family had to come with me, including my grandmother, Rosa, who had flown to New York to be with me at the Princeton graduation and stayed through the summer. We were all very excited because I would now be entering the part of my training where I would actually learn how to cure people. This moment had taken many years, but it was finally here.

We couldn't afford to rent a car from a rental company, so I asked the owner of a local bodega in West New York if he could rent us his van for the weekend. He could, for $100. It wasn't worth much more. The light-green van was falling apart, and it looked like it belonged in a junkyard and not out in the street. But we did not have a choice. So we put everything inside the cargo area of the van. Because the car only had two front seats, we had to improvise a seating area with pillows and blankets in the back for my brothers and my mother, and set up a small stool in between the two front seats for my aging grandmother. The ride up to Boston took several hours because the car shook violently going more than forty miles per hour on the flat road, and it barely made it up on a hill. When we finally made it to Boston and parked outside the dormitories to unload my belongings, our aging van stood in sharp contrast to the more expensive cars of the other students arriving for the school year. As we maneuvered the van into the parking place, I had the impression of the other families gazing with curiosity at this family arriving in this odd, beat-up restaurant delivery van. In fact, one of the friends I was to make at Harvard, Allan Goldstein, told me later he was struck by the van's markings, an advertisement for a Latin restaurant, La Tranquera. He was a Cuban Jew, and he loved Latino food. He was glad that maybe this was a place where he could get some Spanish food.

I had been selected to be part of a highly select group of students at Harvard who had plans of combining a career in clinical medicine and research. This program, called the program in Health Sciences and Technology (HST), was sponsored by Harvard Medical School and the Massachusetts Institute of Technology (MIT). My classmates in the HST program included traditional doctor aspirants, like me, students who were combining an MD with a PhD, and students who were interested in the engineering and physics that advances the frontiers of medicine. At one of our first meetings as a group, we had to introduce ourselves and provide a brief statement about our background.

The accomplishments of my colleagues were daunting. One of the students was a graduate of Notre Dame who had just finished two years at Oxford as a Rhodes Scholar. Another had already started his own engineering company. The most impressive was a young man from Chile named Pedro Huertas, who was something of a political revolutionary. He had been in his second year of medical school in Chile when he was jailed for several years by the government of military dictator Augusto Pinochet because of his dissident ideology. After his release, he had come to the U.S. and had begun a doctorate in cell biology at Stanford. At the age of forty, he decided that he wanted to become a physician and was accepted at Harvard. The most intelligent students, however, were the medical engineering and medical physics students, MEMPS, who had very strong backgrounds in physics and engineering. These students dreamed of one day inventing the next drug or device that would advance medicine to its next frontier.

- - - - - - - - -

At this level of my education, I was feeling more at ease with myself, my accomplishments, and the other students. I no longer had this feeling that I did not belong here. I really didn't care about my accent anymore. I was comfortable with it. As a result, I was able to enjoy and cultivate a more collegial relationship with my classmates. I felt less of a need to prove myself by outdoing others. I may not have been as talented as some of my classmates, but by this point, I knew that my drive might take me places my talent could not.

Life within the walls of Harvard Medical School and MIT was invigorating. Everywhere I looked, I was surrounded by world-class figures in the field of medicine. Just down the hall from our classrooms was the laboratory of Dr. Joseph Murray, who had recently won the Nobel Prize in medicine for his work on suppression of immune systems. Across the yard was the lab of the celebrated geneticist Phillip Leader. And next door at Children's Hospital was the lab of Dr. Judah Folkman who explained the mechanism that helps cancers grow, and who should probably have been awarded a Nobel Prize for his extensive body of work. *Not bad for a kid from Barrio Antioquia*, I said to myself.

The Harvard Medical School quadrangle is in Boston, several miles away from the main university campus in Cambridge. It is surrounded by several world-class hospitals and research facilities, including Brigham and Women's Hospital, the Beth Israel Deaconess Medical Center, the Dana-Farber Cancer Institute, and the Joslin Diabetes Center. Massachusetts General Hospital

(MGH), operated by the medical school, is just across the Charles River. I not only took classes and trailed doctors at all of these hospitals, but I was able to work inside them and at MIT with some top-flight researchers. The students in the Health Sciences and Technology cluster spent the first year at Harvard, the second year at MIT, and then joined the regular medical-school class in the clinical clerkships.

Although we took the same introductory classes as other Harvard medical students, we were in a separate program and our coursework seemed more rigid and theoretical, with a concentration on mathematical equations that underlie the functioning of the body and of disease. For example, in one course on the heart and its diseases, the professor taught us about the electrical impulses that make EKGs possible by asking, "If the letter x is the patient and we look at the patient from infinity, then the following set of differential equations describe the vectors of energy from the heart." In most medical schools, students learned about how the different peaks and valleys of an EKG tracing represent different heart conditions. In my program, we designed mathematical models and used differential equations to explain how the vectors of energy derived from the heart result in an EKG. While I liked to keep my family informed about the mysteries of the human body, that lesson would not be one I would convey.

In the first semester at Harvard, we learned about the normal, healthy processes of the human body or physiology. In the second semester, we learned about what happens when things go wrong—the abnormal processes or pathophysiology. We spent both years almost entirely in the classroom, not in clinics or hospitals, learning how the body functions at the cellular and at the molecular level. We did not just learn that penicillin kills certain bacteria, but we learned how the penicillin compound interacts with the cellular components of the bacteria to interfere with the bacteria's membrane.

Anatomy was the foundation of the training, and all the medical students braced for the day we would be introduced to our cadaver. It is a rite of passage, separating the amateurs from those who will dedicate their lives to medicine. I wondered how I would perform in my dissection of an actual human body. Would I be afraid or sickened? Could I focus sufficiently to master the parts of the body and their functions?

A group of four students was assigned to a single cadaver, which lay covered with a sheet on a gray metal table. My partners in crime were Allan Goldstein, Pedro Huetras, and Sanjoy Duta. An assistant came by and removed the cover and I could see that the white, waxy corpse we had been given was an elderly man. After some light chitchat, we dipped right in, taking apart the muscles of the arm with scalpels and forceps by following the instructions in our dissection manual.

For the next six months, the four of us sliced and picked apart every single organ, muscle, and nerve in that cadaver, naming the parts and trying to understand how each functioned in relation to other parts. I now felt like a student of medicine, and if I had any doubt, the strong formaldehyde preservative smell that lingered long after I left the lab reminded me. Indeed, we all began smelling like our cadaver. It did not matter how many showers we took or how strong a detergent we used, the smell stuck to us. People on the public buses we took seemed to keep a distance, and so did customers in the restaurants we frequented.

In class, Goldstein tried to lighten the atmosphere with occasional stabs at humor. Once, our teacher, Dr. Farish A. Jenkins, Jr., a professor of zoology who also happened to teach our anatomy class, was elaborating on a muscle of the inner thigh called the cremaster and the reflex it causes, called the cremaster reflex, which moves the skin over the scrotum when the inner thigh is touched.

"Who would ever name a muscle the cremaster?" Allan asked aloud. "It sounds like a cartoon character."

Sanjoy and I started laughing, perhaps as a way of relieving the tension of so many days spent with the cadaver, but our laughter seemed disruptive and the professor asked us to be silent.

A few weeks later, Professor Jenkins, a scholarly looking man with a thick mustache and a broad smile, held a special session, away from the cadaver, on the clinical landmarks of the chest. He wanted us to learn where to place the stethoscope to diagnose conditions of the heart. This time, Professor Jenkins brought in two live models, a well-built man and an attractive woman, and had them strip off their clothes. The woman was shapely, with strikingly large breasts. Running a colored marker over her chest with one hand while moving her breast with the other, Professor Jenkins started pointing out the key thoracic locations. The demonstration seemed inherently funny to more than a few of us, and one student could not restrain his laughter, which spread to Allan and Sanjoy and me. "If you guys are not mature enough to be serious, you need to leave the room," Professor Jenkins snapped.

We apologized, but it was clear we had a long way to go to become professionals. That trivial event—our juvenile laughter—brought home how inexperienced we still were, but it began to teach us to isolate our most basic emotions from the earnest demeanor we needed in order to respond to and analyze our patients objectively.

Emotions, it gradually became clear, cannot get in the way of the decisions you make as a doctor. Emotions can cloud your thinking, make the practice of medicine too painful to tolerate. Without an objective steeling of the self, how can doctors keep their wits about them as they treat children who are receiving chemotherapy and who may not survive the cancer? That does not mean we cannot be human, cannot be empathic, but the medical decisions that we make must be made with an objective and scientific approach.

In my anatomy class, I found the dissection of the heart to be particularly fascinating. We all know it as the organ that pumps the blood around the body. It beats because of an internal clock that every second sends out an electrical impulse, which propagates through the muscle so that it opens to receive blood from the veins. The heart then squeezes that blood out so that it can travel to the entire body, down to the toenails. Inside the heart, the blood travels through a series of compartments that open and close in a coordinated fashion so that blood keeps flowing without backing into the previous chamber. Each valve closes at a specific time in the cycle of the heart. It is a masterpiece of choreography that can produce disease and death when it is disturbed.

I would soon learn that the sounds of the closing valves are the first sounds doctors listen to when they put the stethoscope on the chest. Circulation is not a random process. Even within each chamber, there are structures that regulate how the blood is distributed and in which direction it will flow. There is even a little hole inside the heart, the foramen ovale, that is open when the fetus is in the mother's womb and connected to the placenta, which allows the blood to flow into the placenta rather than the lungs. Once the baby emerges from the womb and starts breathing on its own, that little hole starts to close and allow blood to flow into the lungs, which starts them working. Learning this in class, I was amazed—how simple and yet elegant.

One of my teachers was Dr. Seth Alper, a young, energetic physician-scientist who was investigating the molecular basis of hypertension and other renal diseases. Skinny, pale, almost fragile looking, and with a boyish face that made him seem more like a student than an assistant professor of medicine, he projected a strong, captivating personality that spurred on his students and colleagues. I spent many hours in his laboratory, cloning and sequencing a gene found in blood vessels that may be defective in some patients with high blood pressure. This project was later published in *Circulation Research* under the formidable title of "Molecular Cloning, Expression, and Chromosomal Localization of Two Isoforms of the AE3 Anion Exchanger from Human Heart." It was my first significant professional publication.

By my second year at Harvard, my five-year romance with Tina was ending. Without any overt declarations, we had essentially stopped seeing each other. I couldn't get Tina off my mind, but she did not want to see me and for long periods wouldn't answer my calls. I made a conscious effort to stop thinking about her.

Then in the winter of 1991 an unfortunate turn of events brought me again to be with Sandra. I learned that the cancer had progressed inexorably in my grandmother Rosa and that she was very weak and confined to bed. The doctors were trying to temper her pain, but it was clear she had only months to live. I decided to visit for Christmas break and stay for three weeks. Before leaving, I called Sandra to let her know I would be coming. I wasn't sure she even thought about me anymore. Her mother was screening Sandra's telephone calls because two months before she had broken up with a boyfriend, and he persistently kept calling the house.

"I am Harold, Mrs. Rosa's grandson," I said with a nervous formality.

"Yes, my son, I know who you are," she said. "Let me get Sandra for you."

Sandra came on the phone, and she told me that she was happy to hear my voice and that she thought about me often. She seemed delighted that I would be returning.

When I arrived in Barrio Antioquia, I spent the first hours at my grandmother's side, but right afterward, called Sandra. She was going to a graduation party at her cousin's house and invited me to come along. Sandra was now nineteen, a grown woman by Colombian standards, and she looked more beautiful than ever. On this night she was wearing a white silk dress with an exposed back.

As we conversed and danced, I could tell that her friends and cousins were disappointed that I was monopolizing her, but she made clear to everyone that I was her date for the evening.

Although I had spent more years than Sandra in university lecture halls, she was by far livelier and had a gift for animated conversation that made me seem almost aloof. I found her enchanting.

She told me she had started classes at a local community college that would help her become a secretary, and she was taking courses at a modeling school. I was taken by her humility, kindness, and delicacy. During the party, she twice reminded me to call my grandmother because she knew that Rosa would be worrying about her grandson from America staying out at these late hours in the streets of Medellín.

As we swayed around the room to Colombian *salsa*, *porros*, and *cumbia* tunes, our bodies and faces drew close. By the end of the night, when one of Sandra's cousins gave us a ride home, we kissed each other on the cheeks with an ardor I had not experienced before with her. This night and this kiss marked the beginning of our romance.

We saw each other every day of my visit. She would come to my house or I would go to hers. One night, we went to see the Christmas lights and decorations in downtown Medellín. We sat on a bench and I leaned over and kissed her tender lips, and she returned my kisses. Before I returned to America, I told her I was falling in love with her, and she told me she loved me too. I didn't know when I would return to Colombia, but I promised it would be soon.

While I was in Boston, we wrote and called every week, and I felt my love for her deepen. About six months later, in the summer of 1992, I got a chance to return to Colombia for free. A striking bonus to a Harvard medical education is the variety of research activities the school finances. In my case, Brigham and Women's Hospital gave me a grant to spend six weeks evaluating the emergency trauma care in a crowded metropolitan hospital, Medellín's San Vicente de Paul. The study would analyze the response times of ambulances, how people in emergencies were actually making their way to the hospital, and the actual treatment provided for heart attacks and for penetrating trauma.

June and July of 1992, the months I was there, turned out to be a time when violence in Medellín was at a peak. Pablo Escobar, the brutal leader of the Medellín cartel, had recently turned himself in to avoid being extradited to the United States. In exchange, he was allowed to build his own luxurious jail in the mountains of Medellín.

La Catedral, as it was known, sat high on a mountaintop and was more like a fortified country club than a prison. On clear days, it was easily distinguishable from the city's center. Indeed, Escobar's confinement was widely regarded as an embarrassment. There was evidence that he was still running the cartel from prison and was able to come and go as he pleased. There were reports that he was seen at soccer games within the city. When the President ordered the army to move him to another jail, Escobar managed to escape through the lines of an entire Colombian battalion. The violence went on unabated.

During the six weeks of my study, I spent my free time with Sandra. She was now twenty years old, and I was twenty-seven. I sensed that she was the woman I wanted to be with forever. I felt spontaneous and at home with Sandra because she was from my town, my neighborhood, my block. In intimate and romantic moments, we felt at ease with each other, like two lifelong friends.

One day after spending a few hours at a local town pool, we had a romantic dinner at a dimly lit restaurant done up like a Spanish colonial home, and over a glass of wine we murmured matters to each other that we considered our secrets. I confided that I was in love with her. Sandra smiled with pleasure and said, in a soft voice, that she was afraid to tell me her secret because I might get the wrong impression. She then leaned over to my ear, and in a soft voice said, "I have been thinking that I want to be with you." She smiled shyly.

A moment of silence followed. We held each other closely and kissed, and for a while we spoke about other topics. But then I reminded her of her secret and told her not to be afraid because I also had the same thoughts. "Yes, I want to be with you, too," I said. I told her I knew of a hotel on a mountain road outside Medellín that one of my cousins had been to with his fiancée.

We called a taxi and the driver whisked us there in twenty minutes. I was still a student and didn't really have much money for a hotel, but the exchange rate for American dollars worked to my advantage. We stepped into a room with a king-sized bed, a Jacuzzi tub, and a bar. Once inside, we embraced and kissed, and spent time adoring each other, hesitant about what we were about to do. We soon found our way and we acted on our secrets.

"Sandra, my love, this has been a special night and I will never forget it," I said afterward.

"Yes, my love, I trust you," she said, "and I will always love you all my life, even if you cannot return to Colombia."

As we embraced each other, I found myself beset by feelings of guilt. I had not intended for matters to move so far so quickly. However, I also felt deeply in love with her and we both thought that this night was our night and nothing could destroy it. We declared that we would never forget this night, and I found myself promising her that I was going to bring her to America. "I love you, Sandra, and I will do everything that I can to bring you to America." It was almost one in the morning, and I guessed Sandra's parents would be wondering about my intentions, so we called a taxi and returned to our neighborhood.

- - - - - - - -

I flew back to the United States in early August, a week after Pablo Escobar escaped from jail and his organization began a campaign of terror. Hundreds of people across Medellín were slain—policemen, judges, and politicians included. I found the violence disheartening and was happy to be going back to the calm of Harvard where I would witness nothing more explosive than the cloning of a gene.

On the plane, I could not resist reflecting on how much my daring voyage into the United States as a teenager had changed my life and wondering what my life would have been like if my parents had not brought me over. Would I have pursued a medical career or would I have been recruited by Escobar's cartel? I determined that I would do all I could to bring Sandra to America.

I already had experience with the immigration laws in America. So I investigated further what was involved in marrying a citizen of Colombia and bringing her over to America. I filled out the additional paperwork demonstrating that I was an American citizen and had a job and included a reference letter from the chairman of surgery at NYU, where I was an intern at the time. I sent it to the State Department. A few months later, I was thrilled when I received a letter stating that Sandra's application had been accepted. Sandra would be the first in my family to come to America with legal documents. As part of the application, we would have to get married within three months after her entrance into the country.

Sandra arrived at Kennedy International Airport wearing a long black gown, almost as if she were going to a formal ball. She and her mother apparently thought that arriving in the world's most imposing nation required a formal elegance, so her mother had a local seamstress custom-make the black dress. Sandra, with long, lustrous black hair framing her bronze shoulders, looked stunning.

My mother, Alex, and Marlon were with me at the airport and gazed with pleasure as Sandra and I kissed. I could tell my family supported my decision to marry Sandra. They trusted my choice because they could see in my face that this was the girl that made me happy and whom I deeply loved. As we celebrated, I could not help but contrast Sandra's arrival, with a visa that was entirely legal, to my own clandestine arrival fifteen years before at

Newark International Airport. With Sandra, our celebration was free. There was no pretending, no looking behind our shoulders for immigration agents.

Sandra did not have any idea of what was in store for her in New York. I had already started my surgical training at NYU. I lived in a miniature studio apartment on 34th street between 2nd and 3rd Avenues. Because I was seldom home, she ended up spending a lot of time on her own. At first, she was fearful about stepping outside, overwhelmed by the city's clamor and bustle and her inability to let her needs be known in English. She spent hours in our small studio watching television and reading magazines. The rear window faced the yard of an elementary school, and Sandra would sometimes gaze at the children playing during recess. She imagined that one day she would have children who could enjoy such a safe environment, rather than hanging out on the dangerous corners of Barrio Antioquia.

She began to break the ice by taking small walks to the hospital to have coffee or a bite with me. Soon, she felt more secure exploring the neighborhood. Most importantly, she learned how to find her way to the Port Authority terminal, where she could take a bus to West New York and hang out with my parents when I was on call.

We decided to get married on February 12, 1994. We made arrangements to celebrate with a small dinner at my parents' home. That month, I was doing a rotation at NYU's transplant service. I was not only working every day, but was on call round-the-clock in case a transplant needed to be performed. The only day I had free was a single Saturday, so that was the day we chose to get married. City Hall in West New York was closed on Saturdays, so I called my old track coach, Sal Vega, who was now a West New York commissioner, and he agreed to open City Hall for us and bring along a judge to perform the wedding.

The night before the wedding, there was a huge snowstorm. We both got ready in my parents' house. Sandra dressed in my parents' room. We bought Sandra's dress at Macy's for not much more than $100. Her figure was so shapely it made even that simple dress look dazzling. We came down together into the living room, where we both received blessings from my parents. Sadly, Sandra's parents were not there to bless her. Not only was the trip too expensive for them to make, but in those years to obtain a visa it would have taken a trip to the American consulate in Bogota, proof of real estate holdings or a thriving business, and several months of waiting. So Sandra had no family that could accompany her through this milestone. Nevertheless, in the morning she telephoned her mother and asked for her blessing. This was the best we could do.

By the time we stepped outside to head toward City Hall, which was only about fifty yards away, around the corner from my parents' home, the snow had stopped falling. Friends were arriving—even people that we had not invited but who wanted to be at our wedding. Many were immigrants from Barrio Antioquia who had been there for all my graduations from high school and college. The lack of an invitation was not going to keep them away. I had a feeling that our initial plan for a small dinner might change.

We walked hand in hand to City Hall, within the narrow aisle of cleared sidewalk, followed by about ten relatives and friends. We were running late, and I was concerned that we were causing too much trouble for Sal Vega. I prayed that I did not get a call from the hospital. I was anxious, but whenever I looked at my bride, I calmed down. She was bright with energy, laughter, and a zest for life. At City Hall, a cleaning lady directed us to Sal's office, and after a brief greeting, he left to pick up the judge, who lived a few blocks away. Twenty minutes later, the judge showed up and the ceremony got underway. My father took the place of Sandra's father in accompanying the bride.

The judge made some light remarks and then had us begin our vows. I checked on the rings in my pocket, the cheapest we could find. Both together cost no more than $100. As the judge pronounced the oath, Sandra struggled to repeat some of the words. She had barely learned any English in Colombia. We should have given some thought to this problem, but in the frenzy to arrange matters in time we did not. She repeated what the judge mouthed, but could not pronounce the word "fidelity" correctly. The judge had her repeat it several times until her pronunciation came close enough for his taste to make the ceremony legal. As she stumbled her words, my brothers and my mother were also struggling to hold back the laughter that had been building up when they noticed that Sandra was about to repeat the words of the judge in English. After a few moments of anxiety as we promised to love each other for ever, the girl in the school uniform who had enchanted me at the age of sixteen became my wife.

We returned to my parents' house where we feasted on all my mother's specialties: *arepas*, roast pork, a potato salad, and a mixture of rice and beans called *congril*. We drank *aguardiente*, beer, and tequila. I didn't drink because I could yet be called to assist in a liver or renal transplant, but I danced with the others until about four in the morning. A party that was going to be a small family dinner turned out to be a huge celebration with our close friends, many of them with similar experiences as undocumented immigrants in America.

THE MAKING OF A SURGEON

A few minutes before midnight on July 4, 1993, I was startled by the sudden ringing and vibration of the beeper hanging on the side of my surgical scrub pants. I had just sat down on a chair in the on call room on the fifteenth floor of Bellevue Hospital. I was exhausted from running around all day taking non-stop calls from the emergency room, and I was hoping to rest my feet for just a few minutes before seeing my next patient. However, this was an urgent call from the pediatric emergency room, and I had to attend to it immediately. Without hesitation, I sprung to my feet and I rushed downstairs. I was exhausted by the frantic pace of my first night on call.

My first assignment as a surgical intern was in a rotation called the hand rotation. My first weekend on call was the July Fourth weekend, and the patient that I had been called to see was a six-year-old boy who had badly burned his hand in a firecracker explosion. Although I had just completed four years of medical school at Harvard, I didn't really know too much about the hand. I had a basic understanding of its anatomy derived from my anatomy class four years earlier.

In the previous days, I had been arriving at the hospital at five in the morning and leaving at midnight, making rounds with residents and fellows, changing dressings, learning about fractures, learning techniques of splinting, suturing, giving anesthetics, and drawing blood. I was running from call to call without stop. Now I was on call alone and this patient would be my responsibility. The paramedics had dressed and bandaged the hand, but the boy was crying, his mother was sobbing, and his father was terribly nervous. "Doctor, is my son going to lose his hand?" the father asked me as I began examining his son.

The atmosphere around me was frenetic; dozens of people were waiting in their beds to be treated, moaning or screaming. Doctors and nurses were hurrying from one to the other, concentrating on their particular duties without losing themselves in the tumult. My job was to retain my composure and attend to this boy. I had to focus. I wondered what I would find as I took off the dressing. What should I tell the parents? I felt a nervous tingling and drops of sweat forming on my skin. Somehow, I gained my strength as I reminded myself about episodes of my life when I had to be sturdy, like living amidst the violence of Barrio Antioquia or holding myself together when Princeton asked me to produce a genuine green card

I asked the father to be calm and to hold his son in his arms as I worked to get the dressings off. When I removed them, I could see that the boy's skin had been burned away around the palm and fingertips. I cleaned up some of the charred skin, put a fresh dressing on, and asked the nurse to give him pain medication. I told the parents that the hand was going to be fine, but that their son would need some surgery that other doctors would perform. Just at that moment, there was a sharp cracking sound that I instantly recognized. It was a gunshot, right inside the Bellevue emergency room, a sound I had not heard since Barrio Antioquia.

An angry, homeless man being rolled along on a gurney managed to grab the gun of a police officer as he walked by and shot it into the air, injuring a nurse's hand. The nurse became my next patient, though treating her injuries was beyond my experience as an intern, and I had to ask for the help of my senior resident.

The night continued at this pace—surgical consults with one patient after another, my beeper sounding repeatedly, summoning me to another consultation before I was able to complete the one I was involved in. There was no chance to nap. As the first streams of daylight broke through the windows, I roused myself and appeared fresh and intelligent to report to the entire team by five o'clock in the morning.

This was just the beginning of several years of intense training that would get more difficult each year. The first lesson, especially at NYU's program, was to leave your ego at the door. You learn to take criticism, however unsubtly it is delivered. The NYU way of teaching could be direct and sometimes cruel.

"You moron, what the hell were you thinking?"

"Are you sure that you went to Harvard?"

"Why didn't you just shoot him in the head?"

"Is this how you would treat you grandmother?"

"You are not here to think; you are here to do what I tell you."

These were some of the lines that I heard from supervising residents or attending doctors during my training as they expressed disapproval of a medical decision that I had made. The atmosphere was more like a boot camp for Navy Seals than a prestigious surgical program. Notwithstanding, this is the accepted and prevailing method of instruction to turn an inexperienced medical school graduate into a confident and skilled surgeon.

But as with most fine crafts, it is a process of acclimatization and accumulation of small steps that leads to perfection.

For example, as a medical student at Harvard, I was able to hold the heart first of a cadaver and then I graduated to a live heart. The teaching surgeon asked me to put the palm of my hand, softly and gently, on the surface of the heart and hold it up so that he could visualize the vessels he was going to operate on. Later, during my cardiac rotation as a medical student at the Beth Israel Hospital in Boston, I got to hold a live heart many times, assisted in closing the chest at the end of the operation, and helped in harvesting the greater saphenous vein, the vessel in the leg that surgeons transplant into the chest to bypass the blockages of the coronary arteries. Each time I held the heart it was a formidable, awesome moment, but gradually the fright dissipated. That is what training is all about.

In the third and fourth years of medical school, I finally began to see patients on my trips through the different medical rotations—obstetrics, cardiology, internal medicine, and the like— and it was during this time that my decision to become a surgeon began to take shape. Each rotation lasts for one or two months and you become part of the actual medical team. I was now dealing with people, not textbooks. Still, I was there to observe and learn, so my part in every interaction with a patient was limited. It had to be. I was a novice. Even so, I found these limitations frustrating, and I was itching to do things. In fact, even as a young boy I always found fascination and enjoyment working with my hands. In my block in Barrio Antioquia, for example, I enjoyed the distinction of being the best at putting together a go-cart from parts salvaged at a nearby truck factory.

So, it was a natural impulse that when I started spending time in hospitals, I wanted to dive in, repair injured or diseased flesh and ligaments. Surgery offered the best path for me to satisfy that impulse. If someone came into the hospital with an excruciating pain on the right side of the lower abdomen, an internist might diagnose appendicitis. But it was the surgeon working in the operating room who would make a cut over the area of the pain, penetrate the abdomen, remove a small, swollen sack attached to the intestines, and sew up the damage. Two days later the patient would leave pain free.

A classic of medical literature, *The Making of a Surgeon*, firmed up my desire. Its author, William A. Nolen, MD, did his residency at Bellevue Hospital in Manhattan in the 1950s, and I was captivated by his description of the surgical challenges he faced with skill and judgment. I decided that I too wanted to do my residency at a frenetic city hospital like Bellevue, which was run by NYU.

During my day-long interviews at other hospitals run by Columbia and Cornell, I was impressed by the academic and research programs available to their residents, but I was also struck by a remark dropped by the resident who gave us a tour at New York Hospital.

"This is a gentleman's program," he said.

Oddly, I did not want to be in a gentleman's program. I wanted the opposite. I wanted to work really hard. This is what attracted me to the program that had the reputation of being a "malignant program." This program had the nationwide-reputation of absurd demands and sometimes militaristic discipline that bordered on mental and physical abuse.

During our tours at NYU, one of the candidates asked, "What is the call schedule like?"

In a stern voice, the resident leading us around replied, "If you are concerned about the call schedule, this is probably not the program for you."

A dean at Harvard Medical School once said that he would prefer an "intern who would get up in the middle of the night to be at the patient's bedside instead of an intern with straight A's."

I fit his model. I had always pushed myself insanely and seemed to thrive on the challenge. The extra effort that I had to put in in high school and college to rise above my humiliating immigration status prepared me well for the draining effort needed to take care of patients in a grueling environment. Whatever the reasons, NYU's fatiguing hours and battle-hardened instructors were precisely what seduced me.

So, after graduating medical school, I enrolled in the general surgery program at New York University Medical Center, which also furnished doctors for Bellevue, Tisch Hospital, the private hospital in the complex, and Veterans Affairs Medical Center. When I told people I was training at Bellevue, they would look perplexed, thinking I would be treating psychiatric patients. But Bellevue, the oldest public hospital in the country, founded when George Washington was just four, was recognized nationally for its programs in cardiovascular, neonatal, toxicology, and trauma care. Indeed, it was the city's premier trauma center and had been designated as the hospital to which visiting dignitaries, including the president of the United States, would be taken in an emergency. For someone who had recently been an undocumented immigrant, the prospect of treating a stricken president seemed to add an extra level of excitement.

My first impression as I entered Bellevue's main entrance on First Avenue was more of a hectic train station like New York's Grand Central Station than a hospital. Dozens of people, some in white lab coats, some in green scrubs, some in casual street duds, were racing back and forth on urgent missions to who-knew-where. The waiting areas were a jumble of races, cultures, and religions with some people standing in dreary isolation and others in frenzied clusters waiting to see a doctor, their faces twisted in anguish or fear. Now I would have to do what I could to ease that distress.

And yet, this kind of pressure, even torment, was what I had sought. I wanted to demonstrate that I could master the necessary skills without breaking down under the pressure. I had been through such ordeals before and survived and thrived. I would not whine. Whenever my parents would ask me how things were going, I would always say, "Fine, I love it." There were times when I had doubts, when I wondered if I could endure this torment for the five years of general surgery. Not only did I survive, I elected to go into a field that is several degrees more punishing—cardiac surgery.

NYU's heart surgery program was started by the legendary Dr. Frank C. Spencer, a contemporary of all the major heart surgeons who came from a fabled training program at Johns Hopkins— Michael DeBakey, Denton Cooley, and David Sabiston. Intense and fiercely dedicated to his craft, Spencer was known as the toughest of them all. This was not surprising for a man who made his reputation as a battle surgeon in the Korean War.

During combat, he resisted military guidelines that ordered the immediate amputation of a soldier's limb following a penetrating injury. Dr. Spencer felt that he could save some of these limbs by repairing the arteries. Amputation might have made sense during the two world wars where the transport times from the field to a treatment center were long. But in Korea, they had helicopters to ferry wounded soldiers to a field hospital and the short transport period permitted some limbs to be salvaged, especially with a surgeon who had the technical skill to do arterial reconstructions. Because Spencer disregarded the protocols, he was almost court-martialed, but he was able to prove to his superiors that his work had helped a hundred soldiers keep their legs. The military eventually awarded him a medal.

He essentially introduced open-heart surgery to New York and went on to make countless contributions to the field and to write the basic heart-surgery text, sacrificing much of his personal life along the way. Spencer always wanted to be right in the middle of the action in tending to his patients and training his protégés. Right after his appointment as the chairman of cardiac surgery, he chose to live in the dorm with his students instead of moving into a fancy Upper East Side apartment. He also loved Bellevue as an institution and made it the center of NYU's training. When administrators wanted to create a joint ICU at Bellevue for all the separate surgical residency programs at Columbia, New York Hospital, and NYU, he decided that doing so would be inefficient. While the administrators met for months making plans for an ICU, Spencer asked his chief resident to create a sign that said "NYU ICU" and post it the next day in an empty room in the hospital. In the days that followed, he had the necessary equipment gathered from various rooms to create his own ICU exclusively for NYU doctors. This was Dr. Spencer. If he wanted something done, no one could stand in his way.

I felt this intensity when I interviewed with him. He must have sensed by looking at me and hearing my accent that I might have a distinctive story, and he was not restrained to ask about it. I told him about my voyage into the United States on a small boat and he seemed to appreciate what an ordeal I went through. I came out of the room knowing that this was the kind of strict but sensitive doctor I wanted to be and he must have sensed that I had the determination it takes to one day operate on hearts.

Nevertheless, the first time I had to rotate through Dr. Spencer's service, I felt under severe stress. The night before, I could not sleep. I kept turning in bed. *What am I afraid of?* I kept asking myself. *I have been through worse situations. I feel strong. I will make it.*

I got a couple of hours of sleep, then I was up at 5:15 a.m. I took a quick shower, and put on a pair of surgical scrubs. At many hospitals, interns had to wear a suit and a tie, but Spencer wanted to see you in work clothes, ready to get down to the business of taking care of patients. I rushed over to the hospital, getting there on time at 5:45 a.m. As the surgical resident, I was standing next to Dr. Spencer, assisting him in cutting sutures and suctioning excess blood. Although my role was limited, I was right there in the midst of all the surgical action. Dr. Spencer was impressive. He was in his early-to-mid seventies and had slowed considerably from his prime, yet his hands were steady and his ability to make split-second decisions was as sharp as ever. As for me, after being up all night, it was very difficult to stay alert. I had to push myself every second, staying active, anticipating the next move, prepared to cut a stitch even before being called to do it. *Harold, stay awake; don't fall asleep,* I kept telling myself. *This is your chance to learn from the best.*

During coronary artery surgery, there is a point, perhaps the most critical part of the surgery, when the heart is stopped and the surgeon has to drive a very fine needle and suture material to sew the bypass vein onto the artery on the heart. To do this, I had to stand on Dr. Spencer's left side and hold the heart with a steady hand so that he could do his work without movement or interruption. I found this experience daunting but also strangely exhilarating, as if a rush of adrenalin was curing my exhaustion. I was holding a person's heart in my hand and enabling Dr. Spencer to do his life-and-death work. I could see every stitch and every movement of his hand and analyze his strategy, and I realized that one day I would be expected to do the same.

In subsequent surgeries, I would pretend in my mind that I was the one actually performing the operation, following every movement of the chief surgeon, including how he washed his hands, walked into an operating room, positioned and prepared the patient for an operation. Each time I assisted, the anatomy and the physiology of this magnificent organ became better imprinted on my mind. But I wanted to do more. I wanted to tie perfect knots and cut and sew with the fine needle holders.

Precise suturing is at the heart of any successful operation. The needle itself has a gentle half-moon curve, and it needs to take this same direction as it goes through the tissue without causing any damage or extra holes. So, in my free time at home, I practiced suturing on anything that I could find: clothes, towels, shoes, chicken legs, banana peels. I would envision the needle going through in an effortless manner. Sometimes, without actually sewing, I walked around the kitchen and living room with a needle holder in my hand, imitating the movements I had seen Dr. Spencer or his protégés make, moving the needle in phantom motions while eating, watching television, and driving. I wanted this instrument to be an extension of my fingers. Soon, I could tie knots with my left hand, with my eyes closed, and with gloves that I wetted to simulate blood.

At NYU, the cardiac surgeon seemed to rule the hospital. He made his rounds as if he owned the place. Everyone respected him; everyone looked up to him.

Another of these surgical emperors was Dr. Rick Esposito. He was a stocky six footer, a son of Italian immigrants who had been through the entire NYU training regimen himself. He spoke in a commanding and energetic voice, and frequently energized his conversations with strong and picturesque curse words. The first time I met him was at a cardiac arrest. An announcement came over the intercom that an open-heart surgery patient on the fourteenth floor had suffered a cardiac arrest. The cardiac team rushed to her bedside and started the usual protocol of cardiac resuscitation. Two minutes into the code, Dr. Esposito walked in, and in a calm but commanding voice took control of the room. He ordered everyone out, except for two nurses, another intern, and myself. He then directed me to place an intravenous line in the patient's groin, into her femoral artery and vein.

"Come on, Harold, I need that line right now!" I heard him say in a loud voice.

My hands were trembling. Although I was able to regain my composure, I could not help. I could not find her vein. Then I heard him say, "Give me that!" He forcefully took the needle from my hand, and found the vein in a second. We then were able to inject medications, eventually restoring the patient's heart function and vital signs. He then ordered us to take her back into the operating room and commence the procedures required to re-open her chest and massage the heart to revive it. He thanked us and walked out of the room. I had my breath taken away in utter admiration. What had been pandemonium became a piece of exquisite choreography, almost as if it had been rehearsed many times before. Incidents like these only confirmed my desire to become a heart surgeon, to acquire the ability to save people's lives with a set of learnable skills, even if it meant several more years of training.

Perhaps the most important influence on my surgical skills was Dr. Spencer's protégé, Dr. Stephen Colvin. A sturdily built man with a thick neck, thick eyebrows that almost covered his visual field, and deep-set eyes that gave him a penetrating gaze. He too had a commanding presence. He would walk into a room and everyone would know that this was an exceptional doctor and human being. He put all his heart into teaching his fellows; nothing would be ignored or passed over. When one of the junior attending physicians in our group gained too much weight, Colvin even put him on a strict diet. Paradoxically, we were never underfed because Dr. Colvin gave the chief resident access to his personal credit card and he could order food from any local restaurant every night.

Colvin took us through surgical procedures like a drill sergeant takes his new recruits out in the field. He was the all-powerful, all-knowing leader that we all feared and obeyed. He made it clear that we were entering a field where nothing short of perfection would be tolerated. Every stitch had to be cut at the exact length, every knot had to be tied just so. Unlike in most other occupations, errors could cost our patients their lives. He seemed to live at the hospital, sometimes seeing patients in his office into the midnight hours. I never understood how he had the energy to do that. Yet behind this façade of iron discipline, he was a gentle and caring human being who was always willing to help an intern master the details of his profession. He insisted that everyone call him Steve and that everyone—from nurses to medical students to visitors—be given permission to watch him operate.

During my first rotation with him, he yelled at me relentlessly.

"Come on, Harold, this is too long," he would yell about the thread left on a stitch being one millimeter longer than he wanted.

I felt there was nothing that I could ever do right. There were times when I was so sure he hated me that I almost wanted to cry. It almost felt as if he had a personal vendetta against me. Yet I wanted to someday be able to do what I had witnessed doctors like him and Spencer do. I had the firm belief that if I followed Dr. Colvin to the letter, he could get me to where I wanted to be as a surgeon.

Amusingly enough, as the months and years went by, I became one of his favorite fellows. During the summer months, he would often go deep-sea fishing for tuna and leave bags of tuna in a refrigerator in the recovery room, including one for me. He would tell his nurses, "Make sure that Harold takes that bag of tuna." Some friends even began to mock me as his "golden boy" because, to them, I seemed never to do anything wrong in his eyes.

Becoming a cardiac surgeon seemed to require complete devotion and focus, and I, too, found myself surrendering the rest of my life to this new obsession. I found that training in cardiac surgery was as close as I ever came to joining a cult. I was overworked, overstressed, and sleep-deprived, and in this state, I was required to learn the mysterious tenets of what seemed like a new religion with all the attendant fervor.

A typical week would start at five in the morning on a Monday with ICU rounds, reviewing information on the post or preoperative patients with our team of residents and nurse practitioners. Then we might grab a cup of coffee and, by seven in the morning, start the first of the day's operations. Next, we might be asked to perform parts of two or three surgeries. By then, it was nightfall, and our night rounds would start. These were much longer than the morning rounds because they included a more thorough review of each patient. At night, we would undertake the less risky procedures, such as bronchoscopies and tracheotomies. We usually finished our work around midnight. If I was on call, I would stay in the hospital and try to grab some sleep in a large padded chair at the end of the recovery room. The actual amount of sleep I received depended on the severity of the patients' conditions and any unexpected medical complications. Just one critically ill patient with an unanticipated problem would result in a sleepless night.

The next day, Tuesday, the same routine would start at five in the morning, and last the entire day and into the night. I would get home, usually just after midnight, and find Sandra in a deep sleep. As I tried to nod off, feverish with the tense work of the day, I would rehash in my mind every step of an operation I saw or performed before falling asleep. Sometimes, I would wake up in the middle of the night and give Sandra instructions for patients that I had treated that day. The only hours I had that were free were on Saturday afternoon or on Sunday, and I used this time to catch up on my sleep.

Another peculiar aspect of surgical training is that you are not allowed to be sick. There is no such concept as "calling in sick." You simply are not allowed to miss a day, period. More than once, I was dehydrated because of illness—a bout of kidney stones was particularly painful—but I would just have one of the interns insert an intravenous line in a vein and hydrate me with two liters of fluids. Then I continued with my workday. The hospital became my first home, and I averaged over 140 hours per week there.

There was not even time to eat. Instead of taking the time to take a long walk to the cafeteria, I would stroll through the ICU and grab a leftover can of Ensure. Patients were often too sick to drink these cans of flavored protein shakes, so the nurses would leave them on a window sill. Two or three cans were enough to supply the proteins and calories I would need for a day. I even felt anxious taking the time to go to the bathroom, and when I did, my beeper more than once went off.

For two years, I lost contact with my family and my friends. My wife gave birth to a girl, our daughter Jasmine, and between the time she was one and three I doubt I saw her more than once a week. When I did see her, I was too exhausted to play with her.

One Sunday, when Jasmine was about nine months old, I came home after having been on call for forty-eight hours straight without sleep. I gave Sandra a kiss, saying, "Hi my love, how are you?" She remarked how fatigued I looked but said she was going to make us a nice lunch, and asked if while she did I could keep an eye on Jasmine, who was lying on our bed. I lay down next to Jasmine, determined to be a good parent and guard my child for a few minutes. Within seconds, I fell asleep and was suddenly awakened by the sound of my daughter hitting the floor. Sandra rushed in from the kitchen, picked Jasmine up, and held her close. Then she yelled at me, telling me how irresponsible I was. I already felt terrible. I could take care of every detail with patients I knew little about, but could not guard my own child for a few minutes.

By the time Jasmine was a toddler, my alienation from my family was brought home in a powerfully graphic way. Jasmine was asked to draw a picture of the family for her toddler center. In the sketch were figures of my wife, my daughter, and the dog. When the teacher asked her where her father was, she answered, "He is at work."

The fact was that I *was* at work. I was polishing my skills as a heart surgeon. I needed to be calm and deliberate in the face of a crisis, like a sudden cardiac arrest, and in order to do this I needed to be comfortable with my skills and my reactions. I had to be perfect. I needed to be able to tell myself that I had seen these situations many times before. And so I needed to put in as many hours as my muscles, nerves, and mind could tolerate. It is not surprising that the personal consequences of this line of work have ruined many marriages. Fortunately, my wife—who, like me, grew up in the kind of poverty that turned every hour into a struggle to survive—understood this kind of punishing effort and was always supportive.

- - - - - - - -

My return to New York City for my surgical training gave me a sense of fulfillment and accomplishment. In a strange twist of irony and fate, my training in cardiac surgery and experience at NYU would one day bring me back to thoughts of my life as a child in Barrio Antioquia. After all, New York was the city that I used to dream of as a kid strolling along the streets of Barrio Antioquia. This was the skyline that I could clearly recognize because I had seen it many times in the postcards that my father would send when he was living here. The year before I came to the United States, this skyline, without its bright lights, made television headlines around the world due to the New York City Blackout of July 13, 1977.

The images of the city in darkness, as well as the looting and vandalism in some of the neighborhoods, were shown all around the world. As these events unfolded here in New York, I would have conversations with friends about the blackout into the late hours of the night. We would all gather outside and sit on the steps leading to the front entrance of the church. The discussions mostly involved imaginary theories about what had caused the blackout. Someone had started a rumor that it had been caused by an extraterrestrial spaceship that had landed in the center of the city to drain all its energy because it needed the power to return back to its native planet.

The discussions centered on our knowledge of astronomy, science, and the fictional stories or movies that we had seen. The actual cause of the blackout was a series of lightning strikes and the tripping of circuit breakers in several powerful reactors around the city that led to the shutdown of the entire Con Edison power system. This is what they discussed in the news. We found the former arguments about a spaceship more interesting and fascinating than the reality of what occurred. We knew that this was fiction, but we also believed that anything could happen in New York.

The television programs and the radio news shows covered in great detail the 1977 New York City Blackout, as well as the financial crisis of the mid-seventies that almost sent New York City into bankruptcy during the mayoral term of Abraham D. Beame. He was the mayor of New York from 1974 to 1977. Although I was young and didn't have much interest in world news or events, I did follow all the news from New York very closely. After all, both of my parents were living there. Many of my friends in Barrio Antioquia also watched with interest because they had relatives who lived there. Probably because of Beame's short stature (he was about five feet, two inches tall) and his demeanor, which was gentle for a mayor of a big city, Beame generally stood out in the news segments that were shown on television. Ironically, this same powerful person who governed the city that I dreamed of while growing up in Medellín would become one of my patients twenty-four years later when I was the senior cardiothoracic surgery fellow at Tisch Hospital working for Dr. Colvin.

Beame was ninety-four and was very ill, having endured congestive heart failure, renal failure, and poor nutrition. The initial plan was to keep him comfortable during his last few days. But he was a resilient man, and his son, who was always by his side, was not ready to let him go. Colvin thought that if medical management was not working, surgery might present an opportunity—both a coronary bypass and replacement of his aortic valve. Given Beame's age, the surgery would be high risk.

I had the privilege to first-assist Dr. Colvin during Mayor Beame's first open-heart surgery, and I had the honor of directing his post-surgical care. The surgery proceeded flawlessly. Even at the age of 94, Mayor Beame showed great strength, character, and courage as he struggled to recover from multiple medical conditions. I cannot deny that I felt a deep obligation to do my best, not just because this man was my patient, but because this man was a part of the city's history. Over the course of the next few weeks, he improved dramatically—regaining consciousness, absorbing intravenous foods, and later swallowing food on his own. His cheeks regained some color, he started to smile, and, with assistance, he even walked around the hospital ward. Colvin told me once, as we were getting ready for someone else's surgery, how great it would be for NYU to make a television commercial showing Mayor Beame playing golf.

After I moved on from Dr. Colvin's service, one of my colleagues, Dr. Marc Davison, assumed his care. Unfortunately, the artificial valve that we had used as a replacement became infected, and he required a second surgery. As Mayor Beame's medical condition worsened beyond our ability to help him, Dr. Davison became his best friend and companion. Now, in the absence of the cameras, the reporters, the media, and the dignitaries, this historical person who governed the greatest city on earth at one time, spent his last few days in the company of his family and a doctor who was practicing the art of medicine.

LOSING A PATIENT

In October 2007, while I was making my routine rounds in the Respiratory Care Unit (Respi) at St. Francis, I was asked to examine a patient named Alice Stewart to see if she could withstand a tracheotomy. Respi, by the way, is one of the most challenging places at the hospital because this is the place where many patients who have had a difficult medical course may spend weeks or even months recovering from chronic conditions. Many of these patients fight very hard to get better, and many of them never recover.

Except for the sound of the monitors, the unit was unusually silent. As I made my way through the unit, I almost had the feeling that many of these patients were in some sort of vegetative state. This is not unusual in this unit, where many patients are fully dependent on the ventilator and sedated with medication as they cling to their last few breaths of life. A tracheotomy is recommended for patients who are very weak and are probably going to be on the ventilator for their remaining days, or at the very least for a long time. The method consists of making a small opening in the front of the neck at the second ring of the windpipe so a short breathing tube can be inserted in a manner that makes the patient more comfortable.

When I saw Alice lying on her hospital bed, thin, weak, and frail, it seemed immediately apparent that there was not much more we could do for her. She weighed around seventy pounds and her blood pressure was very low. She was sixty-six, but she appeared much older or like a patient with advanced cancer who had not eaten in months. I could glimpse all the bones of her face, neck, and chest pressing up against her skin. I picked up Alice's chart and the notes indicated that she had been brought in to St. Francis for shortness of breath caused by a blockage in her mitral valve, the valve that permits blood to flow from the left atrium of the heart into the left ventricle so it can be pumped into the arteries that feed the body. Her heart and lungs were failing irreversibly. That was the medical information that I obtained from a quick glance at the notes from the different care providers. More important, however, is that I got a sense that many of her caregivers also thought that she was not going to make it. Many of the notes ended with the words, "Her prognosis is very poor." This often means that this person will not make it out of the hospital.

With a sense of helplessness and frustration, I asked her nurse, "What is the plan here?" She told me that her doctors were urging a breathing tube in her neck so Alice could be transferred to a hospice for palliative, end-of-life care. As I held Alice's cold, clammy hand, a hand that lacked all muscle tone, it seemed to me that a permanent breathing tube made sense and would probably ease her last days. In her weakened state, she did not seem like a candidate for heart surgery. Now I needed to relay all this to Alice's family.

Alice was single, but she had an older sister, who happened to walk into the room just after my conversation with the nurse. There was a strong resemblance, except that Alice looked thirty years older than her older sister, who was fit, well dressed, and vigorous. The older sister loved Alice and, with tears in her eyes, she showed me pictures of Alice looking lively and happy just a few months earlier. She agreed that there was not much more that could be done for Alice beyond the breathing tube and a feeding tube that a gastroenterologist would place in Alice's stomach a week later. Alice was ready to be sent to a hospice.

However, as she recovered from those procedures and emerged from her sedation, Alice made gestures and signs to her sister that she was not ready to die. She wanted to live, she told her sister again and again. As a last resort, her sister, who seemed to remain at Alice's bedside virtually round-the-clock, asked the pulmonologist and the cardiologist if there was any way heart surgery could still be done. That meant that I would have to evaluate Alice again, this time as a candidate for open-heart surgery.

"She's not going to make it, no way," I told the cardiologist when he called me.

"Well, could you just come by and explain that to Alice and her sister?" he asked. "Just as a courtesy."

I examined Alice once more and told her sister that the odds were nine out of ten that she would not survive surgery. Yet, those odds did not deter the sister; she saw something we weren't catching: a strong flicker of life in Alice's eyes. That seemed to give her the confidence that she could put her sister through such a procedure.

"Doctor," the sister said. "My sister is a fighter; I can't let her go without a fight."

She managed to persuade me. I scheduled Alice for surgery the next day.

The most difficult part of the procedure was enduring the skepticism of my surgical team when they gazed at Alice lying on her gurney. I was also skeptical. I had extreme confidence that I could get her through the technical aspects of the surgical procedure, but could she possibly recover from the weeks and months of pulmonary and physical therapy? As she was brought into the operating room, there were many doubts that she would get better. It is very unusual to perform open-heart surgery on a patient who is attached to both breathing and feeding tubes. These patients are often too ill to survive the procedure.

"Harold, what are we doing here?" Dr. Allan Resnick, the anesthesiologist and the medical director of the operating room, asked.

I had no sensible answer. I could tell by the look on their faces that the nurses and technicians felt the same way. I tossed some doubts around in my mind. *Am I wrong to be doing this? Am I being grandiose, acting the part of the surgeon glorying in making life and death decisions? What am I trying to prove?*

In the minutes before the surgery, as I often do during times of difficult surgical decisions, I thought of one of my greatest mentors, Dr. Colvin. What would he have done? The answer seemed clear. He would have operated. He would have done everything he could for this woman, just as he had for Mayor Beame at the advanced age of ninety-four. She still had a chance at living. In American medicine, life is sacred until God finally takes it from us, and we do everything that we can to make people comfortable and help them.

On a more personal and philosophical side, I understood why Alice wanted to proceed with the high-risk surgery. At times, we are all faced with taking risks to enrich our human existence. For example, I thought of the chances my parents took when they arranged to put me and Byron on that boat, of the gambles my grandmothers took to let us go, of the gambles Byron and I, small and mindless as we were, took to endure that voyage in 1978. There are gambles in not acting, as well. Perhaps, Byron and I could have grown up in immense poverty that would have seriously limited our existence. Or even worse, we could have ended up in a coffin surrounded by four candles in the middle of our living room, the casualties of another vendetta in Barrio Antioquia.

From thoughts like these I gained strength. By the time I entered the operating room and looked down on Alice covered with a sterile sheet, I focused all my energy on mending Alice's heart; God would take care of the rest. I had to persuade my team, and I tried to do it by the power of my work. I tried to make every cut, every suture, and every stitch as close to perfect as I knew how. I sensed that there was no room for even a single error; Alice was not strong enough to endure complications. Dr. Resnick and the nurses were on the same page. Everyone in the room was striving for perfection.

The surgery was as fine as it could possibly be. I had replaced her mitral valve and her heart began pumping strongly. After the surgery, and after a few days in the intensive care unit, she started to make progress toward regaining her health. On December 10, she was stable enough to be transferred to a rehab center. Five months later, on April 25, 2008, I saw her in my office. She was ambling clumsily with a walker, but she was dressed in street clothes and her cheeks were pink; she had gained twenty pounds and was on her way to resuming the normal life of a sixty-six-year-old woman. She had one question for me.

"Dr. Fernandez, when can I drive?"

"You can start driving now," I responded

She looked at me with a smile on her face and a bright glow of life in her eyes. She gave me a hug and kissed me.

"Thank you doctor," she said. "How can I ever repay you?"

I told her it was God who had decided to give her more time. I was just privileged to be a witness at the miracle of her recovery. I had done the easy part. With her will to live and spiritual strength, she had done the hard work to get better. Now she sends me a card several times a year to mark the holidays she thought she would never enjoy again. Alice Stewart's card for the last Christmas read, "Dear Dr. Fernandez, thank you again for allowing me to see this Christmas. I wish you all the best."

Unfortunately, my life as a heart surgeon is not always this happy. At times, we try to help and we cannot. Other times we try to help, and we may inadvertently cause harm—not as a consequence of negligence, as many lawyers would like to think, but as a result of the fact that medicine is not an exact science. At times, success makes us happy, proud, and fills us with confidence, and always, our failures bring distress and heartbreak. There are situations that really can bring us to tears and tear us up inside.

A couple of years later, as I was again walking through the same unit making rounds, a nurse stopped me so that I could see a patient who was dying in the same room where I had seen Alice. The patient's name was Janice. She had been a beautiful teenage girl growing up in a prominent family in Long island. Now she was on life support because she had an infection in one of the valves inside her heart, the Tricuspid Valve. Janice was now twenty-two years old, and most likely, only had a few days to live. A few years earlier, she had befriended a drug dealer who introduced her to heroin. In just a few years of her addiction, she had injected drugs into every possible vein in her body, including the veins in her neck. She was now a slave of her addiction to drugs. Her heart valve was infected with bacteria, and she was dying of failure of her heart, lungs, and kidneys. Pictures of her heart showed a vast infection inside.

As I looked at this young woman lying on this bed, unconscious, on a ventilator, and on a dialysis machine, my heart dropped to the floor. I wanted to cry. I thought of my own daughter. I wanted to help this girl. I really hoped that there was something that I could do to fix her problem and give her another opportunity. Unfortunately, the answer was no. Her best option at this point was for her to get better with medicines. She needed to have antibiotics and many prayers to get better.

After a few weeks of treatment on antibiotics, she improved and was able to come off the ventilator; however, she was still having fevers, and her infection inside the heart was still going strong. Now, because she was slightly better, she was a better candidate for open-heart surgery. I felt that we had a small window of opportunity to perform surgery. I discussed the procedure with her father and her aunts. They realized that it was very risky, but they also understood that this was her only chance. They agreed to proceed, and we scheduled her for surgery.

Once again, we had doubts about how she would do. I had confidence that she would do fine, but the bigger question was whether she would stay away from drugs after her recovery. Her surgery went well. Janice recovered and left the hospital after several weeks of antibiotics in her veins. I saw her in the office a few months later. Everything seemed to be getting better. Both of her aunts accompanied her to the visit. They were very happy. She had not returned to her old friends. She had not returned to her drug abuse. With a wide smile on her face, she thanked me, and she said, "Dr, Fernandez I finally found a boyfriend who has a job for the first time in my life." I felt great. We discussed her life for several minutes. I listened to the details of her new friends. I wished her well, and I reinforced the importance of staying away from drugs. She gave me a big hug before she left my office.

It was all great, until two months later, when I received a call from the hospital. Janice had been readmitted to the hospital again with very high fevers. Her valve was infected again, and she was once again very ill with failure of her lungs, kidneys, and liver. Once again, we attempted to treat her with medication first. This time, it did not work. She was getting worse. Her doctors and her family wanted another attempt at surgery. We all thought that this was her only opportunity. I was sure that I could get her through the surgery. I was confident that I could go in and remove all the infection and fix her heart. I was wrong. Her infection was now much worse. Her infection now involved all the valves in her heart. I worked on her heart for several hours; however, I could not get her better. After correcting all her problems and removing all the infection, her heart was too weak at the end, and her lungs were no longer working. She expired on the operating room table.

I felt awful. I wanted to cry. All my efforts, all my years of training, all the technology we had, and I could not help this young girl. The family was aware of the extreme risks of her surgery, but they were still hopeful that a miracle would occur. This time, it was not to be. Janice's body was lifeless, and I had to tell her father and her aunts. As I walked into the waiting room to inform them, I walked in with my head down. The family was silent. They knew that I was about to give them the worst news of their lives. However, they waited until I finally said, "I am sorry to tell you this, but I could not help Janice; she has died."

The family started crying. "Oh, my angel. My angel!" her aunt exclaimed. "Why, God? Why have you taken her away from us?"

I did not know what to do or say, except tell them that I was sorry that I could not help her. It was a desperate moment. The father had lost his little girl. She had been through so much, but he had not given up on her. As he heard my explanation of what transpired in the operating room, the tears flowed profusely down his cheeks. He could not comprehend why his daughter had suffered so much.

We were there for several minutes as the family expressed their grief. Even at this moment of terrible tragedy, the family found a place in their hearts to thank me for my effort to help her.

"Oh, Dr. Fernandez, thank you for helping Janice." One of her aunts told me that Janice had been really happy with her care at the hospital and had even thought about doing something in the medical field.

I felt powerless. I was in the room with the family, sharing my suffering with them. They had lost a daughter and a niece, and I had lost a dear patient. I had used all my ability to help and I could not. All my years of training at Princeton, Harvard, MIT, and at NYU Medical Center were not enough. Now the only thing that I could do was to be there with the family and share my pain and suffering with them.

This is the part of being a heart surgeon that I dreaded. You feel like running away, but you cannot. This is the most difficult part of the medical profession because at the end of the day, the doctor becomes one with the patient and the family. We share in their pain and suffering.

This aspect of medicine is what makes this field unique. You are not dealing with objects or money, you are dealing with someone's life. And as a heart surgeon there are times when we lose the battle and we lose a patient. I have learned through my years in practice that although there are times when the science of medicine fails and I am not able to heal, I need the personal comfort that I have done everything that I can possibly do, and that I have treated people with compassion, kindness, and decency.

I think that Dr. Joseph B. Martin, the dean of Harvard Medical School, put it well in remarks to the entering class of 2009. He told these prospective physicians that he wanted to emphasize "the art of medicine and the art of communication in medicine." This is the arena of medicine that most doctors find elusive, but when it works, it is most rewarding. The challenge is that, in reaching out to patients as other human beings, a doctor inevitably shares in their suffering. The rewards come when the relationship with the patient and the family brings consolation in the face of medicine's powerlessness.

In practicing medicine all these years, I have found that there are two essentials to being a competent doctor. First, there are the facts and the science. This is what you learn from the books. In the medical lecture halls at Harvard, I learned about every disease, the options for treatment, and the way to apply those options in real-life situations. Gaining that knowledge may require long hours of study, but most people, I believe, can do so with some perseverance. Perhaps even a computer or a robot can. Far harder to master is the second ingredient for skillful medicine, the ability to reach out to the patient as another human being and become the patient's advocate and partner. This is a skill that is learned not from textbooks but that comes from within your own inner compassion. There are doctors who can spout all the facts but cannot empathize with or relate to the people they treat. There is a stone wall between them, and the patient is deprived of the human connection. Another dean at Harvard once stated that "the art in caring for the patient is caring for the patient."

This skill is useful when we reach the limit of medical capabilities. Still, there is comfort and healing that can happen from simply holding a patient's hand or spending time at the bedside. I began to learn this lesson even before I received my medical license, at the deathbed of my grandmother Rosa. She had suffered from uterine cancer, and in her last months, when cancer reached an advanced stage, her doctors no longer had medical solutions to offer. When I took my trip to Medellín after finishing my third semester at Harvard Medical School in 1991, I spent a couple of weeks with her, often sleeping at her bedside. She had lost over sixty pounds and was constantly nauseated. With the wide array of theoretical medical facts and science that I had learned up to that point, there was little I could do to help her. In fact, there was not much anyone could do. She had lost the battle to cancer. The only thing we could all do as a family was to love her and be at her side.

Until her last hours, my grandmother displayed the kind of wisdom that you don't learn in school, but that you acquire through years of coping with hardships like the violence in Barrio Antioquia and the murder of a granddaughter. Even as she lay writhing on her bed, unable to get up because of malnutrition and bone pain, I could see a delighted sparkle in her dark-brown eyes each time she heard me using medical terms in my conversations with her doctor. This is what she had dreamed of for many years. My grandmother had seen me graduate from Princeton, had visited the Harvard campus, and seen that I was well on my way to completing medical school.

Even in her moments of delirium, my grandmother would repeat the advice that she had already given me in countless letters about my becoming a doctor. She knew very well that I was infinitely much better off strolling through the halls and laboratories of Harvard Medical School than the treacherous streets and alleys of Barrio Antioquia. When she died on February 27, 1992, she seemed at peace. In the way she lived and died, she taught me to hold life precious and to take the risks needed to keep a life vital. This viewpoint is what allowed her to send us on a risky journey across the sea so that we could enjoy a better life. That lesson of holding life precious and vital is a lesson I take with me every day.

A BOUQUET OF FLOWERS

On a warm day in October of 1994, Arancy Chica, one of my dear cousins, was working part time at her family's supermarket. She was helping out as a cashier at the entrance. As she attended to the customers paying for their groceries, she noticed that two young men, whom she did not know, entered the front of the grocery store. One of them was carrying a bouquet of flowers. As he approached the counter, he said that he had a delivery of flowers for Arancy Chica. Delighted, Arancy smiled and acknowledged that she was who they were looking for. When she reached for the flowers, the other man shot her in the chest. As Arancy flailed to the floor from the impact of the bullet, he leaped over the counter and shot her once more in the head. The two assassins dashed out of the store and drove away. The killers were never found.

Arancy occupied a special place in my heart. When I had returned to Colombia as a medical student to analyze emergencies in Medellín's hospital, I stayed in my Aunt Gilma's house and Arancy and I had become close friends.

She was an attractive, humble, lively young lady, with dark hair cascading down to the middle of her back. However, by twenty-eight years of age she had still never married and lived at home. She was the nucleus of that house, doing the cooking and cleaning and working part time at a local grocery store owned by the family, the *E & W Supermercado*, to bring in extra income. She did all those monotonous tasks with a cheerful, kind spirit. Her smile seemed to ease the cares of my day, just as it did for others in her life. Indeed, she treated me like a younger brother and made sure that all my clothes were ironed and all my meals were warm and that the uniform I wore when I visited the hospital was spotless. She even strolled places in Barrio Antioquia with me so neighbors would know I belonged in the neighborhood and was not an easy target or an intruder.

Arancy did not deserve this, nor do the thousands of Colombians who are the victims of senseless violence each year. She did not have a mean bone in her body, and she had never done anything against anyone. Although in Colombia the assassins are rarely brought to justice, many of the local residents have information about the proceedings or the criminals. In Arancy's murder, it is believed that one of the customers at the grocery store had flirted with her across the counter and the man's wife found out about his infatuation and hired two *sicarios* from another town to kill her.

The murder left a deep hole in Aunt Gilma's home and we worried she would never recover. But she had to pull herself together because, as a widow—Jose Chica had died a few years previously—she was the anchor of her family of nine surviving children. This was not the end of great loss for her, and in less than two years after Arancy's death, she lost a son, Guillermo, to the same rampant violence. He was gunned down just two blocks from her house after a night of dancing and drinking at a local bar that ended in an argument. It was Aunt Gilma herself who called to tell us the horrible news. Now her family could not ignore the ever-looming threat of violence that was so pervasive in Barrio Antioquia.

A few years later, my aunt's business suffered some bad spells and her two sons, who ran it for her, had to close it down. Some of the creditors threatened the sons and she insisted they flee to the United States. She had lost a son and a daughter and could not risk any more of her children. So she moved out of Barrio Antioquia to a safer neighborhood, and her two sons moved to America with their families.

Senseless violence and crimes have touched the lives of almost every Colombian family, and mine was not an exception. Sometime after my parents left for America, my grandmother Rosa took in her second daughter Nubia and baby granddaughter, Ericka. Byron and I treated her like a little sister. We heard her speak her first words and saw her take her first steps. She was two when Byron and I left to join my parents in New Jersey, and the next time I saw her was in 1988, when we returned to Colombia for the first time. On a sunny day, from the balcony of our house, she introduced me to the girl in the school uniform who later became my wife. At the age of twelve, she was a typical rebellious, dark-eyed, gawky teenager trying to figure out who she was and would be.

Yet, even under my grandmother's watchful eye, Ericka had befriended a rough crowd, just as I had done when I was her age. One night, on July 3, 1989, she got into an argument with a young man over a friend's bicycle that had been stolen. He demanded Ericka tell him where it was. That young man turned out to be an assassin for a drug gang, and when he did not get the answer he wanted, he shot Ericka to death just a few blocks from our house. He cowardly shot her in the back as she tried to run away and hide in a house.

My grandmother was visiting us in West New York when she learned of Erika's sudden and violent death. It had been a rich interlude in which she saw me graduate from Princeton, and toured the Harvard campus at which I would be spending four years studying medicine. And then came the shattering news. My grandmother sobbed for days. "How can anyone hurt my little girl?" she cried. "How can anyone be so cruel?"

She could not be consoled and berated herself for leaving Erika behind to take the trip to America. Though everyone knew who the killer was, no one was ever charged, and it was little consolation that just a few years later the killer was himself murdered in a gang war. That was how pervasive violence was in Medellín in the early nineties.

The reality was that not just my family but many families in Colombia experienced the pain and agony of losing their loved ones to senseless crime and, furthermore, continued to live with the anguish that the killers just walked away. We lived with it as a fact of life, like the occasional thunderstorm that blew throughout the streets in the rainy season. When I was growing up, my grandmothers had casually given Byron and me detailed instructions about what to do if we were caught in a fight. "Run as fast as you can and go into the first house that is open," Rosa would say.

That sense of vulnerability and helplessness that one feels as a young boy or girl growing up under such conditions is what my parents and grandmothers wanted to protect us from. They had seen many young boys and girls follow a path that led to death, or to prison. They had seen innocent young men get murdered because of their entanglement with violent relatives and friends, and they did not want to have their lives scorched by such incidents. That is why they decided to drag us away from such an ambiance at all costs, even if it meant a hazardous midnight voyage across the sea in a small boat.

This is the explanation that I could have given to my daughter Jasmine one night when she naively asked me, "Why do they come here, Daddy?" This question was motivated one night while we were watching a news report on "illegal immigration." As part of the coverage, they showed several angry picketers shouting and brandishing signs that read, "Deport All Illegal Aliens" and "Illegal Aliens are Criminals." My daughter, Jasmine, who was eight at the time, seemed unusually captivated and asked me, "Daddy, what is an illegal alien? Why are those people so angry?"

I'm guessing that because she comes from an affluent Long
Island town with parents who stick out because of their accents
and their appearance, the word "immigrant" might have had a
special resonance for her, particularly when paired with the omi-
nous word "illegal." I told her in simple terms that an illegal alien
is a person who is living in the United States without the government's authorization. I added that these people have commit-
ted an illegal immigration act, but that they are not criminals.
I also explained that the picketers were angry because they felt
threatened by the presence of people who came from a different
country without permission, and were competing for jobs at a
time when the economy is not doing well. My simple explanation, of course, stirred more questions than it answered. This is
why she asked, "Why do they come here? Shouldn't they stay in
their own countries?"

My daughter was very young, so I realized that I could not
give her a comprehensive explanation of why we search for a place
where we can live with dignity, and have better opportunities. So
I simply replied that the immigrants come here because they are
searching for a better life for themselves and for their families.
Often, as was the case for my parents, they are motivated by desperation, by fear, by hopelessness, and by poverty so unrelenting
that they will risk their own lives to come to America. I let her
know that her own parents and grandparents had left their native
Colombia in search of work and a better future. I explained that
they found opportunities in the United States because its economy is one of the strongest in the world and there is a huge need
for manual labor.

The immigration debate is obviously far more complex than
the explanation that I gave Jasmine. She did not, for example,
ask, "Why didn't you come here legally?" Had she asked, I would
have told her that it is almost impossible to receive a permanent
visa to come to the United States if you are from a poor Third-
World country. In fact, it has become hard to get even a tempo-

rary visitor's visa unless you have sufficient assets, like a house or a business, to show that you are not likely to abandon those possessions and remain here permanently.

Recently, my story was published in the New York *Daily News*, "Smuggled as a Child from Colombia, Now He's a Harvard Grad and a Doctor," and the *New York Times*, "An Undocumented Princetonian." Many of my older patients who were part of the wave of European immigration of the early twentieth century were overjoyed when they read my story. As I examined some of these patients in my office, they would share some of their own stories of hardship when they came to America. Nonetheless, they are grateful for the opportunities they had when they came to the United States and happy that America welcomed them with open arms. These immigrants left behind their families, culture, friends, and possessions and came to America in search of freedom and opportunity. Many of them would not have been welcomed under today's immigration laws. What a loss that would have been for the country! Because of today's policies, people striving to enhance their lives often have no choice but to find their way here without the required entry documents. My parents, my brother, and I needed to escape Colombia's everyday violence and stifling, feudal economy. We would have preferred to arrive here with our papers in order, but this was not realistic.

Immigration reform is clearly one of the greatest challenges that we are currently facing. Yes, the United States needs to have the power to control its borders, particularly in the post 9/11 age of terrorism. And, yes, American workers also have a right to protect themselves against a flood of workers who will underprice them in the job market. American taxpayers need to be concerned with the amount of costly social services undocumented immigrants may consume, especially if they are not paying taxes. Nevertheless, America continues to be the land of dreams, justice, and opportunity for all, and we need to find a solution to these difficult problems.

UNDOCUMENTED

So what is the solution? We can spend billions solely on racist enforcement laws or a fence across land, air, and sea, or we can be more practical and find a way to incorporate them into our country in a humane fashion that makes sense to both sides. The inescapable fact is that there are millions of undocumented families living among us who have been here for many years and who are an integral part of our daily lives, with deep roots in our own personal lives and our social and economic institutions. Can we throw them all out? I think most reasonable Americans will concede that this is impossible, let alone cruel to the children born here. So the only real option is to find a way to offer them a sensible path toward emerging from the shadows of society. The solution to this dilemma will only come when we open our minds and our hearts and realize that this is a great human tragedy.

A perfect example is the judge who handled my family's immigration appeal. He could have strictly adhered to the letter of the immigration law and told my parents, "I am deeply sorry, but you have broken the law and therefore you have to leave the country." But he tempered his decision by taking into account my parents' two sons who were American citizens by birth and raised here and spoke fluent English, not to mention his awareness of their older brother who was getting A's at Princeton and would likely be a valuable addition to American life. The judge allowed an element of human compassion to influence his decision. He had the gift of empathy and did not simply follow a set of guidelines that would have forced him to kick my family out. I strongly feel that all of us who intimately know undocumented immigrant families in America develop a sense of compassion towards them because they are not criminals. Most of them are exactly like my family.

This is exactly how one of my American patients, Mr. Justin, felt toward his workers. He was a robust man in his early sixties who had undergone quadruple bypass surgery. Four weeks after his surgery, he came to my office for the usual post-operative visit. When I was done with the examination, he asked, "Doctor Fernandez, when can I return to work?"

"What kind of work do you do?" I responded.

He told me he was a landscaper, which his thick, muscled hands and arms seemed to confirm. I recommended that he not take up such physically demanding work for at least six weeks. He then revealed that he didn't actually do any of the heavy toil, but supervised twenty workers. Without knowledge of my background as a previous undocumented immigrant, he confided to me that most of them were undocumented, but were thoroughly honest, dedicated, and reliable. "In all my years in this business, I've never employed people who work as hard as they do," he said. "I don't know why we cannot help them. It makes me very sad."

Whatever doubts he felt about their legal status, he had become emotionally embroiled in their lives and realized it was a waste of human life to force them to live a fugitive existence. Given the long history and tradition of America as the most generous country in the world, I feel that most Americans would feel similar to Mr. Justin if they truly examined the humanitarian side of the immigration debate.

A CHILDHOOD DREAM

One ordinary day in the spring of 2005, I came to do my job as a heart surgeon at St. Francis Hospital on Long Island, New York. I was now an attending surgeon at one of the premier hospitals in America. This was my childhood dream. As I walked from my office to the main hospital building, I stopped briefly to admire the blossoming flowers and the view of the well-manicured lawn and gardens that surround the brick pathway connecting my office to the main building. Although I could have walked through the narrow labyrinth of indoor hallways that led to the hospital, I instead took this outdoor path to enjoy a few breaths of fresh air and sun. Often, this would be the only ray of light that I would see all day. For a heart surgeon at a major medical center, the work can become extremely intense. I realized that once I crossed the doors into the main hospital building, I would be occupied all day and possibly not see any sunlight for the rest of the day.

However, on this day the sky was clear, the sun was shining strongly, and I was prepared for a light day at the hospital. I had just finished a weeklong rotational shift and had not scheduled any elective surgeries. I was planning to see my patients in the intensive care unit (ICU), make my daily rounds through the hospital, catch up on some reading, and clean up my desk from work that had accumulated there over the last few weeks. If all worked out as I planned, I could go home early and have dinner with my wife, Sandra, and my two kids, Jasmine and Brandon. The idea of sitting down with my family for dinner was very exciting because I had been home late every night for the last several weeks. As I left my house earlier that morning, my wife had asked me if she should make dinner tonight. I said, "Yes, my love, today I will be home early. I promise." The daily routine of a heart surgeon, however, is often unpredictable, and on this typically light work day my routine was about to take a dramatic change.

The serenity of the garden, the gentle, unassuming redbrick architecture of the grounds that surround the main hospital building at St. Francis, and the variety of religious statues almost give the appearance that this is a monastery or a center for religious retreats instead of a major heart center in the Northeast. This sense of tranquility changes completely once you enter the main cardiac intensive care unit. Once inside, a complex of individual ICU rooms surrounds one with state-of-the-art medical equipment to treat patients with heart conditions. In addition to the patients, there are numerous health care providers working tirelessly to make people better. At the center of the team doing this work is the heart surgeon. This person has the training and ability to literally open a person's chest and work directly in the heart to correct problems. In simple words, this is, in fact, what I do every day. I have spent all my life learning everything there is to know about this important part of the body so that I can repair some of the problems that might develop. As you may imagine, this has required many hours of training, commitment, and missed opportunities in many other areas of my life. However, having the great opportunity to help my patients when they have life-threatening diseases fulfills my childhood dream of being able to help people. This was the case on this typical spring day in 2005.

As I briefly visited each patient during my morning ICU rounds, I stopped at each nurses desk, made some light talk with the nurses, and evaluated each patient's vital signs. When most of the patients are doing well, this daily routine may appear monotonous, but it is necessary so that subtle changes in a patient's condition can be detected early by the attending surgeon.

The quiet baseline noise of beeps in the unit was suddenly interrupted by an urgent call over the hospital's intercom system: "Doctor Fernández, CATH LAB STAT!"

This is an urgent call placed when a cardiac surgeon is needed immediately in the catheterization laboratory. This is the place where invasive cardiologists perform the diagnostic procedures that provide a picture of the vessels in the heart. It is also the place where lifesaving procedures are performed to open up blockages in the arteries that bring blood to the heart muscle. By and large, these are very safe procedures that have revolutionized the way we treat coronary artery disease. On some occasions, however, a cardiologist may not be able to open the artery because it is too complicated. Less frequently, the small wires that are inserted into these tiny arteries may cause damage.

One dreaded complication occurs when the artery perforates, causing a leakage of blood into the pericardial sac that surrounds the heart. This is a life-threatening emergency because the accumulation of blood into this small space leads to a condition where the pressure around the heart builds up to the point where the heart is compressed and fails to pump blood. In medical terms, this is called tamponade.

When I heard this call, I rushed to the catheterization unit. I was dressed in a white shirt, red tie, and my long white coat. I was holding my pockets as I ran down the long corridor that leads to the catheterization laboratory to prevent the contents from spilling out. Although I was running, I was composed, and I was already thinking in my head of the possible emergencies that I would be dealing with, as well as their treatments. I did not want any surprises when I finally reached the patient. Although I had only been in private practice for a few years, I had already seen it all after many years of training at NYU's Bellevue Hospital. I was confident of the training I had received from the best surgeons in the world, Dr. Frank Spencer and Dr. Stephen Colvin.

As I opened the wide set of double doors that lead to the laboratory, I was directed into suite number two by some of the nurses. As I hurried in, the attending cardiologist, Dr. Asif Rehman, said, "Harold, this is Mrs. Smith. She is in cardiac tamponade. You have to bring her to the operating room right away." Mrs. Smith was a pleasant woman, a mother of four. She had a history of high blood pressure and had recently had a positive stress test. Because of her medical risk factors and the results of the stress test, she was electively scheduled for an angiogram.

The night before coming to the hospital, she had been slightly nervous but confident that her procedure would just be another routine angiogram at the heart center. She had relaxed in her living room, watching her favorite television programs in the company of her family. Although she was retired, she was active with her community and family. As she enjoyed the warmth of her company and her surroundings, she'd had no idea that the next day she would be in cardiac tamponade.

Any time there is a cardiac arrest in a hospital, a sequence of maneuvers are used to attempt to revive that person. We follow the guidelines of Advanced Cardiac Life Support (ACLS). This includes securing the airway with a breathing tube and external cardiac massage (CPR). As you may imagine, and have probably seen on medical television shows, this also involves many people working feverishly to save this person's life. This was the scene as I approached my patient for the first time. The cardiologist had done all that he could to help this woman. From this moment on, she would become my patient. It was now my turn to use my knowledge and skills learned over many years of training. I was now at the center of a massive attempt to return life to Mrs. Smith.

At first, I noticed that although one of the nurses was doing adequate CPR, the blood-pressure monitor was not recording a pressure tracing. The red tracing of her arterial blood pressure tracing on the monitor was flat. She was dying. The reason for this was that the pressure inside her pericardial sac had become so great that, even with CPR, the heart was not pumping blood. I instructed one of the nurses to open up one of the thoracic trays.

This set of surgical instruments has the basic tools to perform an open resuscitation at the bedside. Briefly, I needed to open her chest. I quickly needed to get access to her heart to save her life. I realized that I needed to drain some of the blood from the pericardial space as quickly as possible to allow room for the heart to beat. With the help of one of the physician assistants, John Thoresz, I quickly prepared the patient and performed a pericardiocentesis. This is a procedure where a large needle is inserted through the lower aspect of the breastbone and directed posteriorly into the pericardial sac to drain the fluid.

I was able to remove about a cup of blood. Mrs. Smith's heart regained some function with the help of CPR, but this was only a temporary fix because the artery on the surface of the heart was still bleeding.

Two minutes later, she was in cardiac arrest again. During this time, I had arranged to have an operating room ready. Because the bleeding appeared to be very severe, I made the decision to open her chest in the catheterization laboratory.

Typically, this is done with a special saw that cuts through the middle of the breastbone; however, I did not have this tool available in the bedside tray. With John assisting me, I proceeded to open the bone with a large pair of scissors from the tray. Mrs. Smith's bone was fragile enough that I was able to do this without difficulty.

I then placed a retractor to separate the bone, opened the pericardial sac, and removed all the blood that was compressing the heart. With this maneuver, and a brief episode of open cardiac massage, her heart started to beat again. I could see the tiny perforation in her coronary artery. It was in the anterior vessel of the heart. I was able to control it with a light amount of pressure. Mrs. Smith was now stable. Her tamponade had been released. This was not the end, however; she had several blockages in her coronary arteries that would need to be fixed. With her heart in my hands and my index finger controlling the loss of blood, we proceeded to one of the cardiac operating suites.

Considering my beginnings in America as an undocumented immigrant, who would believe I was now a specialist in the modern treatment of a heart attack in one of the premier hospitals of America? Nonetheless, there I was, in the center of a colossal attempt to help this wonderful lady.

With the help of a very experienced and knowledgeable team of laboratory technicians, nurses, physician assistants, perfusionists, and a great anesthesiologist, Dr. Joel Baskoff, I was able to bring Mrs. Smith into one of the operating rooms. A few minutes later, I had placed her on artificial support with the heart-lung machine. This gave her heart the opportunity to rest, and it gave me the time that I needed to restore blood flow to the heart muscle, which was dying. Following this dramatic rescue operation, Mrs. Smith had a prolonged but successful recovery. Four weeks later, she was back in her house with her family, ready to start cardiac rehabilitation.

Although I broke the promise that I had made to my wife and did not make it to dinner with my family on this ordinary night, I was happy that I was able to help my patient and that my actions made it possible for her to enjoy another day with her family. My wife understood when I called her and said, "My love, I am sorry, but I am very busy tonight and I cannot make it to dinner. I am taking care of a very sick lady and I won't be home until late tonight."

After many calls like this, my wife has grown accustomed to them. I am fortunate that she is very understanding. Without requesting any more details, she said, "I will make dinner anyway, and I will wait until you are home."

- - - - - - - - -

When I reflect on some of the events in my life, I realize that I have been extraordinarily fortunate. I am convinced that I would not have become a heart surgeon if my parents had not made the decision to bring me to America at a very early age. In fact, I always think of this action as one of those events that suddenly changes the course of our earthly existence. I have often wondered about the root of these actions. Are they random events? Or are they part of a greater destiny that has already been written? This is obviously a philosophical question for which there will never be an answer.

For many of us, including me, faith in a greater purpose explains the events in our lives that may at times appear chaotic and unjust. In a letter to Max Born in 1926, Albert Einstein wrote, "At any rate, I am convinced that He [God] does not play dice." The greater context of this document is that there may be a universal order and arrangement of nature and our existence that has been deliberately planned. Unfortunately, our intelligence is too limited to even begin to understand this universal order. Quoting again from Professor Einstein, "My religion consists of a humble admiration of the illimitable superior spirit who reveals himself in the slight details we are able to perceive with our frail and feeble mind."

Through my own limited study and understanding of molecular biology and medicine over many years in the classroom, the laboratory, and the clinics, I have been privileged to get a glimpse into some of the details. The discovery by James Watson and

Francis Crick of the molecular structure of DNA on February 28, 1953, revolutionized our understanding of life, genetics, and inheritance. Since then, we have gained an understanding of the exact process by which a particular sequence of molecules or bases in a strand of DNA becomes a protein. Furthermore, we have the methods to manipulate genes and proteins to make better medications and help patients. We even have the methods to reproduce and clone other living species in the laboratory. Yet, we have not been able to understand the reason why the same set of instructions that produce healthy processes most of the time can become defective and lead to a brain tumor in an innocent young person who has not had the opportunity to enjoy life.

So it was that in the early months of 1978, my parents made a decision that changed the course of my life. Was this action a random decision that resulted from their personal needs? Or was this an act of destiny? I will never know, and I do not think that it matters. Nonetheless, the sequence of events since then has given me the fantastic opportunity to perform one of the most humble professions on earth. As a heart surgeon, my duty is to help, as best as I can, people who are in need. It can be the greatest and most satisfying job when I am able to bring relief, and it can be the loneliest and most devastating job when my actions are not successful.

As immigrants, we all have different stories of success here in the United States, and each story represents our own individual American Dream. Even though this book relates my personal story, it will undoubtedly be linked to the current struggle of undocumented immigrants in America. These are people who are living in the shadows of American society. They are looking from the outside, waiting and hoping to be invited in.

The last few years have been difficult for millions who live in America without legal immigration documents. Many are the families with strong ties to the United States who have lived here for a long time, have American-born kids, and have contributed positively to the well-being of America. These are people who have, for many years, lived in the shadows of society with the daily fear that one day their American Dream might be taken away. I know exactly how this feels because my family and I lived this way for many years.

The human and moral aspects of the immigration dilemma now facing millions of upright families have been lost in the current debate on immigration reform in which one side passionately argues for increased border security, and the other side cries for acceptance. The extreme depiction of undocumented families as criminals is often displayed or vaguely implied by some popular media personalities, who do not see a difference between an illegal immigration act and other more serious criminal acts. My journey as an undocumented immigrant in the shadows of American society shows the human struggle of such families, and it confirms that most undocumented families are indeed very similar to a typical modern American family.

In the darkness of the early hours of October 26, 1978, I was a thirteen-year-old boy crammed in a small boat with other undocumented immigrants, crossing the treacherous waters of the Bermuda Triangle. I did not do this because I was looking for adventure. My parents would have given all their wealth so that we could have properly obtained legal visas to enter the United States. However, this was not possible. If there had been a line or a waiting list for us so that we could come here legally, we would have done it. Unfortunately, some people cannot get on that list. As we stared at each other inside the cabin of this small boat, we were all terrified, praying, crying, and thinking that this was our last day on earth. I feared that I would never see my parents and grandmothers again. I asked God, as I tried to stay calm during that trip, *Please, my Lord, give me one more day in the arms of my mother; let me feel her kisses and her arms around me just one more time.* I had not seen my mother in over two years.

Nearly thirty years later, that same boy made his dream of becoming a doctor a reality. Although some dreams often occur overnight, my dream of becoming a heart surgeon took place over many years. This was all made possible because I had that first opportunity to be accepted in America, where all dreams are possible.

As a small boy growing up in a humble town in Medellín, Colombia, I had seen doctors come to help my grandmothers, Rosa and Alicia. Although relatively young, they suffered from uterine cancer and diabetes. Doctors would make house visits to help alleviate their pain. I was always overwhelmed by their power, by their ability to bring hope and relief to the patients and their families. As a young boy, I decided that this was my dream. I wanted to help. My grandmothers knew this, and they would buy me doctor-instrument toys for the holidays. They would proudly tell friends and family that this is what I wanted. Of course, no one really believed it could happen. My parents were not even in Colombia. They were in America, living as undocumented immigrants, trying to make some money so that we could eat and eventually buy a house. I clearly remember the faces of disbelief when my grandmothers talked about my dreams and my aspirations. Although very young, this would only make me more determined that I would make it happen. Yes, although my parents were far away, they were in a land where we all believed anything was possible. They were in America. This is where we all wanted to be. So each time that I spoke with my mother on the telephone, I would tell her, "Mom, we need you. We need to be with you. Please bring us to America." My parents listened. They brought me to America and gave me the opportunity to fulfill my dream of helping others.

I sometimes wonder about what my life and that of my brother would have been like had we stayed in Barrio Antioquia, come of age there, and raised a family there. Although there are some exceptions, social class determines the arc of a life in many countries in South and Central America. Those who do go to college and graduate to a successful career usually come from families that have enough wealth to support such an education. My parents did not. My father could not even find a job. Furthermore, I think that the violence that plagued our neighborhood would have also put us at great risk of becoming another victim of a vicious act of violence. I need only reflect on the toll of what happened to so many young cousins and dear friends who remained in Barrio Antioquia.

Instead, we had the extraordinary opportunity to come to America. Here we have all lived with dignity, justice, freedom, and most importantly, the prospect to dream. Until he retired at the age of sixty-three, my father worked in embroidery factories in West New York, including one factory where he toiled for twenty-eight years. In each job, he was able to walk to work from his home. But his last job was in Jersey City, three miles away, and I learned from his friends that in his early sixties he was bicycling those three miles.

By that point, I was a staff surgeon at St. Francis Hospital in Long Island, earning a good salary, and I decided to buy him a car—a new, small Mitsubishi costing $11,000. I drove the car up to my parents' house and had Jasmine, who was then four years old, run into the house to give them the keys to the car.

As they came outside, we all looked on with great fascination as they stared at the surprise gift. They could not believe their eyes. My father was overjoyed and my mother had tears in her eyes. We were overwhelmed with joy as my father squeezed into the Mitsubishi and drove it once around the block. He had never owned a new vehicle before. I felt moved to see this tender man of modest, precise habits indulge himself in this gift—a minute reward for all the sacrifices he and my mother had endured for their children.

My brother Byron, who took that dangerous voyage with me in 1978, had some difficulty adjusting to the demands of his high school curriculum. While I was starting Princeton, he was dropping out of Memorial High School. My brother evolved into loving a life of easy pleasure, of nighttime and weekend parties, of drinking and smoking and sleeping until noon. But he also had to contend with the hurt of falling short of the achievements of a star older brother.

In high school, teachers he had would sometimes compare Byron to me. Once he was conjugating Spanish verbs on the blackboard and made some errors. The teacher told him, "You know, Byron, the difference between you and your brother is like the difference between night and day."

Byron has a short temper. He threw the chalk across the room, told the teacher to leave him alone, and stormed out. There were other blow-ups like this, and finally, in the middle of his junior year, Byron stopped going to school. It took months of pleading and weeping for my parents to convince him to return and finish getting his diploma.

"If you can't follow our rules, then you cannot live in this house," my father would admonish him. My mother, preferring a more diplomatic, tolerant approach, would argue with my father. "Alberto, we cannot be so hard on him. He is going through very difficult years," she would say.

After many heated discussions, Byron abruptly moved out of the house, stuffing all his clothes in a suitcase, and telling no one where he was heading. We did not see him or hear from him for several months. We learned that he spent time bunking with different friends, supporting himself by pumping gasoline or bell hopping at a hotel. My mother was crushed and felt helpless. When I would call her on the phone from Princeton, she managed to appear calm, but her voice betrayed her pain.

Then, after a few months, he called and asked if he could return home. My mother didn't bother to check with my father, knowing that he was suffering as much as she was. Over the next few years, Byron put his life back in order. He didn't go to college like me, but he started working in construction and found it to his liking. Showing a late-blooming tenacity, perhaps a trait he absorbed from my father, he moved through the ranks of a company that restores landmark buildings like the New York Public Library on 42nd Street. He ended up as a foreman, one of the few Hispanics in management. He also found in Johana a strong and gentle wife, a Colombian native who has kept him resolutely diligent, despite the loss of her own parents to senseless violence in Medellin. They live on the second floor of my parents' house with their two boys, Andres and Michael.

In the basement of that vibrantly crowded house lives Marlon, with his Cuban-born wife, Marisol, and their daughter, Emily. Marisol, who was Marlon's high school sweetheart, married him after she finished her college degree. She is a first-grade teacher at the very first school I attended in America, P.S. #1 in West New York. Marlon had shown promise as a young technology whiz, constructing computers in the basement out of simple components and fixing the new computers that he bought. He had a special talent for writing up computer programs as well. However, he dropped out of the New Jersey Institute of Technology after completing a semester. Still, with his self-taught mastery of computers, he was able to find a job at the Internal Revenue Service as a computer and information technologist and supervises employees who are college graduates. He knows that his prospects are limited without a degree in computer science and is aware of what a mistake he made dropping out of college.

Alex, 16 years younger than me and the one who most looks like me (in Spanish, we call him *el repetido*, the repeated one), lives with my parents on the first floor. He graduated with a degree in economics from William Paterson University and works for a finance firm in New Jersey. He also had a rough time in college. When he was a junior, he suddenly lost his interest and love for academics. He failed all his second-semester courses and dropped out.

He did not inform me that he had broken off his college career, but I found out that he had when I applied for a loan to buy my first house on Long Island and discovered that I had a horrific credit score. Student loans that I had co-signed on for Alex were delinquent. I was surprised because I thought that Alex was still in school and not yet liable for paying off those loans.

"How can these loans be in delinquency if you are an active student?" I asked.

He eventually confessed to what he had done. Beyond my disappointment at this waste of talent, I was very upset with him because he had not given me the opportunity to be of assistance. When he had been a small child, I spent hours teaching him to read and helping him memorize the multiplication tables. Innately intelligent, he was an outstanding student, even if he didn't work terribly hard. Of course, in some ways he reminded me of myself. I too kept my problems to myself, never letting on to my parents that my status at Princeton was jeopardized until the storm had passed.

During our conversation, Alex was clearly upset with himself and said he wanted to return to school. I said I would help him get back. Alex set up an appointment for the two of us with his dean and with the school's financial officer. I took a day off from work, met with the deans, paid all of Alex's bills, and helped him pick his courses for the next year. I told his advisor to keep a close eye on him and keep in touch with me if there were any problems. Alex earned straight A's in his last year.

Like other immigrants who feel themselves adrift and quite alone in this vast, teeming country, our family has always been very close, in good times and bad. Our hard-fought experience as undocumented immigrants has served to strengthen those bonds. Similar to many immigrant families today, the discussion at our dinner table was often centered on our identity as undocumented immigrants, changes in the immigration law, rumors about people or families that had been deported, towns where it might be relatively easy to secure a genuine social security card, etc. We talked at length about the relatives who were far away, living lives we could not witness. Even thousands of miles apart, we shared moments of happiness with them, and we suffered each time we received news of tragic events. Often, we talked about education as the only vehicle for achieving success in this country. The hardships of surviving in this country without documents gave us all a deeper tolerance for one another's struggles, flaws, and setbacks without feeling that we must ever surrender to failure. All of that bred a deep love. We helped each other through whatever problems we faced. We celebrated all triumphs and special occasions as a family. Although undocumented, my family was just a typical American family.

In the preface to Rudolph Giuliani's recent book, *Leadership*—a signed copy of which was given to me by one of my patients who worked for him—he describes with pride the story of his father's experience coming from Italy as an immigrant. America received him with open arms. This gave Mr. Giuliani the opportunity to be the mayor of NYC, play a key leadership role in the aftermath of the greatest attack against our country, and even be a candidate for president of the United States. By example, we need to open our society once again in the true tradition of American ideals and generosity to the millions of lawful but undocumented immigrants who are already in our country. I started my existence in the United States as an undocumented immigrant, and America opened its doors. This gave me the honor and privilege to help Mrs. Smith when she was dying. This allowed me the great opportunity to fulfill my childhood dream of helping others. Someday, the son or daughter of one of today's undocumented immigrants may become a heart surgeon who helps patients or may run for president of the United States of America.

CPSIA information can be obtained
at www.ICGtesting.com
Printed in the USA
FSHW01n2034010618
48719FS